POSTCARD HISTORY SERIES

Thief River Falls and Pennington County

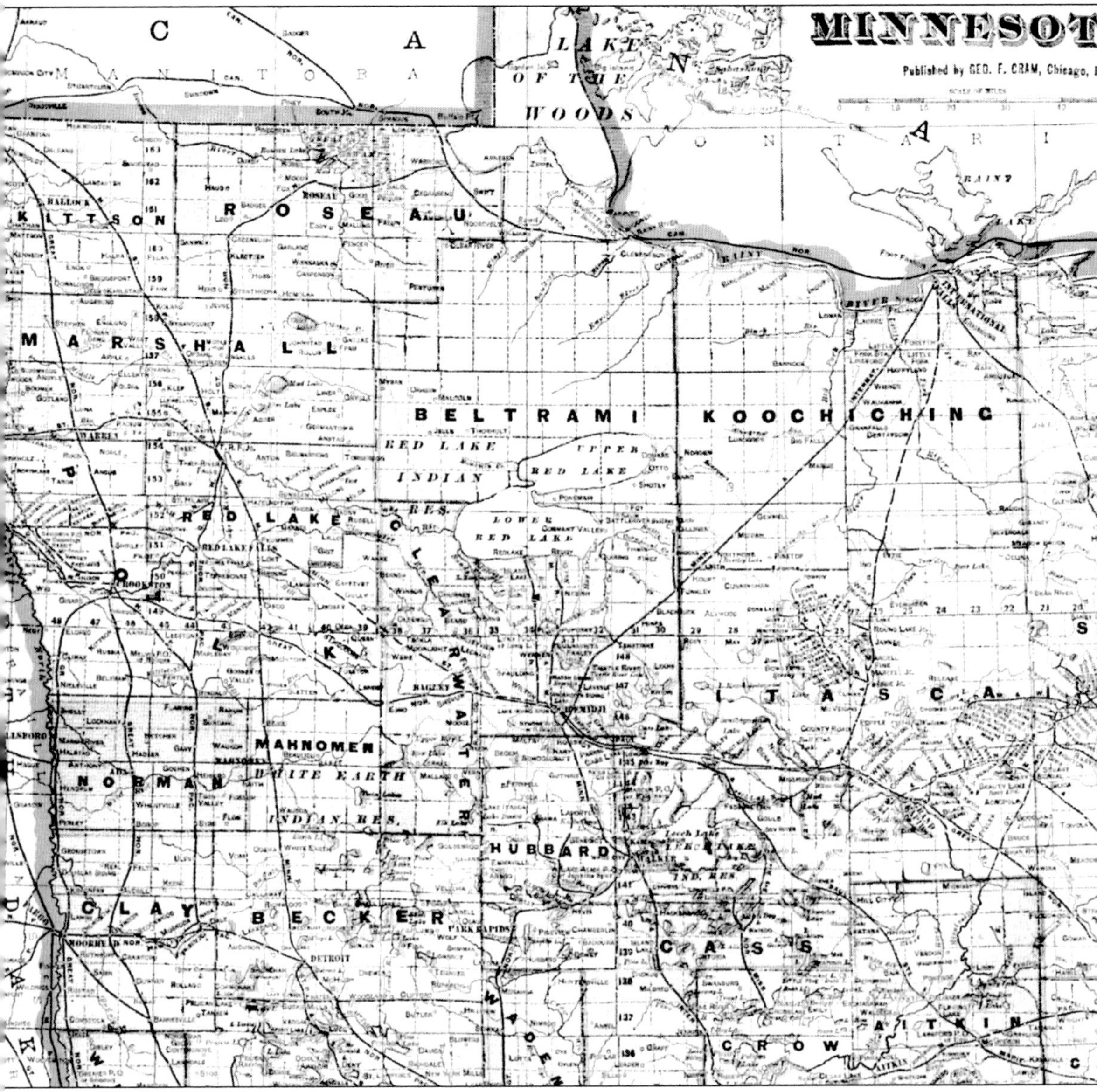

Minnesota 1910 Map. Thief River Falls and Pennington County were part of Red Lake County in 1910. In 1897, both counties were a part of Polk County. The eastern part of Pennington was in the Red Lake Indian Reservation until 1904, when the 93,000 acres were sold at public auction from the high school in Thief River Falls.

On the front cover: Shown in this picture looking north from the east side of the river, the Thief River Falls power plant, sawmill, log chutes, and the Hanson Barzen Milling Company were on the west side of the river. (Courtesy of the Pennington County Historical Society.)

On the back cover: Shown in this picture looking west from Main Avenue South near First Street, the Thief River Falls Great Northern Railroad Depot and water tower stretched along the tracks. The first Great Northern depot, located near the current fairgrounds, burned. Replacing it, this depot was built in 1894 and moved to Main Avenue in 1904. A third depot was built on the east side of Main Avenue and later moved to the Peder Engelstad Pioneer Village. (Courtesy of the Pennington County Historical Society.)

POSTCARD HISTORY SERIES

Thief River Falls and Pennington County

Pennington County Historical Society and Caryl J. Bugge

ARCADIA PUBLISHING

ISBN 978-0-7385-4025-0

Published by Arcadia Publishing
Charleston, South Carolina

Printed in the United States of America

Library of Congress Catalog Card Number: 2005938284

For all general information contact Arcadia Publishing at:
Telephone 843-853-2070
Fax 843-853-0044
E-mail sales@arcadiapublishing.com
For customer service and orders:
Toll-Free 1-888-313-2665

Visit us on the Internet at www.arcadiapublishing.com

This postcard book is dedicated to the photographers. Jacob Borry recorded the early history of the Thief River Falls. He was followed by Sigurd Salveson, Alfred Lundgren, Thomas Waale, Neal Fox, and Walter Kavanaugh. The works of other photographers from Northwestern Minnesota are recorded in our collection. Some of them are Orville Ellingson, John A. Hansen, Olaf Holm, Richard Nieland, Margaret Peterson, and Larry Rude.

Contents

Acknowledgments

First and foremost of those deserving credit and thanks for this work are the contributors of the postcards included. A large number of the cards used are from over 400 postcards donated to the Pennington County Historical Society by Dr. Ernest Padilla in 2005. Some of the other donors are unknown and some of them are no longer living, but those who are known are Violet Anderson, Patricia Bader, Gene and Gretchen Beito, Mark Borsheim, Bradley Brouse, Orville Christianson, James Dalager, Pat Dunning, Ole Granum, Phyllis Gustafson, Norma Hanson, Jerry Haugen, Avis Hoium, William Holmes, Bernice Lafrenz, Doris Langerud, Joan Lochrie, Stuart Nelson, Darrel Nicholson, Marion Prichard, Marjorie (Wangenstein) Radi, Rolland and Enid Sande, Conrad and Patricia (Jackson) Swanson, Linda Swanson, Dale and Linda Wennberg, Fern Williams, and Alan, Bruce, and Daryl Williamson. The collection of the society regrettably does not contain postcards depicting the American Indians who first lived in the county.

Without the assistance of the Pennington County Historical Society Advisory Committee, the identification of each scene depicted would not have been possible. The members of this committee met regularly to assist in the identification of images. The author's appreciation and applause are deserved by Art Buringrud, John Jaranson, Inez Mostue, Stuart Nelson, Marion Prichard, and Fern Williams. In addition to the committee, Rufus Olson supplied the identification for St. Hilaire, and Arlo Rude was invaluable in assisting in dating scenes. The work of this group of people and the author was not to write history but to simply identify and date the images as completely and accurately as possible. There were even disagreements as to specific details, so there is no claim that there are no errors.

Special recognition is deserved for Andy Filer and Fern Williams. Filer first suggested this project and is a computer programmer who has constantly prodded and provoked the use of technology in preserving history. Williams has answered endless telephone calls and has loved helping with the project.

For information on the content, contact the Pennington County Historical Society at:
Mail: P. O. Box 127, Thief River Falls, MN 56701
E-mail: pchstrf@mncable.net
Telephone: 218-681-5767
Website: http://www.pvillage.org

INTRODUCTION

The Thief River Falls of today is located where Thief River and Red Lake River converge. The earliest settlers, the Ojibwe, named their village Negiddahmitigwayyung—"Where the Two Rivers Meet." During early European settlement, the site was divided into three villages, including that of the Ojibwe. In 1889, the settlers on the southeast side of the rivers formed a village called Red Lake Rapids in honor of the river that supported their sawmill. In 1890, settlers on the west side of the rivers named their village Thief River Falls, although the Thief River ended north of where the village was platted.

Economics and practicality led the two European villages to merge in 1896, and there was controversy over the name. The citizens of each village preferred to retain their name, but agreed to compromise on a name. Strong contenders were Beau Falls and Twin Falls. However, when the question was taken to the polls, Thief River Falls was elected, receiving 78 votes (versus 52 for Twin Falls). The Red Lake Rapids newspaper was already called *The Thief River Falls News*, and most of the businesses and population in town were in the original Thief River Falls area.

Why was Thief River so named in the first place? An early English translation of the Dakota name occurred in 1823, when army Major H. S. Long labeled the river "Thief R." on a map made during an excursion up the Red River to Winnipeg, Manitoba. Although he never saw the river, he took his information from Giacomo Constantino Beltrami, a 44-year-old Italian army officer, adventurer, linguist, and political exile. Beltrami, a member of Long's party, had become disgruntled due to the meager supplies and strict regimen. He set off with three guides to find the source of the Mississippi. He did not succeed, but he did find the Thief River and traveled down it to the present site of Thief River Falls.

According to Native American legend, the name thief or robber was applied to the river because of conflict between the Dakota and the Ojibwe. The Dakota occupied the territory first but were driven out by the Ojibwe. However, not all the Dakota left their homes. Those who stayed built a high embankment around their village. When the Cree and Assiniboine informed the Ojibwe of the Dakota village's existence, the Ojibwe destroyed the village and its denizens. The Ojibwe then named the nearby lake and its river Ke-moj-ake-se-be, or Secret Earth River. The French mispronounced it Ke-mod-ske, or Stealing Earth; and it was finally translated into Thief River on explorer Joseph Nicollet's map in 1839. Other legends refer to a maiden who leaped into the river after her lover was killed and a Dakota warrior who lived alone, robbing and pillaging for several years.

Pennington County has a similarly colorful history. When Thief River Falls and Red Lake Rapids were discussing their union, both towns were located in Polk County. Polk County was established in 1858, when Minnesota entered the union, and comprised much of northwestern Minnesota—people had to travel over 100 miles just to get to the country seat. In 1896, voters created three new counties: Mills, Columbia, and Red Lake County. Columbia County never officially organized, but the other two succeeded in establishing themselves. However, Red Lake County and Mills County overlapped. Red Lake Falls became the county seat for Red Lake County; Thief River Falls became the county seat for Mills County. Eventually, Gov. David M. Clough declared Red Lake County the legal entity because its petition had been received prior to the Mills County petition.

Red Lake Falls was a smaller town located 18 miles south of Thief River Falls. Thief River Falls, due to its advantageous position on the two rivers, grew more rapidly. As a result, in 1905, Thief River Falls gathered 2,006 of the 2,365 voters in the county to sign a petition to claim the county seat. However, Red Lake Falls managed to gain a court order to block the county commission vote, so the petition was denied. More court and commission activity occurred over the next year. At one point, a petition disappeared under suspicious circumstances from the county auditor's safe. A new petition with even more names in favor of the move was presented to the county commissioners. The State Supreme Court ruled that a new petition could not be considered until the old petition's fate had been determined. The courthouse building purchased by Red Lake Falls in 1905 mysteriously burned to the ground a few months after the Supreme Court ruling.

In 1909, tiring of controversy, 899 voters drew up a new petition asking for a county wide vote on a decision to split the county. The vote was taken in November 1910, with 1,942 voting for division and 1,801 against. On November 23, 1910, Gov. Adolph O. Eberhart declared the establishment of Pennington County, with the county seat in Thief River Falls. The county was named after Edmund Pennington, the president of the Soo Railroad Line, which had been instrumental in the formation and growth of Thief River Falls. Pennington, once a mere section boss on the line, had worked his way up to lead the company. Pennington's rise from obscurity into prominence seemed to mirror Thief River Falls's rise into importance as a county seat, and so the citizens of the new county found him an appropriate person for whom to name their new county.

—Dr. Diane Drake

One

Farming, Logging, and Railroading

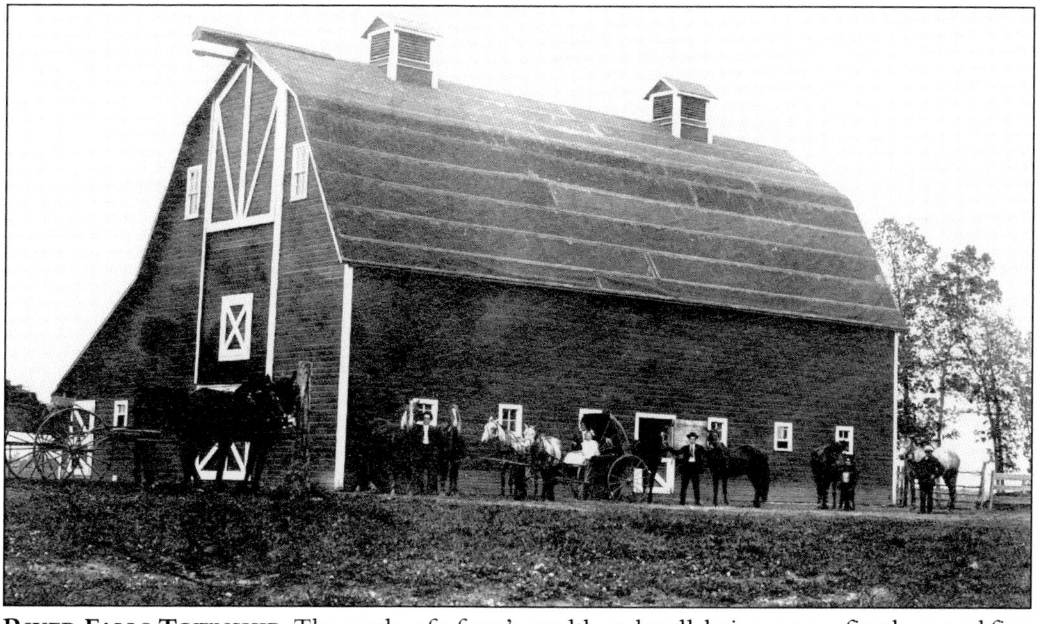

River Falls Township. The marks of a farm's wealth and well-being were a fine barn and fine horses. This barn belonged to Peter Johnson, who farmed near St. Hilaire in about 1910. Proudly displayed in front of the barn are the horses and, possibly, the entire family of this farmer.

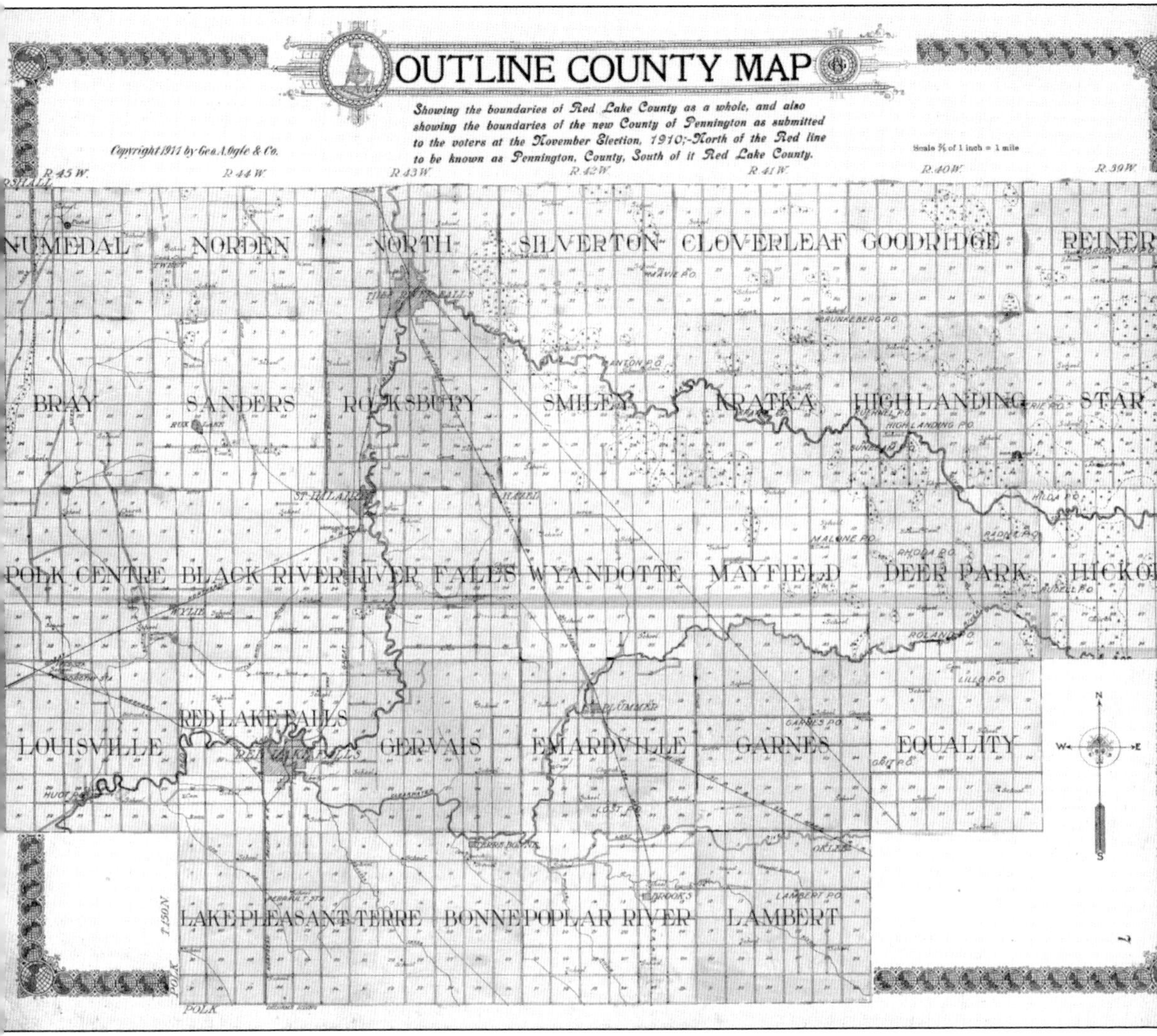

PENNINGTON 1911 COUNTY ATLAS. This map shows the division of Red Lake and Pennington Counties in 1910.

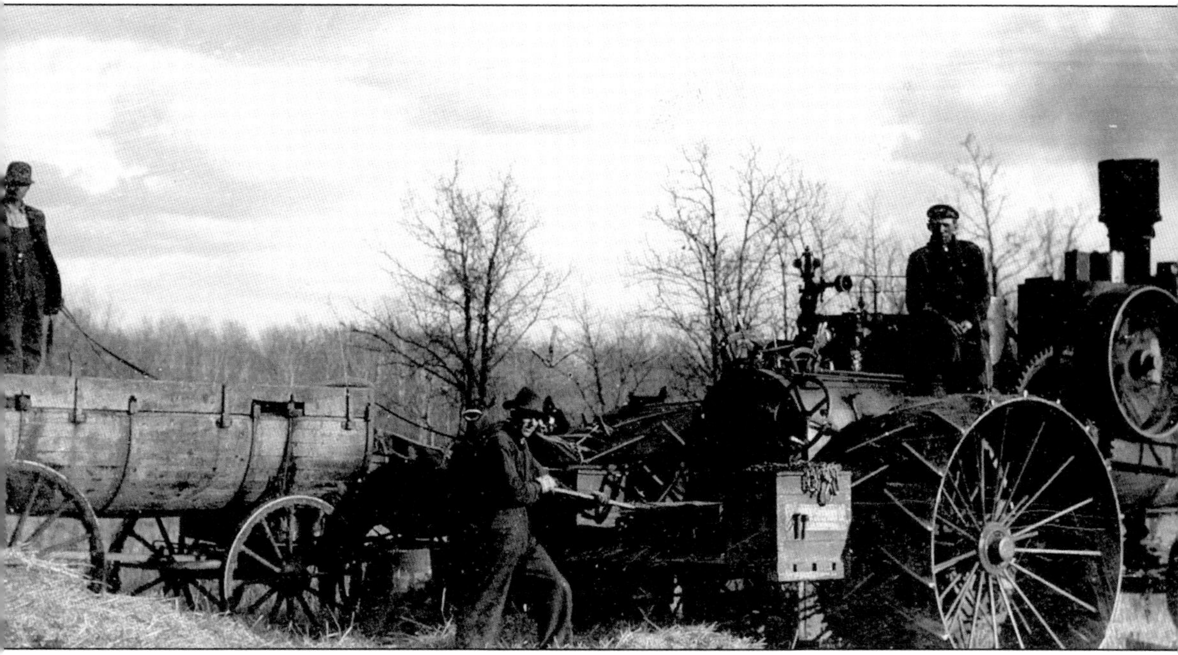

ROCKSBURY TOWNSHIP. Arnt Loberg feeds the engine, and Martin Loberg stands on the engine powering the grain separator on the Lars Loberg Farm in Section 30.

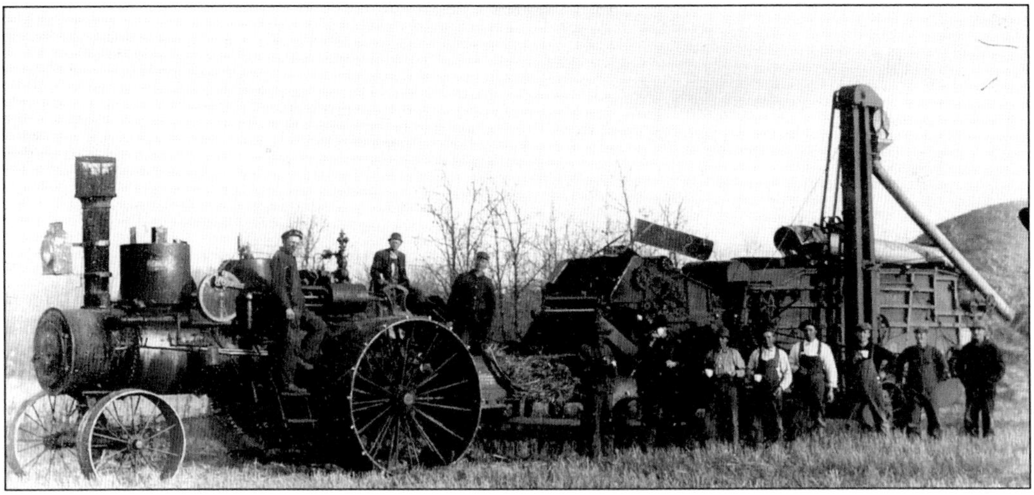

ROCKSBURY TOWNSHIP, THRESHING. Martin, Arnt, and Lars Loberg thresh on the Loberg farm along with other farmers, including Arnt Branum.

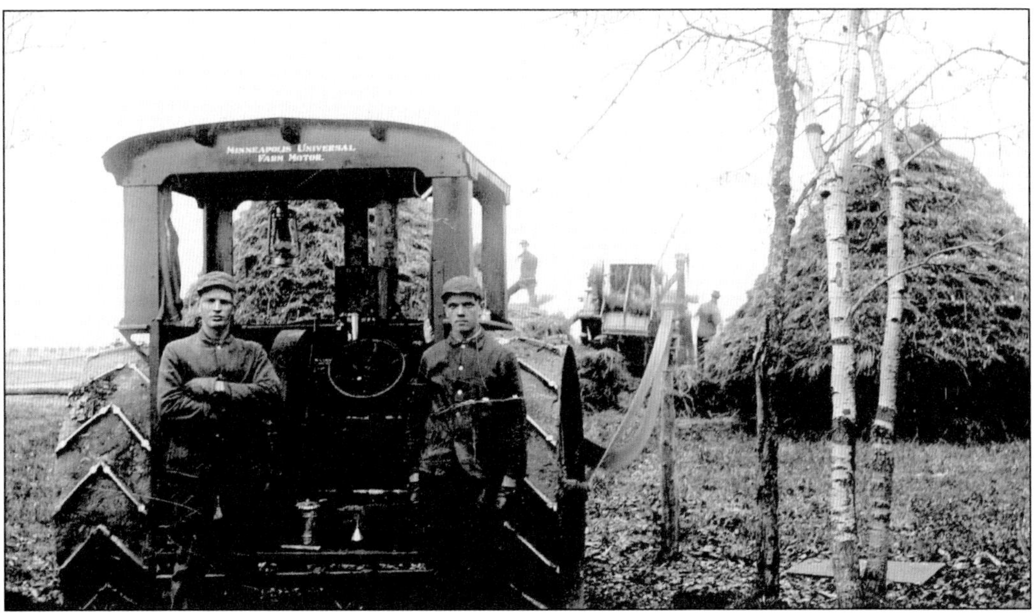

ROCKSBURY TOWNSHIP, MARTIN AND GEORGE PETERSON. Martin (left) and George Peterson stand at the rear of the farm engine that powered the belt to the grain separator on the Peder Engelstad farm in Section 14. Grain shocks were stacked on the right, and the threshed straw is on the left.

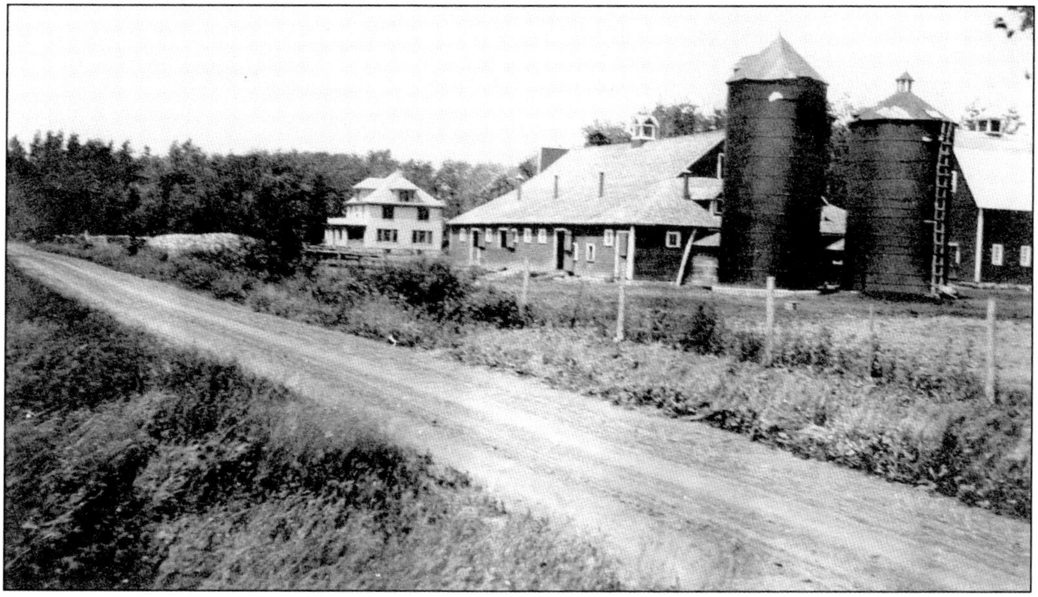

ROCKSBURY TOWNSHIP, CLOVERLEAF FARM. Peder and Mathilda Engelstad owned the Cloverleaf Farm. Peder and Mathilda emigrated from Norway and made farming history by planting alfalfa instead of grain. The house was built in 1912 and still stands.

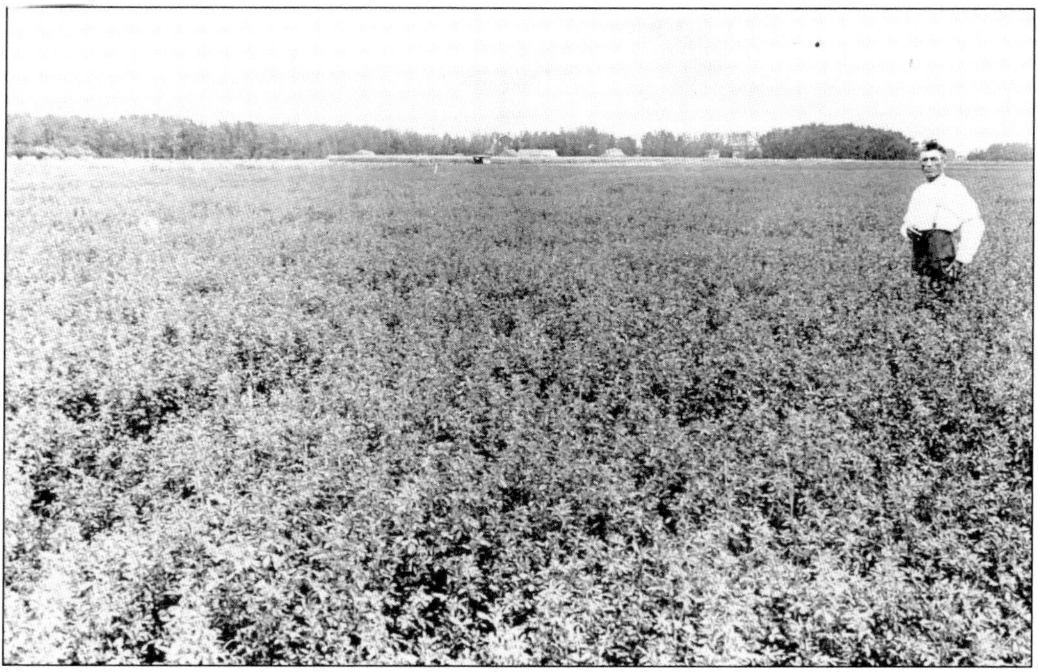

ROCKSBURY TOWNSHIP, ALFALFA FIELD. Peder Engelstad stands in an alfalfa field north of the farm. He was a leader in the improvement of the dairy industry and an early innovator in farming. The buildings for the farm are in the background. Peder and Mathilda had 13 children, 10 of whom lived to adulthood.

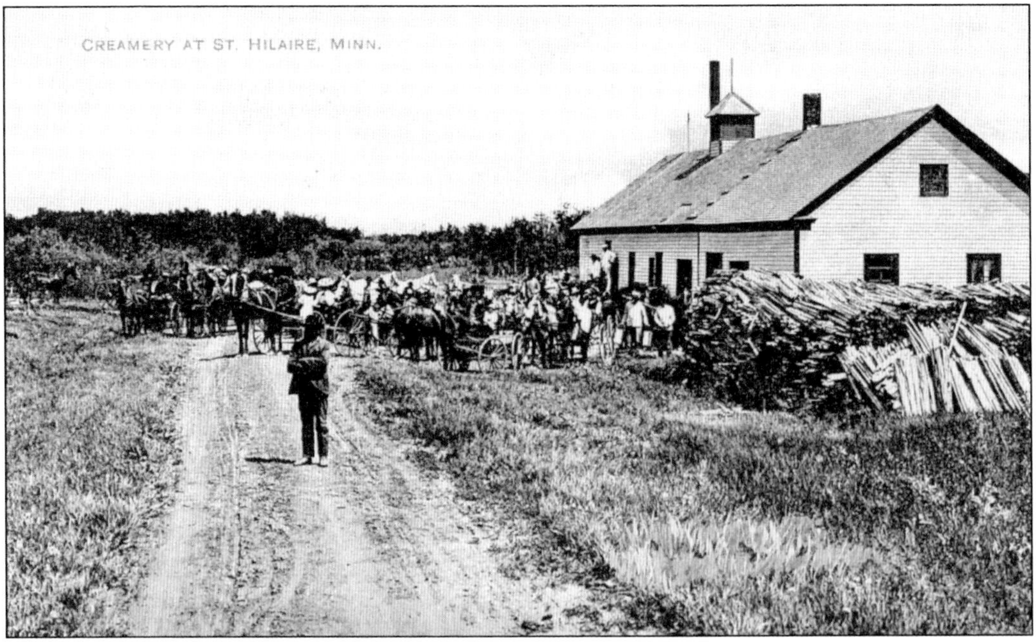

ST. HILAIRE MINNESOTA AVENUE. The Cooperative Creamery was organized in 1902, and a new creamery building was constructed in 1921 when cooperative creameries were organized and legally recognized by the Minnesota legislature. The co-ops trimmed the cost of shipping butter to the eastern area of the country by filling entire railcars with tubs of butter. The postmark is 1915.

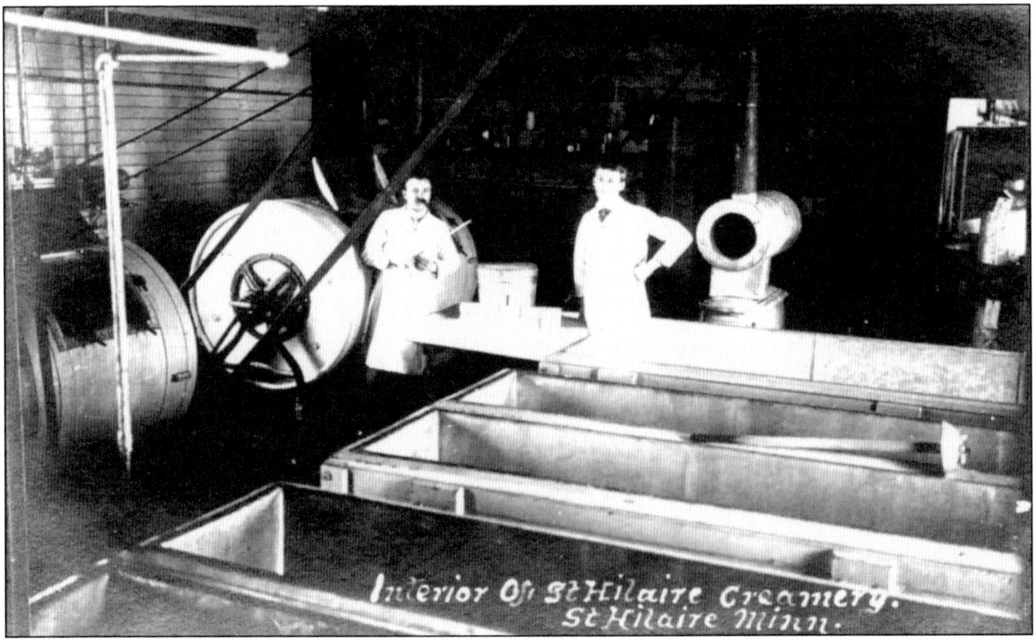

ST. HILAIRE CREAMERY INTERIOR. John Waage, on the left, was the Minnesota Champion Buttermaker from 1921 to 1923. The St. Hilaire Creamery was the largest cooperative creamery in Minnesota. A banner day of production was two tons of butter.

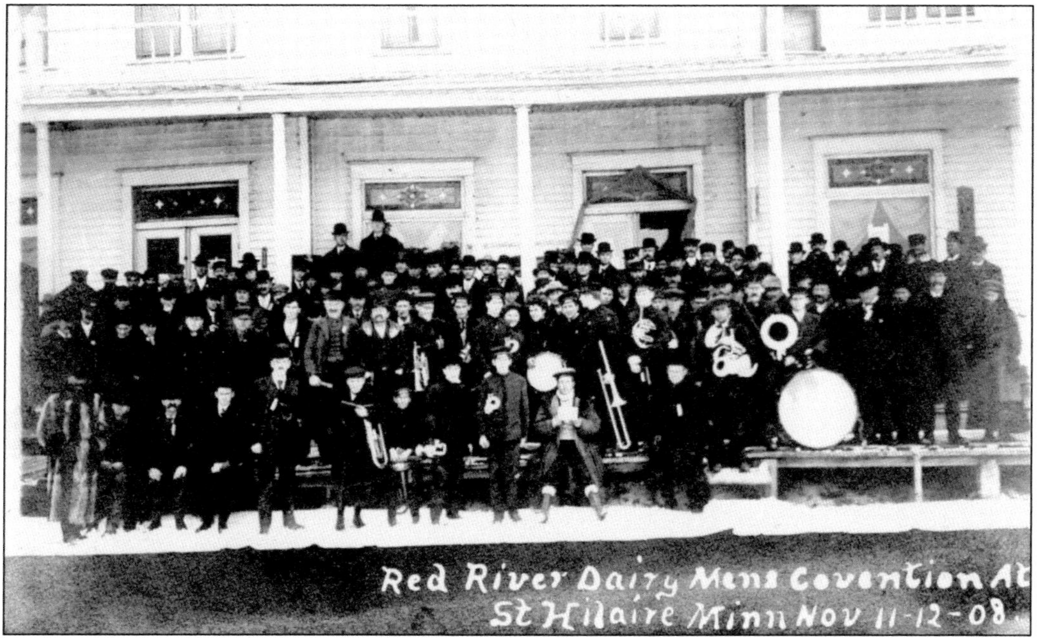

St. Hilaire Broadway Avenue, Hotel Markham. The Red River Dairy Men's Convention was held on November 11 and 12 in 1908. Attendees are pictured on the front porch of the Hotel Markham.

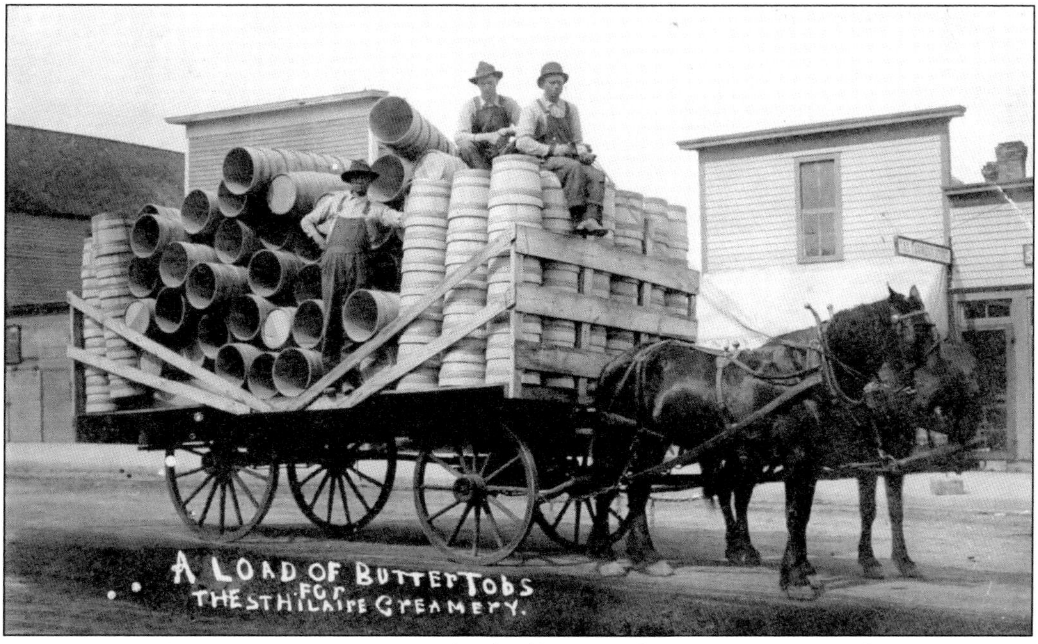

St. Hilaire Broadway Avenue. A load of butter tubs is on its way to the creamery in St. Hilaire. The postmark is from Hazel in 1915.

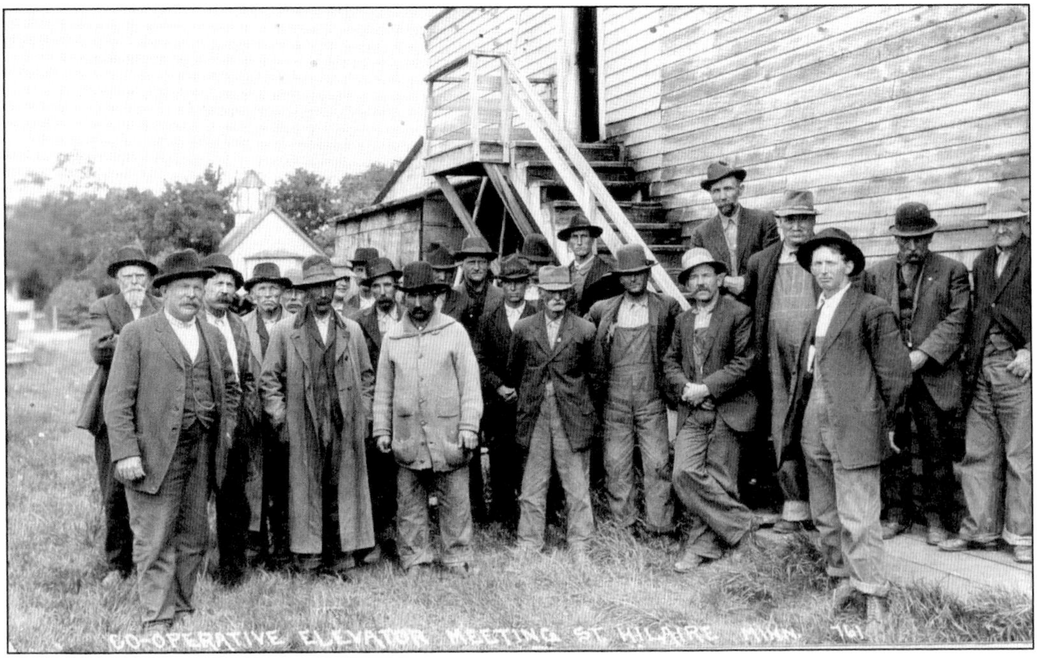

St. Hilaire Cooperative Elevator. Grain farmers joined together to market their crops. Among the members were Ed Aubol, James Roy, Norm Beebe, Nels Anderson, Ole Larson, Andrew Odegard, Swan Johnson, Andrew Soderberg, Fred Soderberg, Fred Rux, Emil Just, Albert Nelson, Ira Carpenter, Peter Lundberg, Martin Olson, Ole Loberg, and Andrew Mortenson.

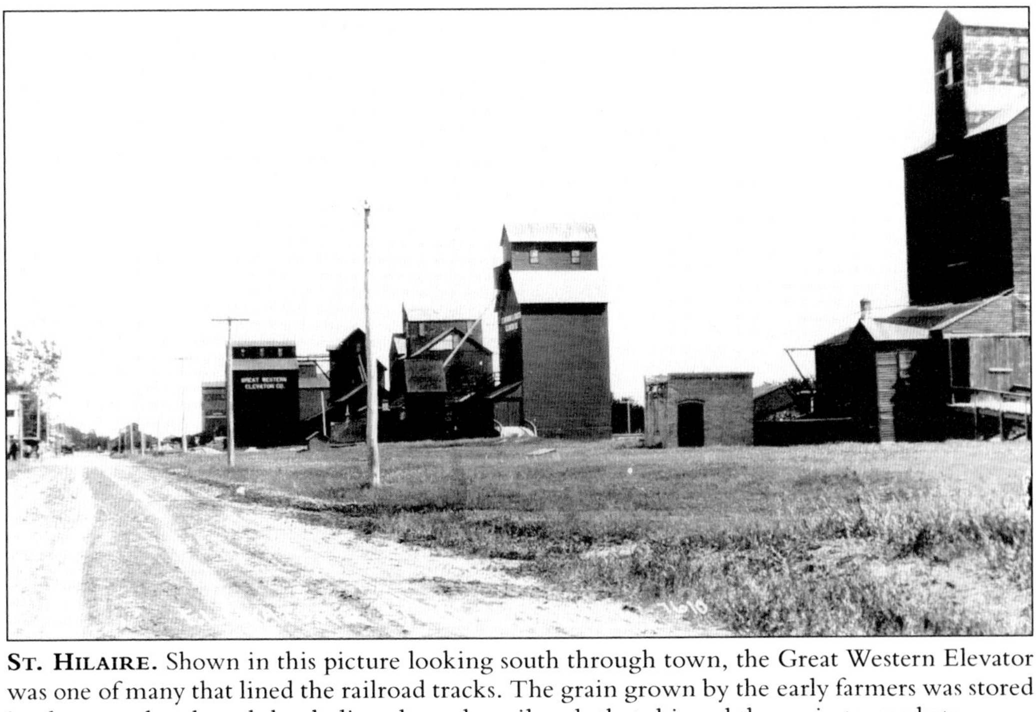

St. Hilaire. Shown in this picture looking south through town, the Great Western Elevator was one of many that lined the railroad tracks. The grain grown by the early farmers was stored in elevators that dotted the skyline along the railroads that shipped the grain to markets.

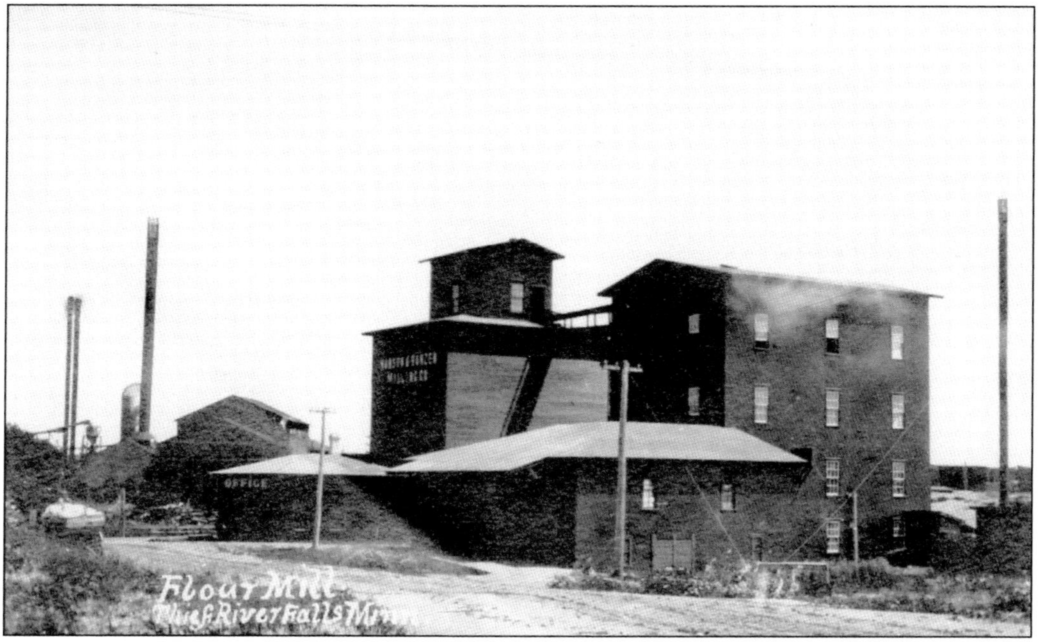

THIEF RIVER FALLS LA BREE AVENUE. Shown in this picture looking southwest, the Hanson Barzen Flour Mill (manufacturer of "Vivo" flour) was at the foot of La Bree Avenue, south of where the hospital complex is currently located.

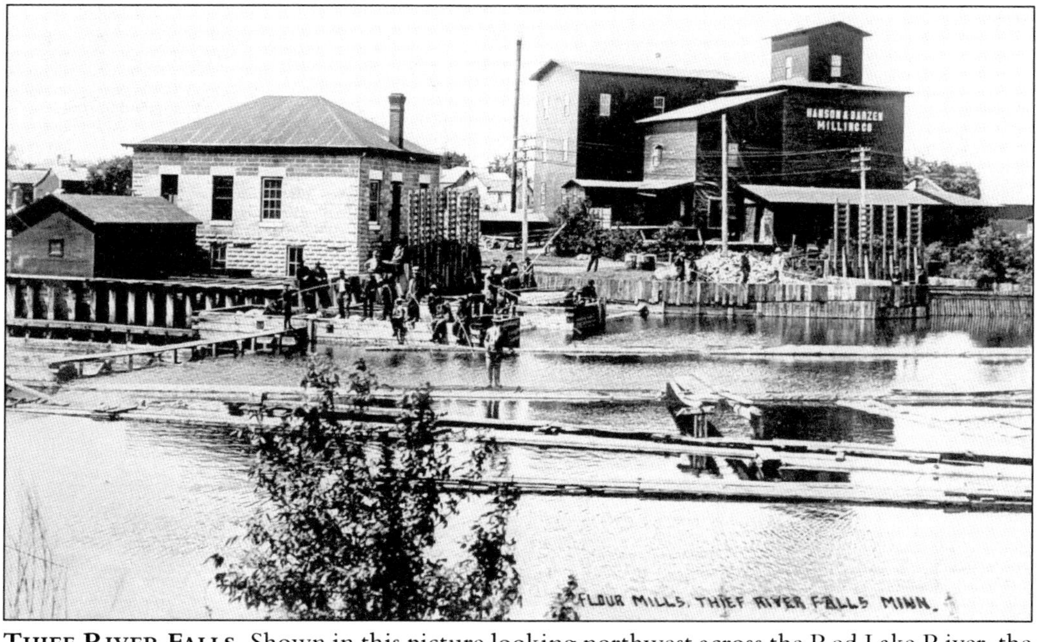

THIEF RIVER FALLS. Shown in this picture looking northwest across the Red Lake River, the City Power Block House and dam provided power for the sawmill and, on the east side of the river, the Hansen Barzen Milling Company in the early 1900s.

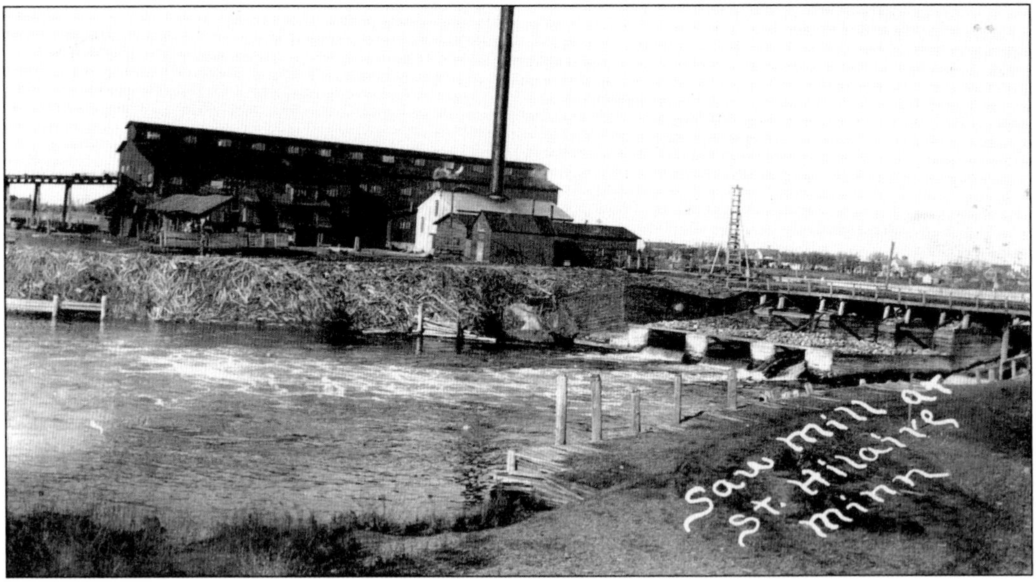

St. Hilaire Sawmill. Shown in this picture looking northwest from the east on the island in the Red Lake River, the mill was located on the west side of the river. Owned by the Shevlin and Carpenter Company, the mill opened in 1897, running day and night until the river froze over. At times, there were 500 men employed at the mill.

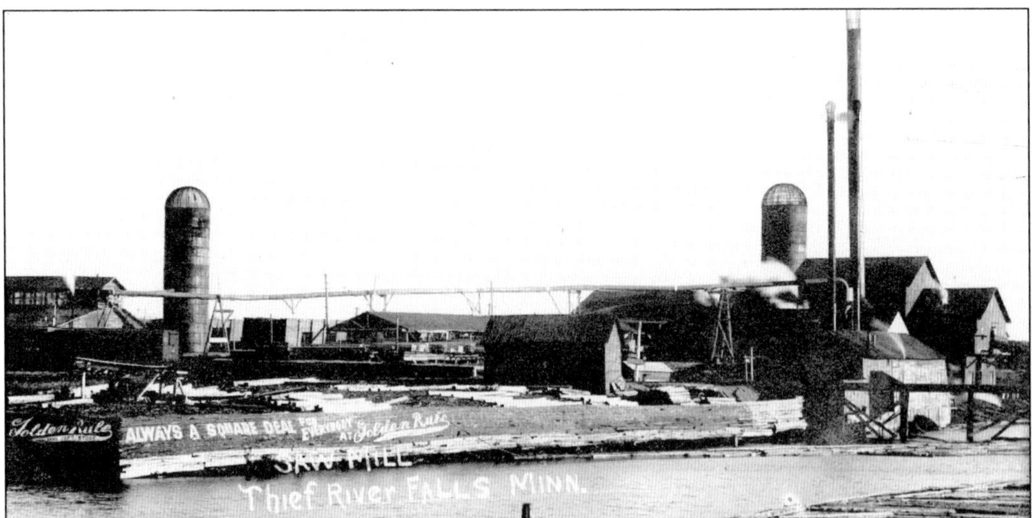

Thief River Falls Sawmill. Shown in this picture looking southeast across the Red Lake River from First Street, the mill was on the west side of the river. Patrick and James Meehan opened the mill in 1892.

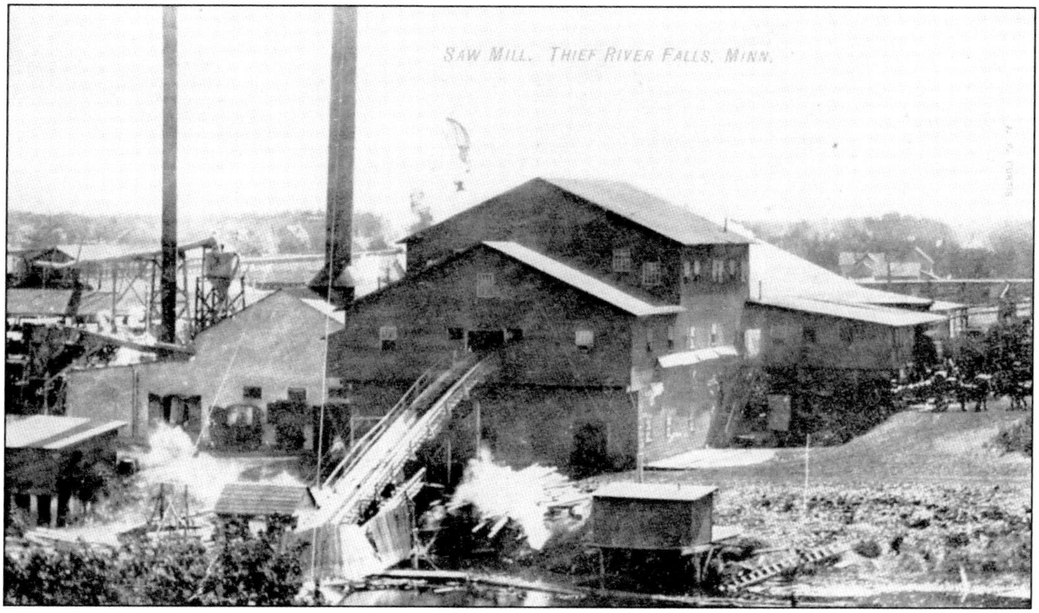

THIEF RIVER FALLS SAWMILL, EAST. Shown in this picture looking east from the river's edge, the mill ran day and night in two 10-hour shifts, employing between 300 and 400 men between April and October. The population of the city was 3,500 in 1905.

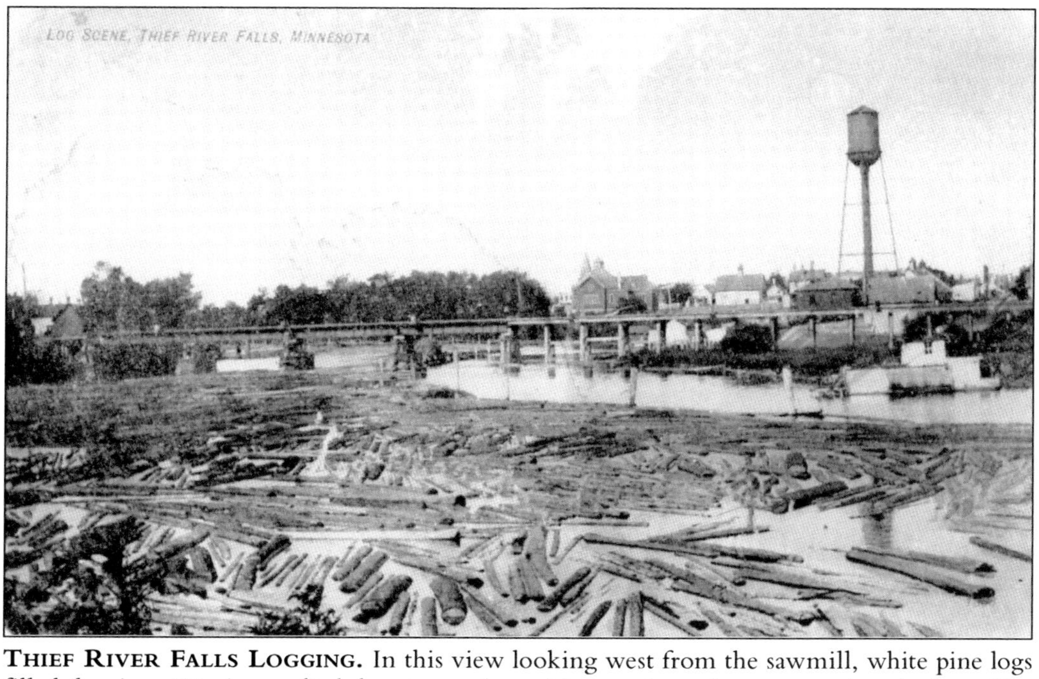

THIEF RIVER FALLS LOGGING. In this view looking west from the sawmill, white pine logs filled the river. Wanigans plied the river and provided meals to the men moving the logs. The Great Northern Bridge, Methodist Episcopal Church, and city water tower are in the background on this card postmarked 1908.

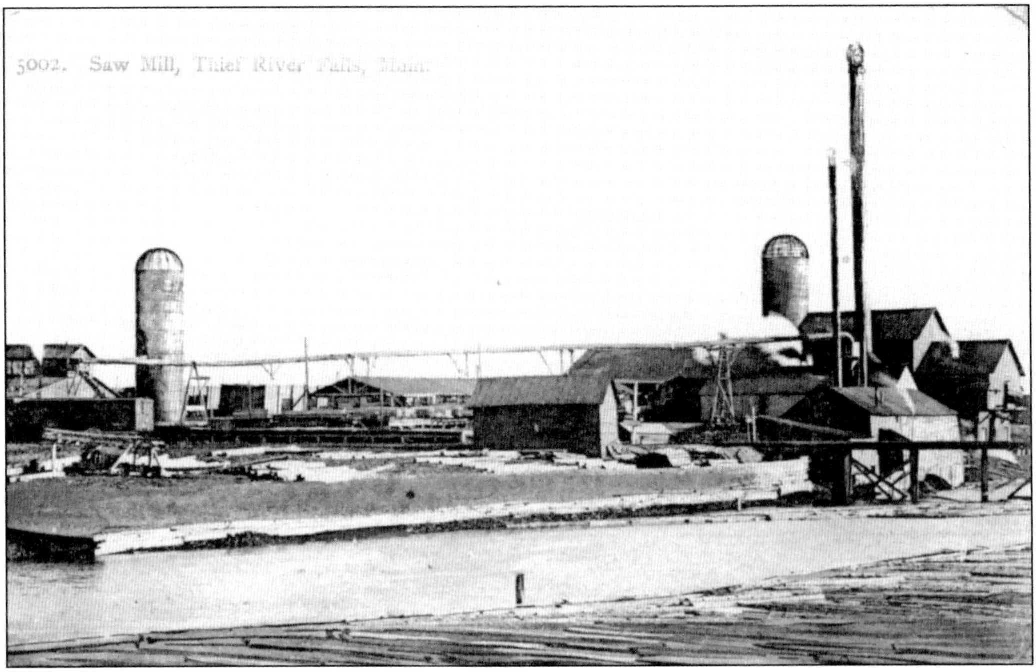

THE GREAT NORTHERN RAILROAD. The Great Northern Railroad served the sawmill with a spur from the west side of the river. Currently, Hugo's No. 7 is located where the mill operated, and the pilings of the railroad bridge pictured on the far right can still be found along the edge of the river.

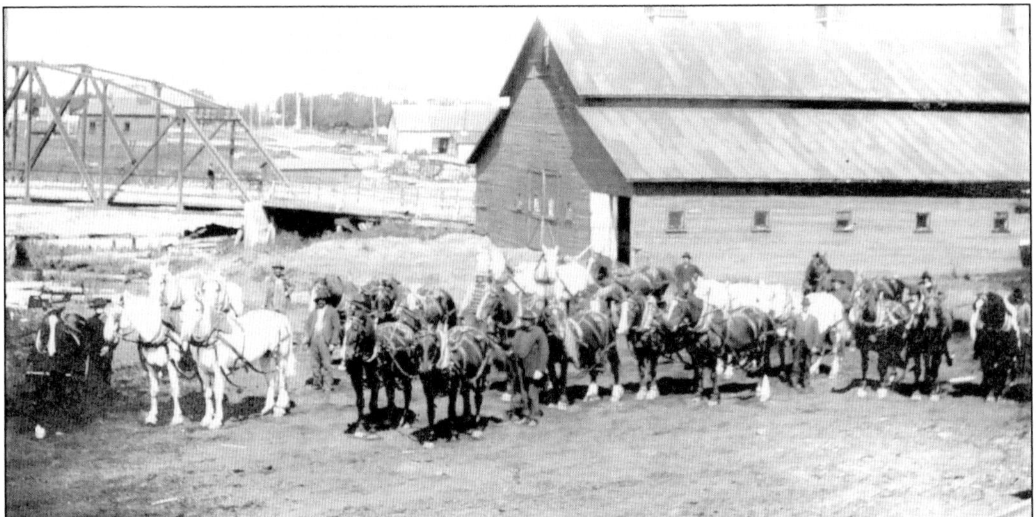

THIEF RIVER FALLS SAWMILL LIVERY BARN. In this view looking northwest from the mill, the horses and the men handling them are lined up in front of the livery located near the east end of the old iron bridge.

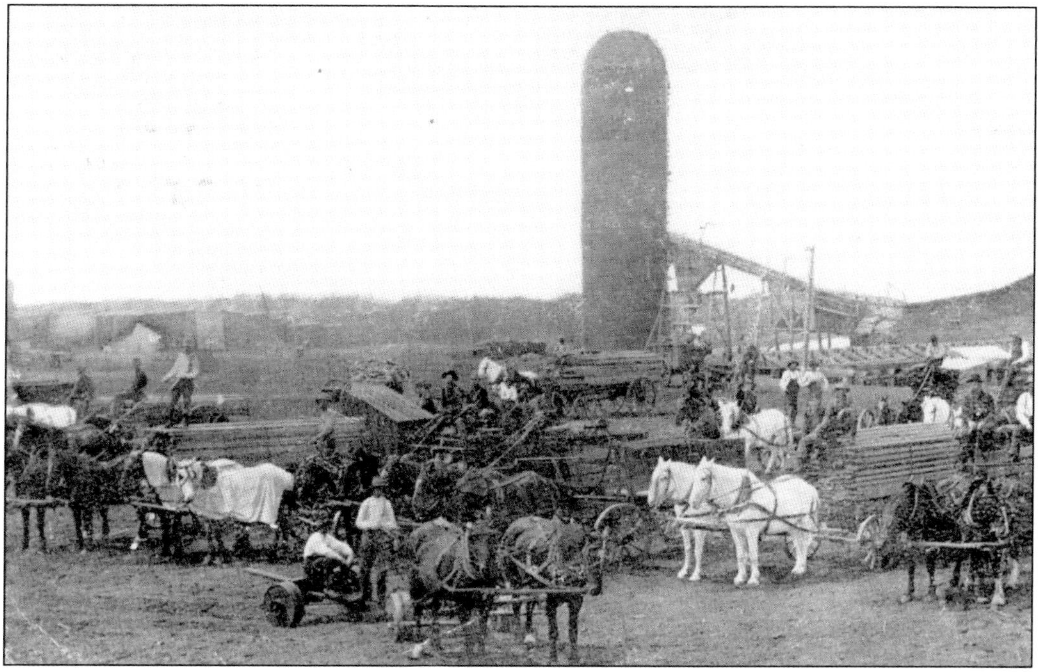

THIEF RIVER FALLS LUMBER COMPANY. The Meehan brothers sold the sawmill in 1899, and it was then run under the name of the Thief River Falls Lumber Company until it closed in 1914.

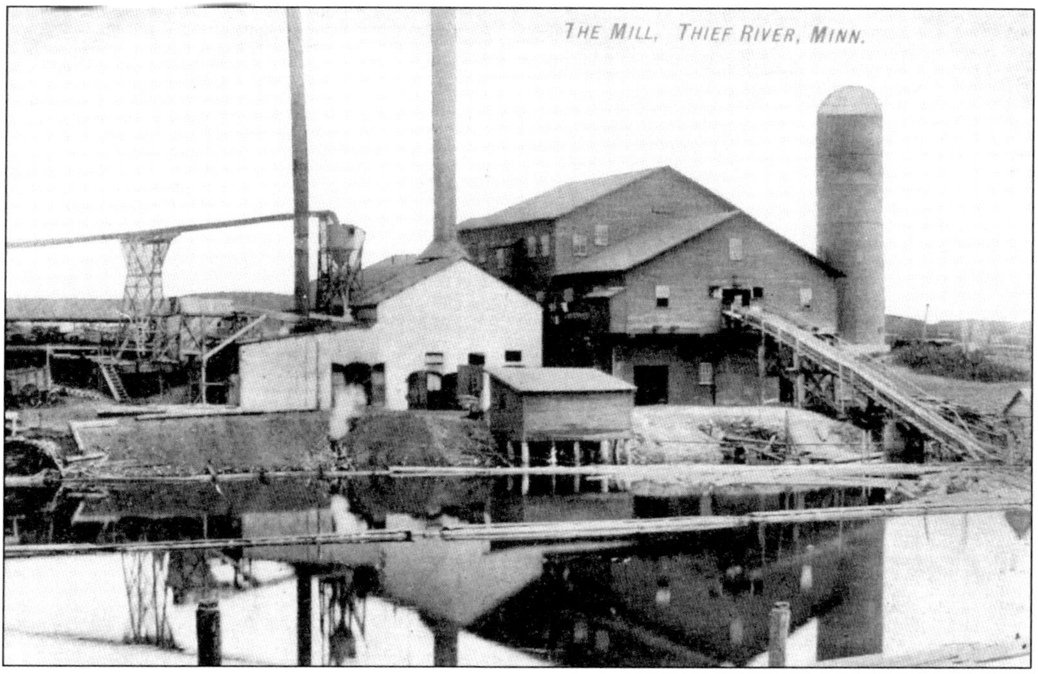

THIEF RIVER FALLS SAWMILL AND RED LAKE RIVER. Shown in this picture looking east from South La Bree Avenue, the mill buildings are reflected in the Red Lake River. The mill produced over 300 million board feet of lumber between 1899 and 1908. This card was postmarked 1907.

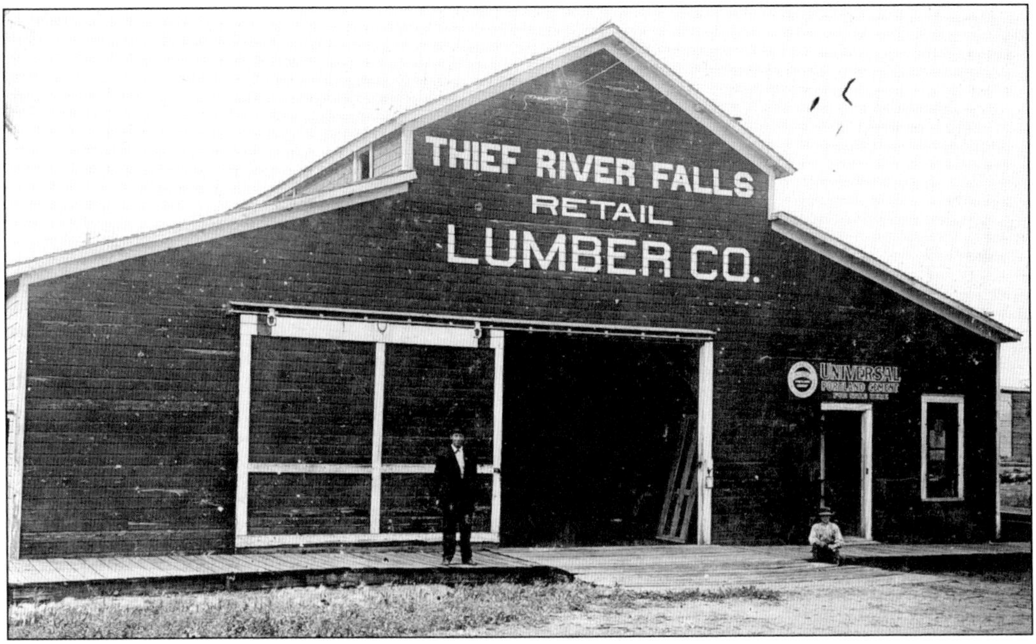

Thief River Falls Retail Lumber Company. The retail yard was located at 320 Bridge (now First) Street. When the business was sold, it included standing timber, logs, the saw and planing mills, shore rights, three steamboats, and a number of lumberyards. The value of the exchange was $500,000 in 1899.

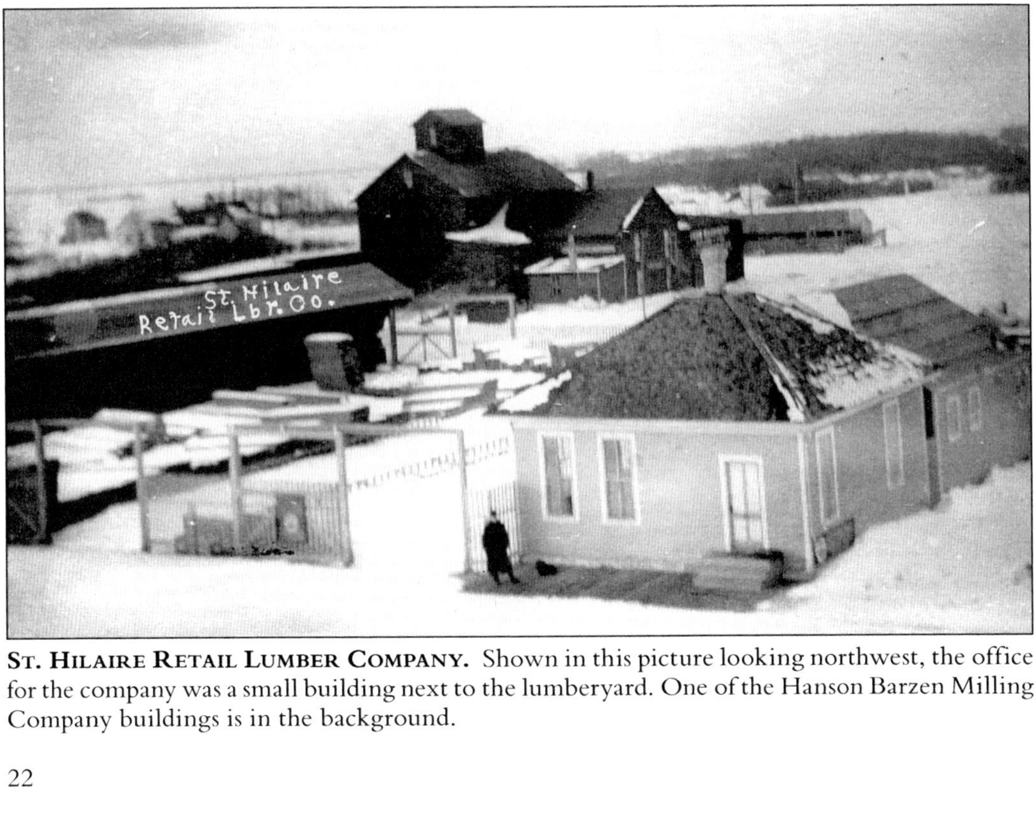

St. Hilaire Retail Lumber Company. Shown in this picture looking northwest, the office for the company was a small building next to the lumberyard. One of the Hanson Barzen Milling Company buildings is in the background.

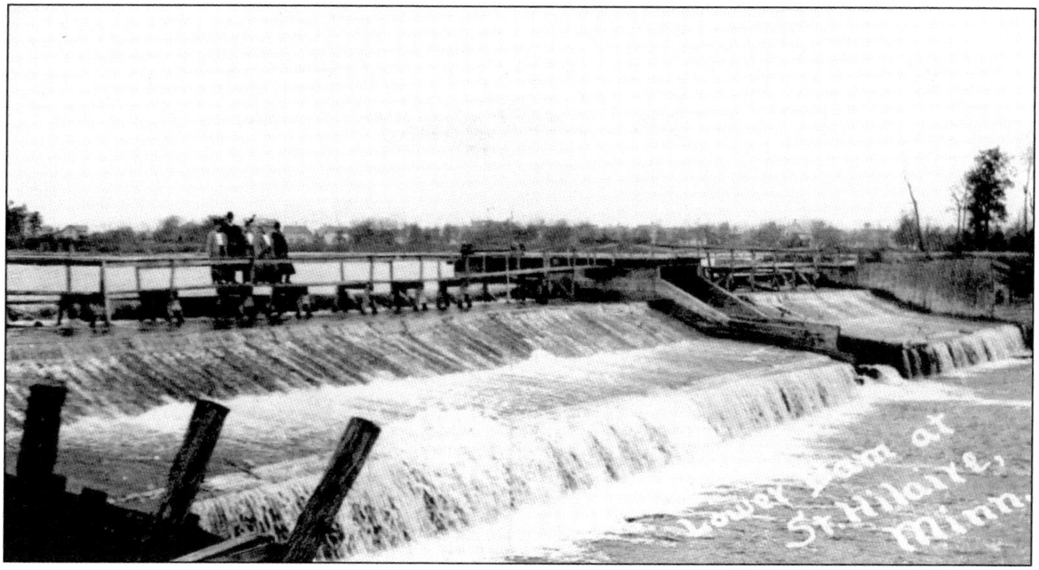

St. Hilaire Lower Dam, Looking Northwest. In a view looking northwest, this dam was one of two that were built in 1897 to create a backwater pond for log storage and to create a race for processing the logs. This card is postmarked 1907.

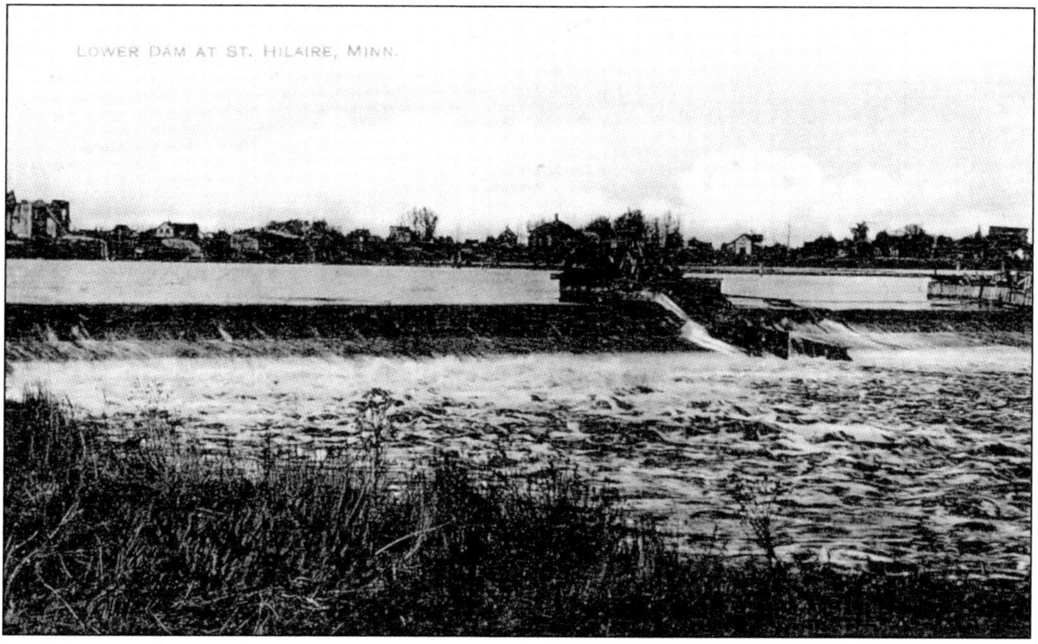

St. Hilaire Lower Dam, Looking West. In this view looking west, the skyline of the city is pictured on this card. The population of the city in 1905 was 911 people. At the height of the mill days, the city included several dozen retail stores, four churches, two hotels, four taverns, two banks, a creamery, and a flourmill.

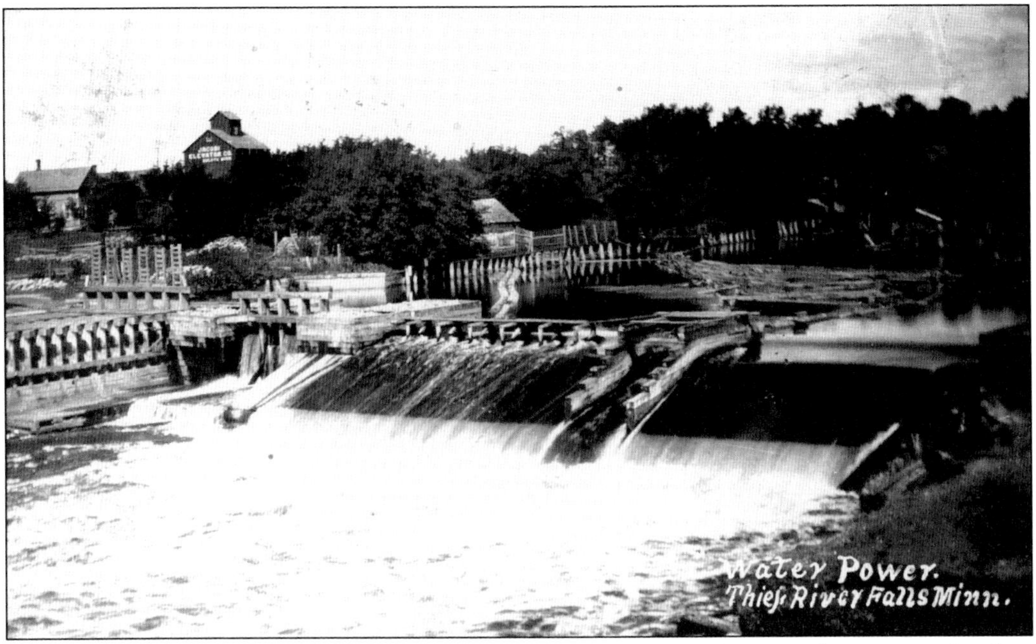

THIEF RIVER FALLS WATER POWER. Shown in this picture looking northwest over the dam and log chutes along the Red Lake River, the Jacob Elevator Company stood across the river. This card is postmarked 1908.

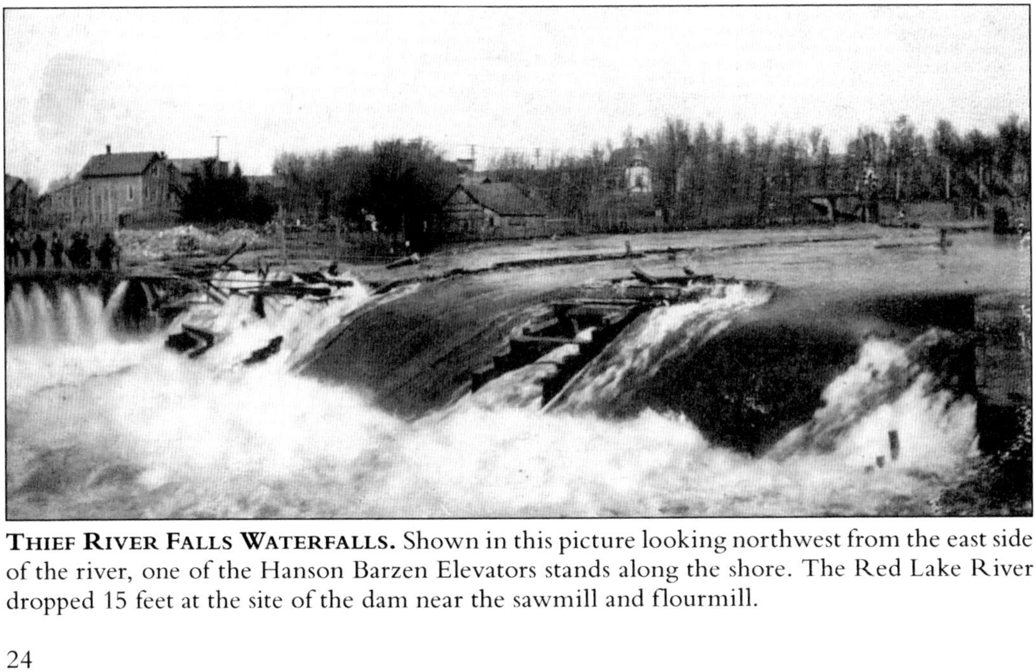

THIEF RIVER FALLS WATERFALLS. Shown in this picture looking northwest from the east side of the river, one of the Hanson Barzen Elevators stands along the shore. The Red Lake River dropped 15 feet at the site of the dam near the sawmill and flourmill.

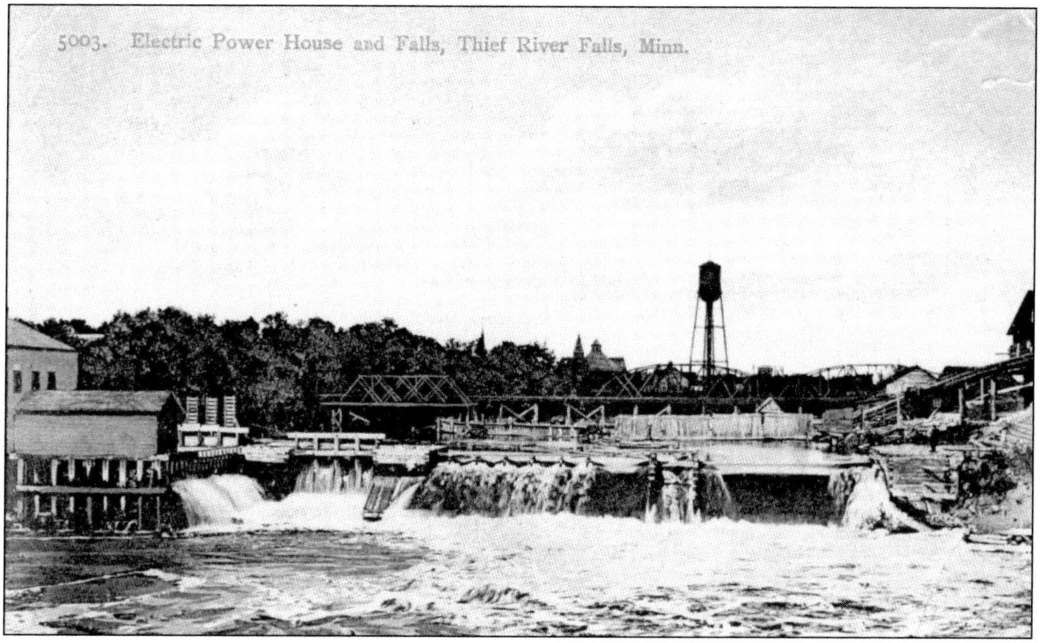

Thief River Falls Electric Powerhouse and Falls, Looking North. In this view looking north from below the dam, the blockhouse for the power plant is shown on the left. The Great Northern Bridge and the First Street Bridge spanned the river beneath the city water tower.

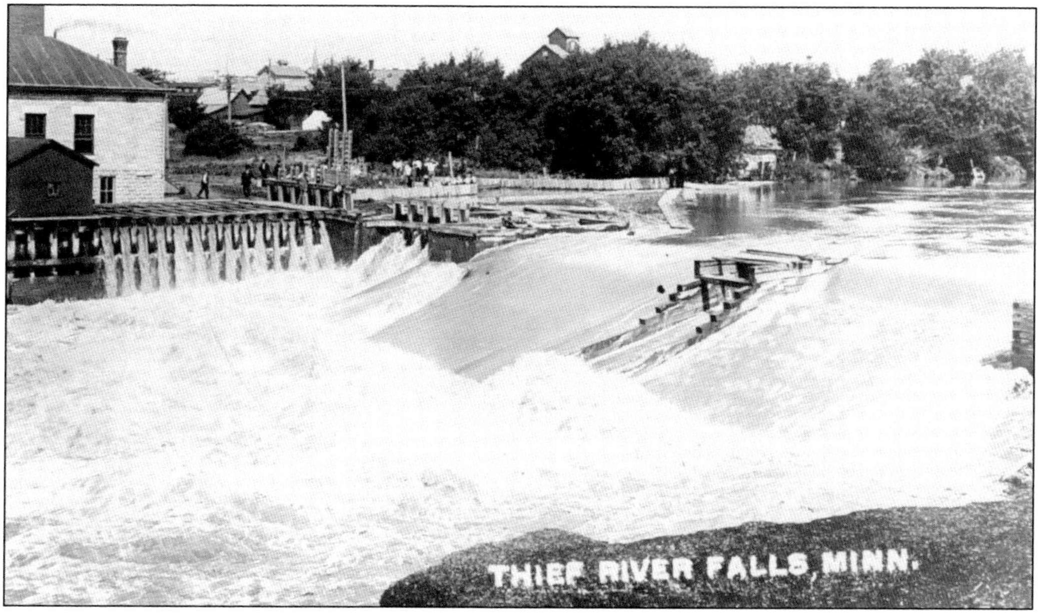

Thief River Falls Electric Powerhouse and Falls, Looking Northwest. The picture looking northwest from the east side of the river shows a slightly different view of the dam and the grain elevators.

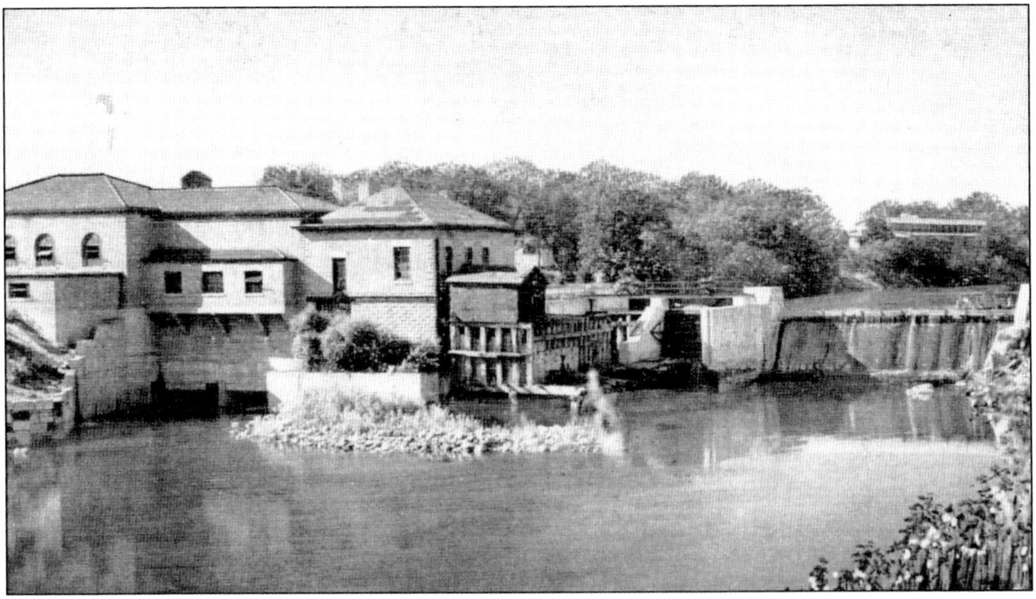

Thief River Falls Powerhouse and Dam. In this view looking northwest from the east, the stone and brick powerhouse were on the west side of the Red Lake River. Part of the stone structure still stands today.

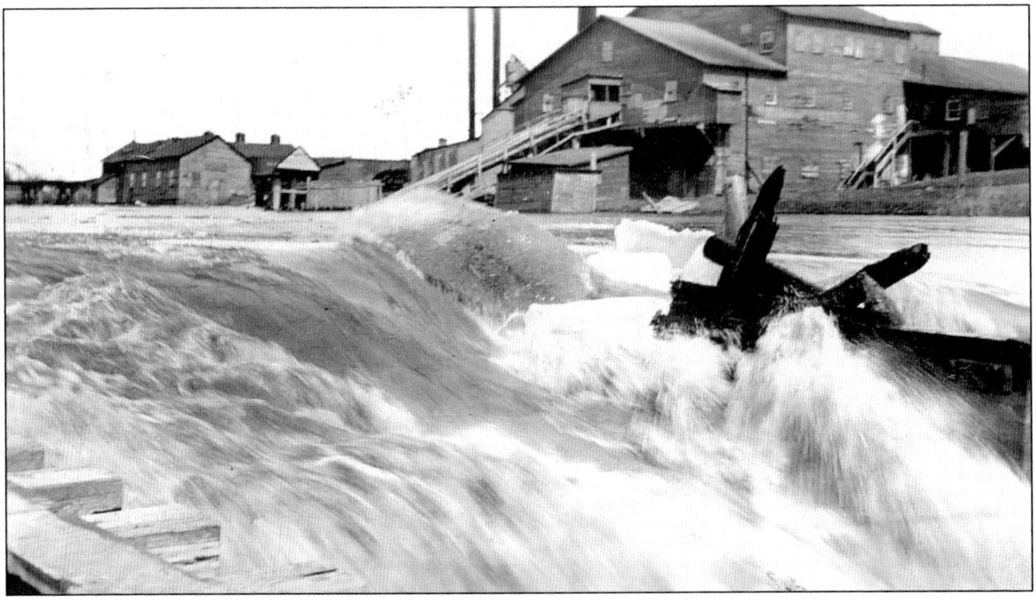

Thief River Falls Spring Breakup on the Red Lake River. In this picture looking northeast, the sawmill is seen across the river. The trees cut during the winter were stacked along the rivers and floated to the mills when the ice broke in the spring.

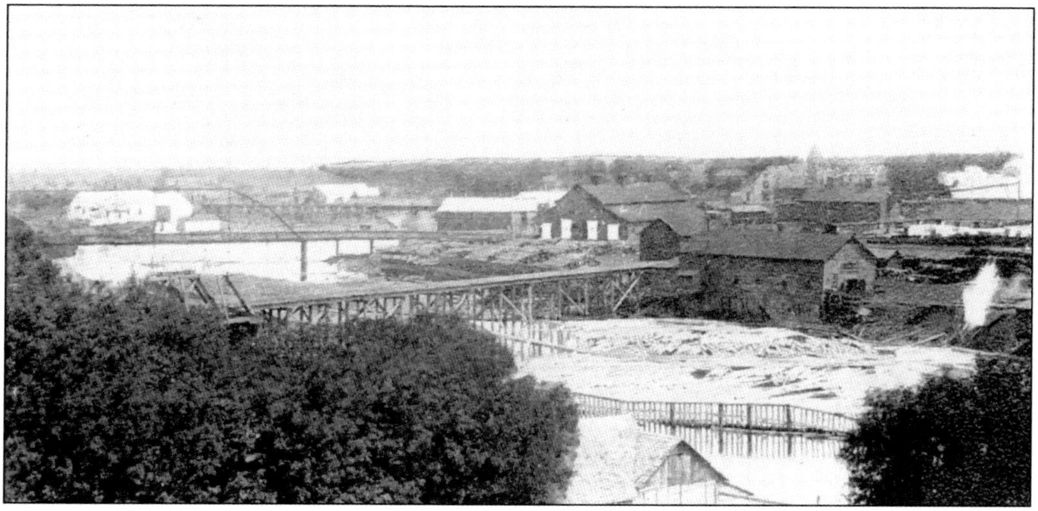

Thief River Falls Red Lake River. The branded logs floated to Thief River Falls, St. Hilaire, and Crookston, where the mills cut them into one-inch boards of varied lengths that were mostly one foot across and placed in huge piles to dry outside of the mills. After dried, the lumber was moved to the planning mill and loaded on boxcars for shipment.

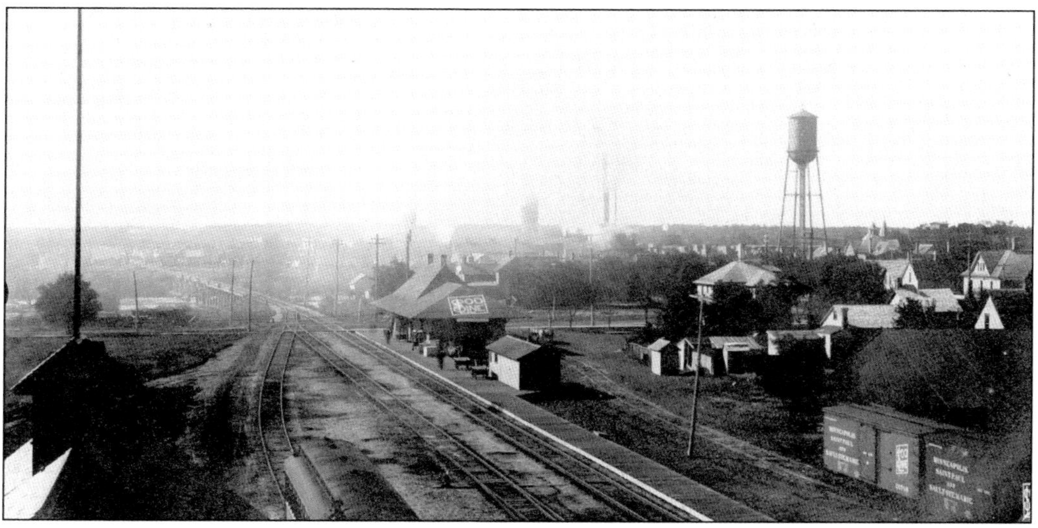

Thief River Falls First Soo Line Depot, Southwest View. In this view looking southwest, the wood combination building was on Third Street. The Minneapolis, St. Paul, and Sault Ste. Marie Railway came to Thief River Falls in 1904. The division headquarters was located in a residence on the corner of Atlantic Avenue and Third Street.

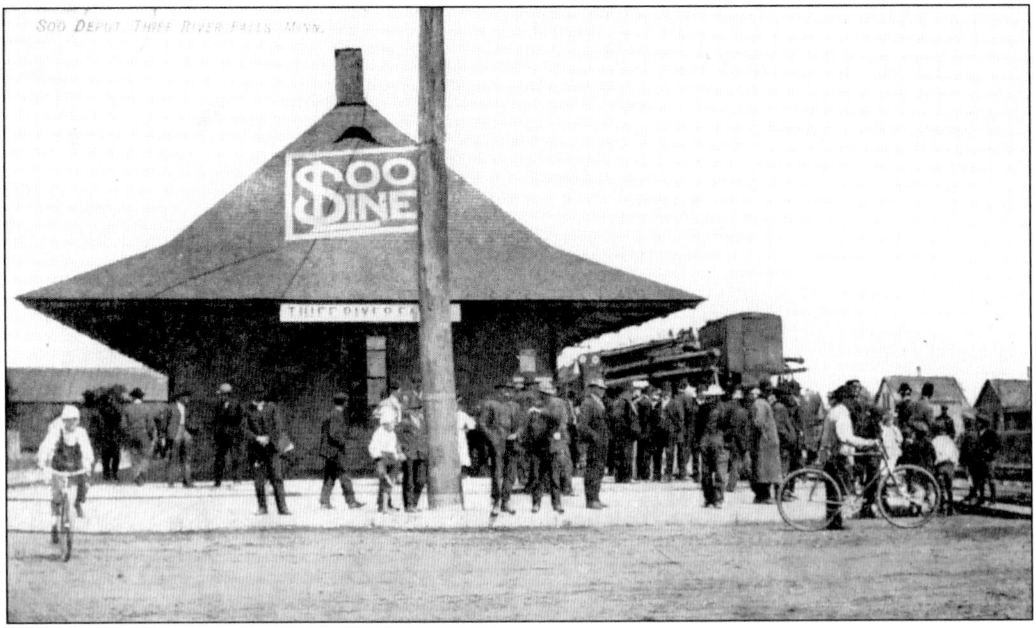

THIEF RIVER FALLS FIRST SOO LINE DEPOT, NORTH VIEW. This view looking north on Third Street shows the front of the depot. The depot served both freight and passengers. The building was moved north down the tracks and was finally razed in 1988.

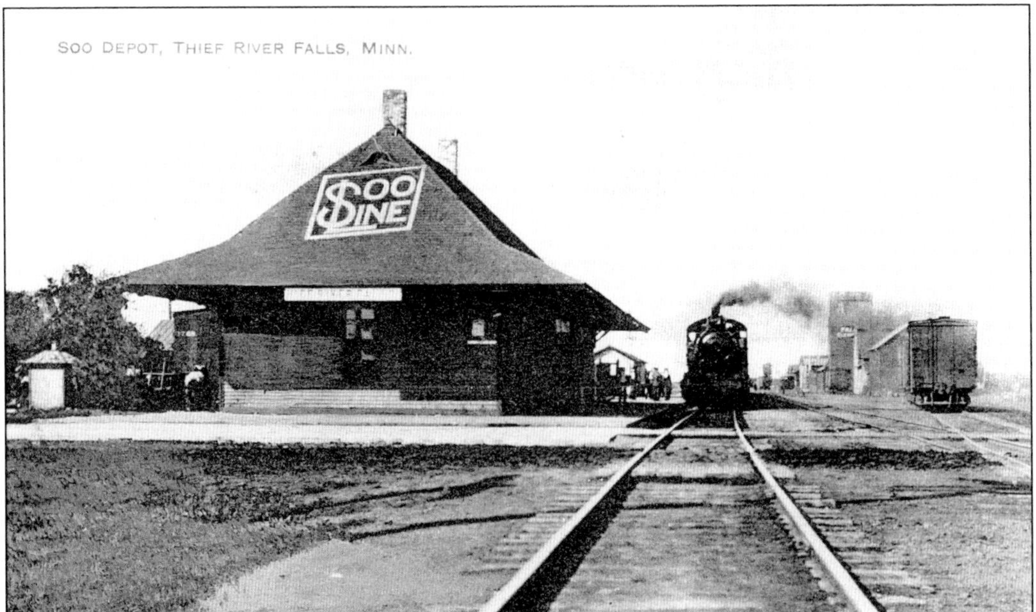

FIRST SOO LINE DEPOT. Looking north, this view shows the further growth in the area of the railroad tracks. In October 1912, the depot was moved north to Sixth Street and converted to a freight depot. The city was considered to be located in a strategic position to command the trade for hundreds of miles around it.

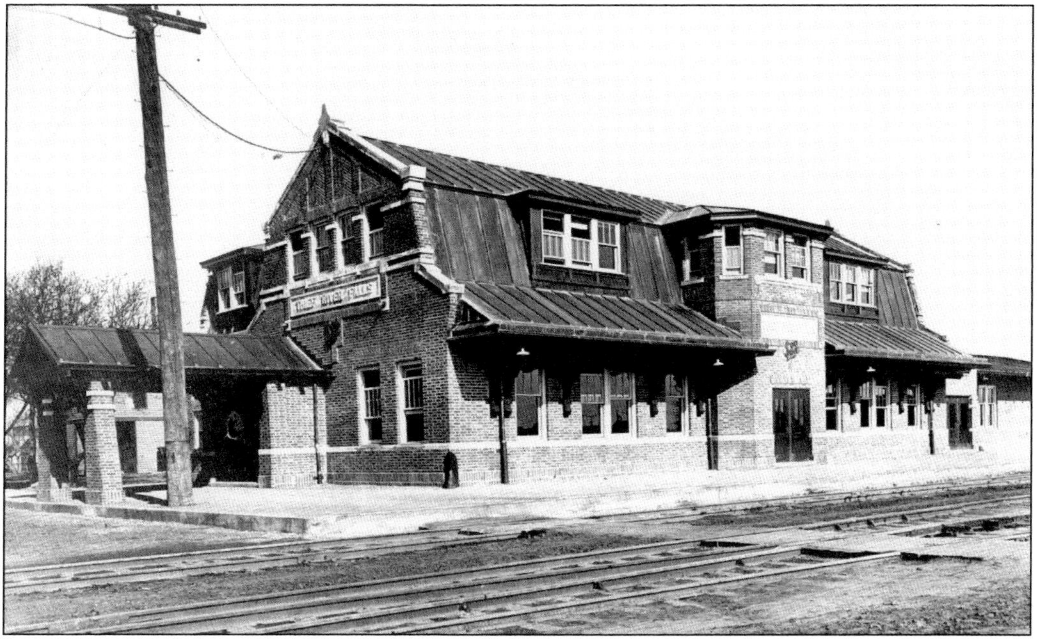

THIEF RIVER FALLS SECOND SOO LINE DEPOT, NORTHWEST VIEW. In this view looking northwest on Third Street, the house that served the first depot can be seen through the front overhang. Construction began for the new depot in 1913 and was completed in 1914. This depot housed the division offices, superintendent, train dispatchers, and other supervisory personnel.

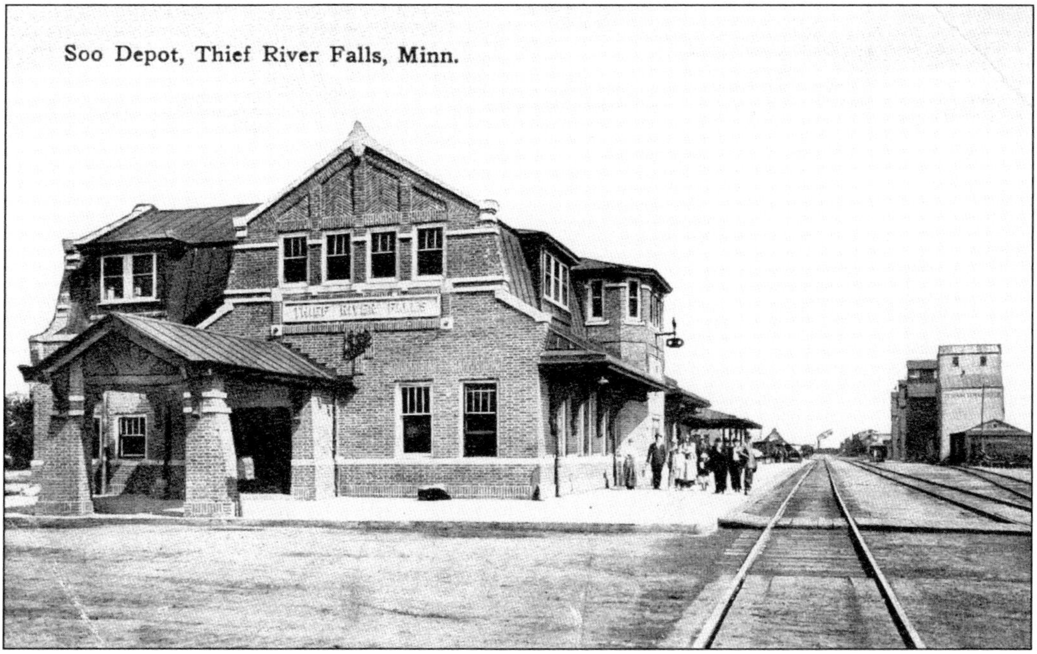

SECOND SOO LINE DEPOT. In this view looking northwest from Third Street, the first depot can be seen down the tracks to the north. A distant train is also approaching the depot. Grain elevators were built along the railroad tracks. This postcard is postmarked 1919.

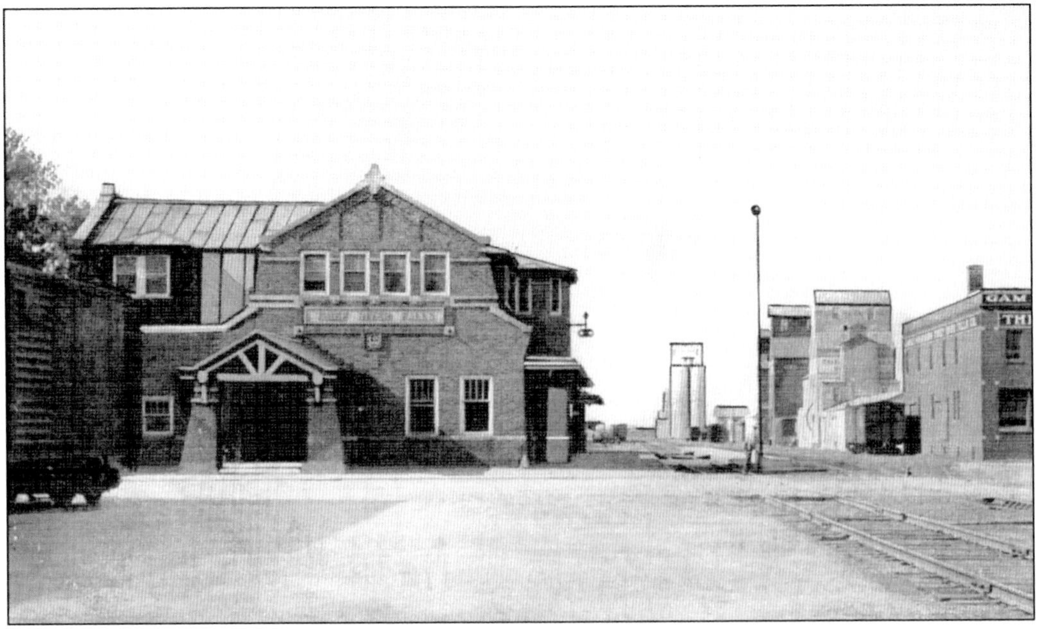

THIEF RIVER FALLS SECOND SOO LINE DEPOT AND GAMBLE-ROBINSON COMPANY. A freight car stands on the far left across Third Street, and the Gamble-Robinson Company is on the far right. The depot was a unique structure and was the largest depot on the Soo Line west of Minneapolis. At one time, 17 trains passed through the city each day.

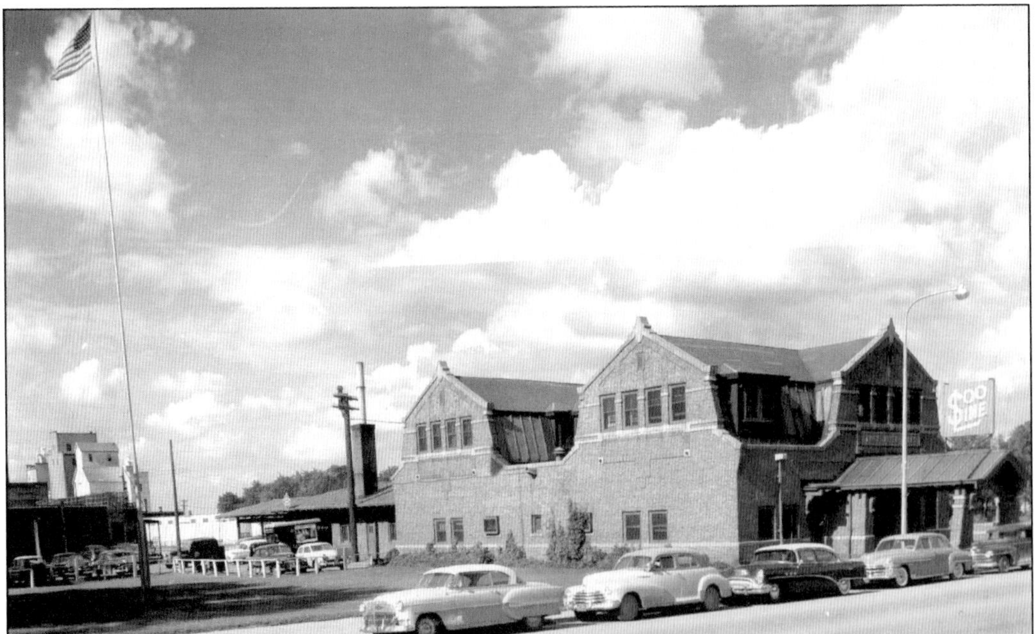

THIEF RIVER FALLS SECOND SOO LINE DEPOT, 1950S. In this view looking northeast, the depot is seen as it was in the 1950s. The last passenger train left the depot in 1967. The depot was abandoned in 1987 and scheduled for demolition in 1993, and the Save the Depot campaign began in 1994. City possession and addition to the National Register of Historic Places both occurred in 1995. The depot was reopened in 1998 as the Thief River Falls City Offices.

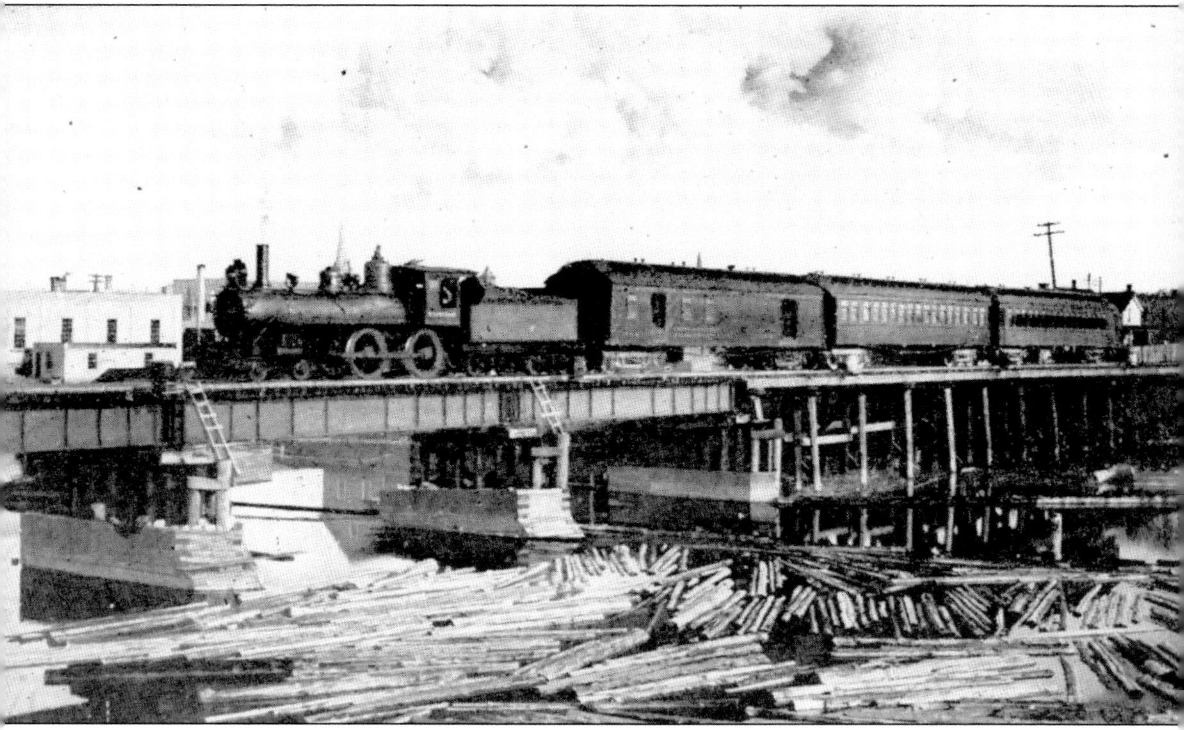

THIEF RIVER FALLS SOO LINE TRAIN NO. 162. In this view looking northeast, the Thief River Falls–Duluth train crosses the Red Lake River at 7:00 a.m. in the middle of the second decade of the 20th century. The city water tower is on the left, and the logs in the river are en route to sawmills down the river.

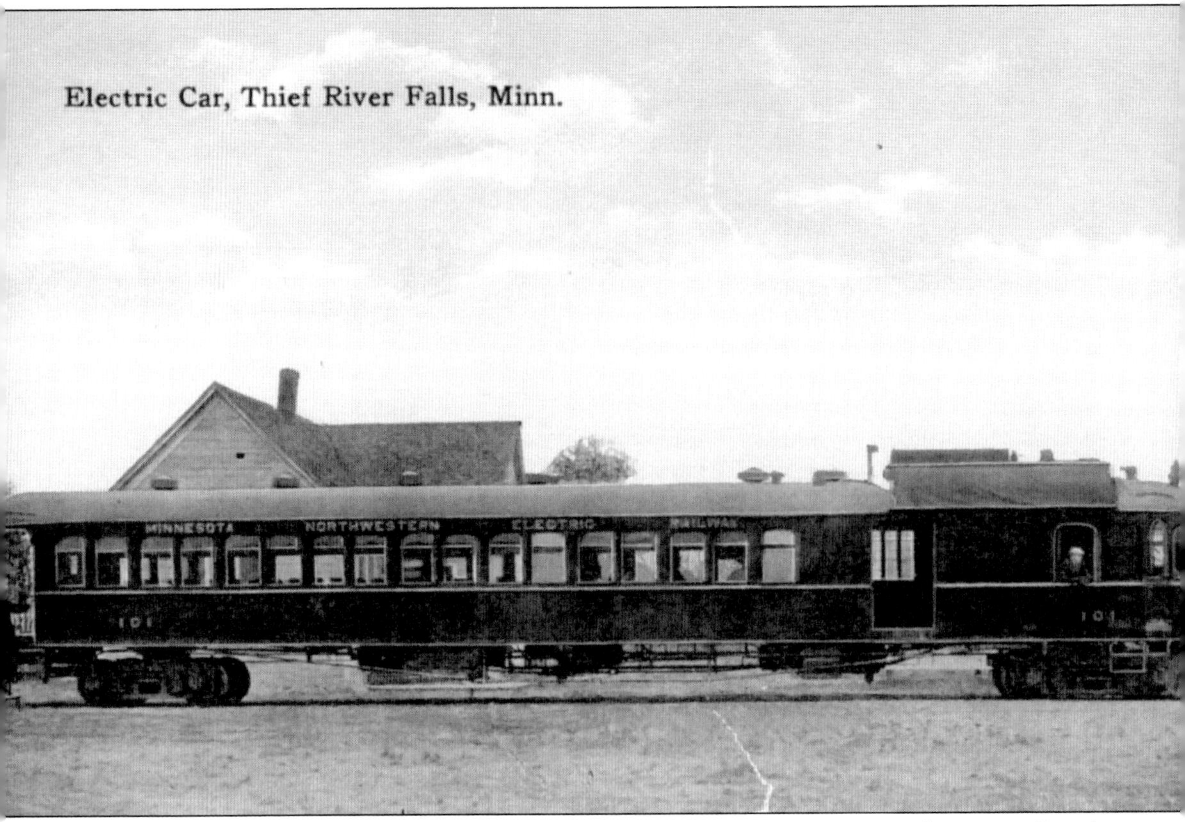

Goodridge and Thief River Falls. The Minnesota Northwestern Electric Railroad ran six trains daily between the towns from October 12, 1914, until March 15, 1940. The first conductor was Leon Babcock, and later Joe Zavoral served as conductor until the company went out of business. This card showing a car from the train is postmarked 1917.

Two

Thief River Falls, St. Hilaire, Goodridge, Hazel, and Mavie

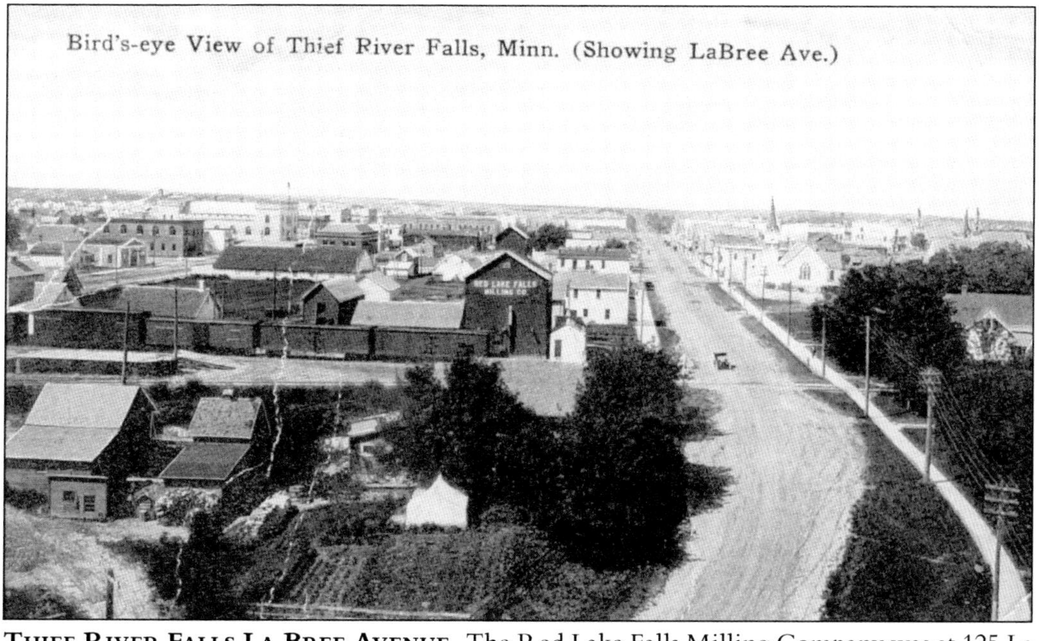

Thief River Falls La Bree Avenue. The Red Lake Falls Milling Company was at 125 La Bree Avenue South. The white spire on the right is the Hauge Synod of the Lutheran Church, located on the corner where the Northwest Medical Center is now. The first courthouse, library, first auditorium, and the Dobner-Meehan buildings are on the far left.

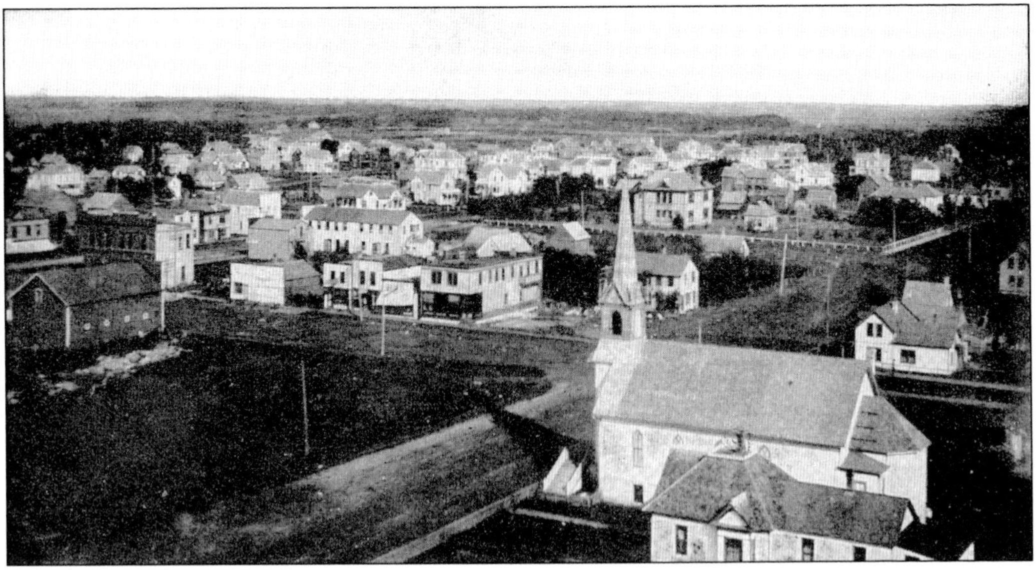

THIEF RIVER FALLS HORACE AVENUE. In this view looking northwest from Second Street, the Scandinavian Evangelical Church and parsonage are located at 214 and 218 Horace Avenue. The parsonage is currently being restored. Central School, on Fourth Street, can be seen on this card, postmarked 1908.

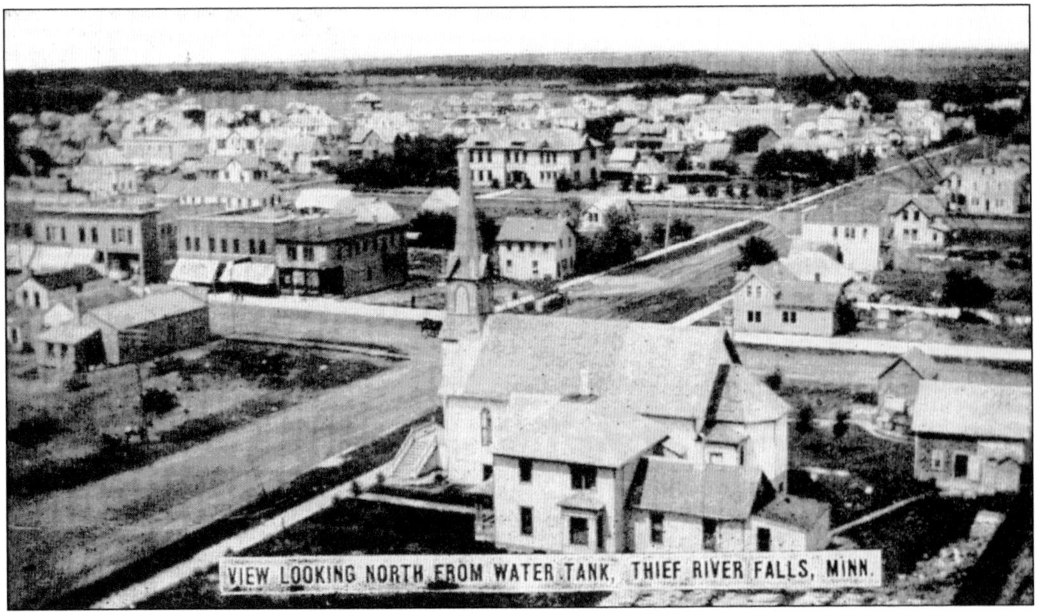

THE SCANDINAVIAN EVANGELICAL CHURCH. Looking northwest from the city water tower, this is a later view of the corner at Third Street. The Scandinavian Evangelical Church was built in 1893, sold to a private party in 1931, and later burned down.

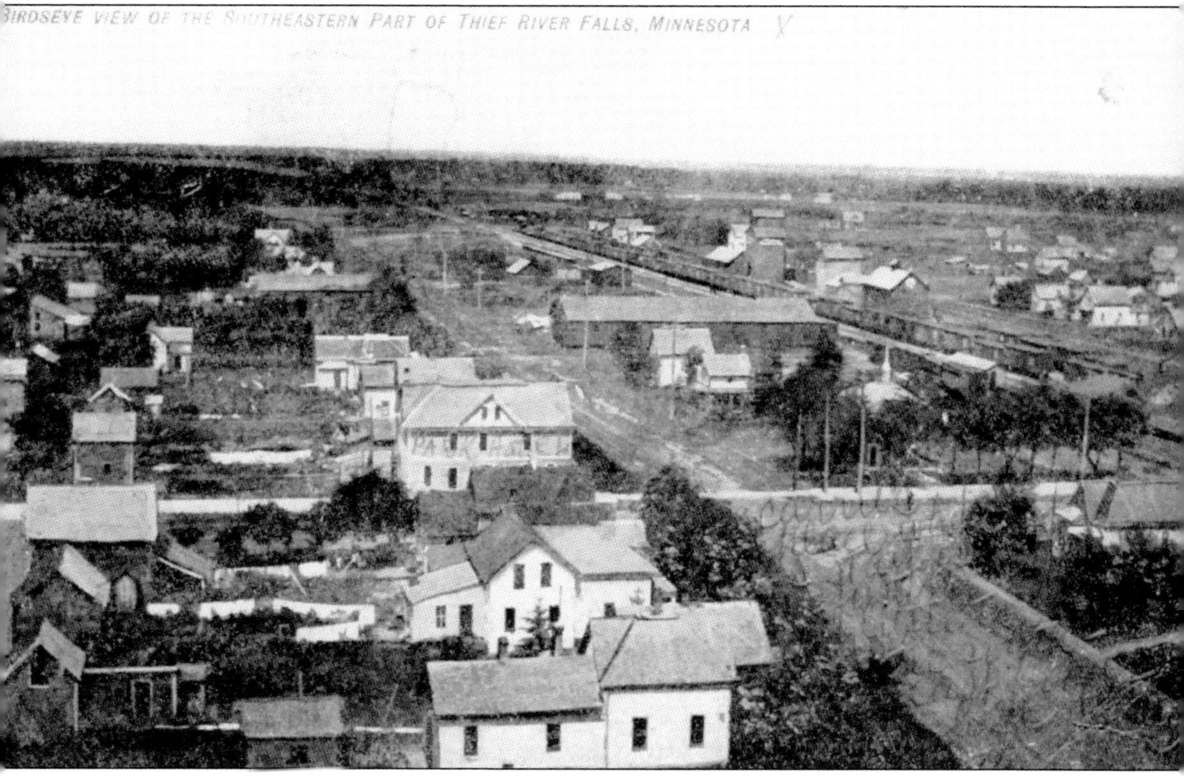

THIEF RIVER FALLS ATLANTIC AVENUE. In this picture looking northeast from the water tower, the Park Hotel (the center building) is at 301 Atlantic Avenue. The first Soo Line depot is on Third Street on the far right on this postcard postmarked 1908.

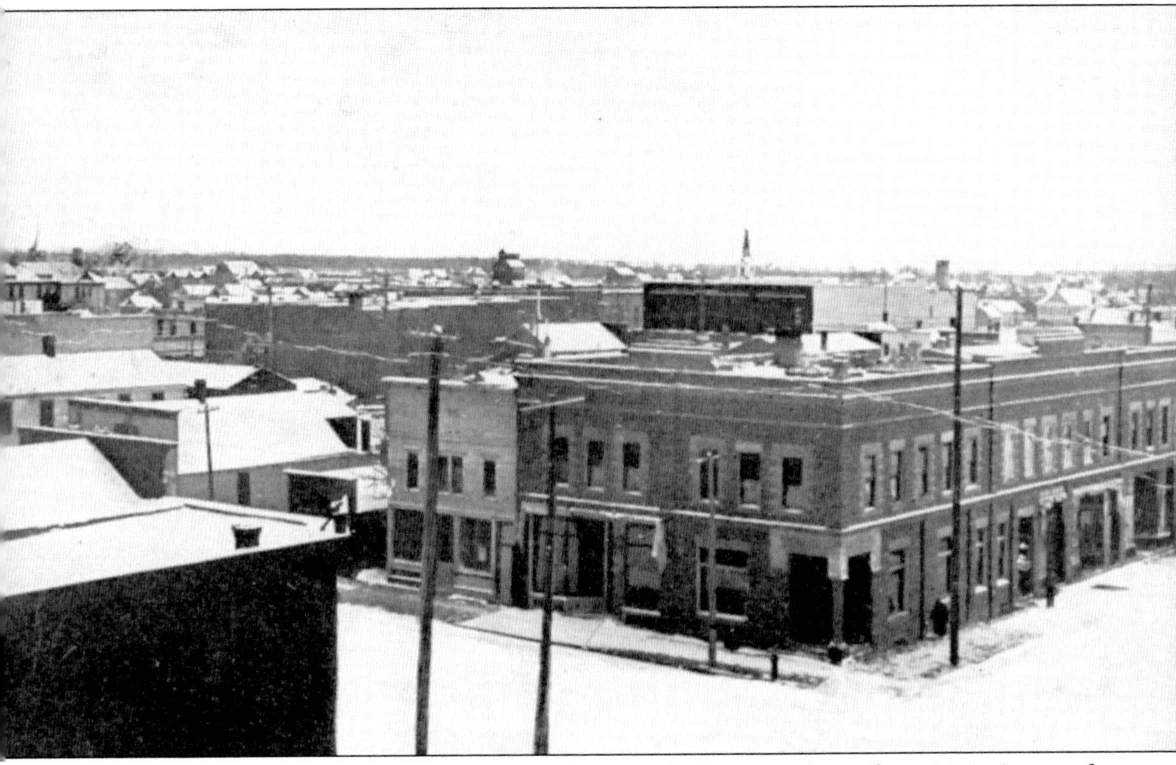

THIEF RIVER FALLS MAIN AVENUE. In this view looking northeast from Main Avenue from the top of the auditorium, the buildings on Second Street are covered in snow. The corner of the Dobner-Meehan Building is on the far right, and Central School is in the left background.

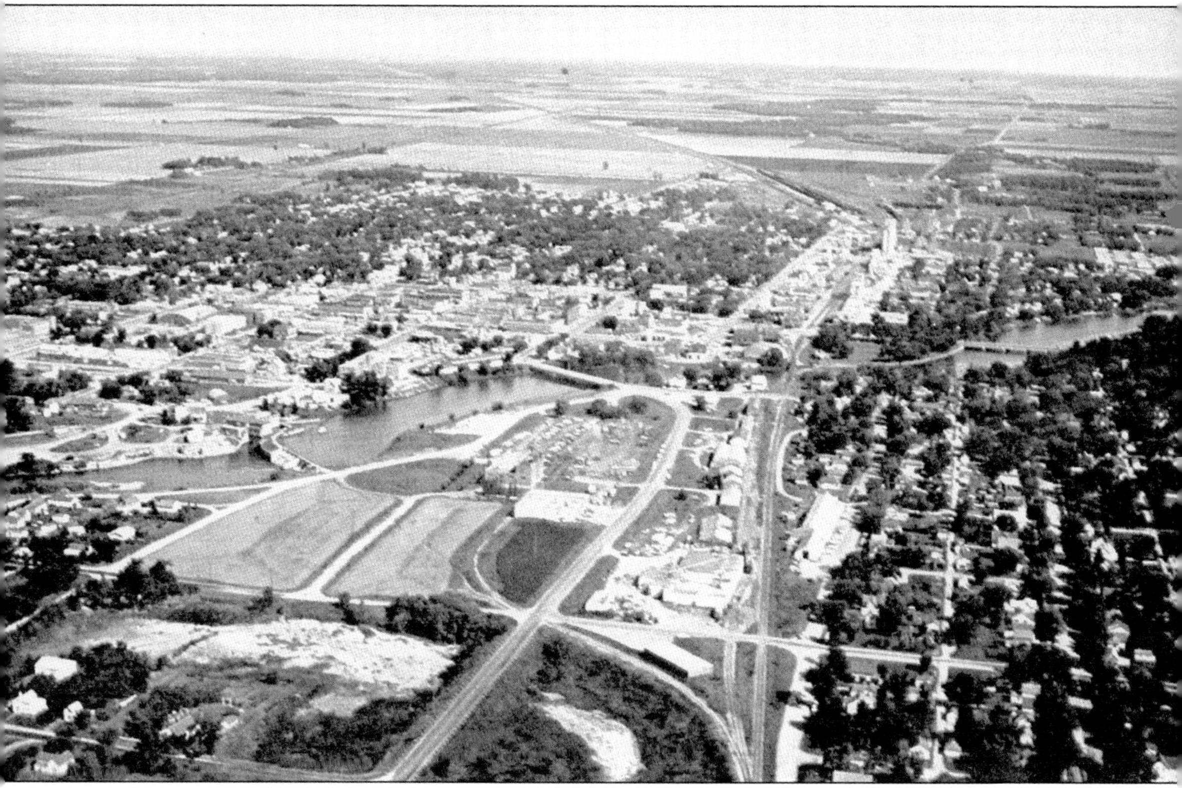

THIEF RIVER FALLS AERIAL VIEW, 1950. In this picture looking northwest, the railroad tracks and Pennington Avenue divide the view of the city in the fall of 1950. The large open area in the foreground is a field of grain.

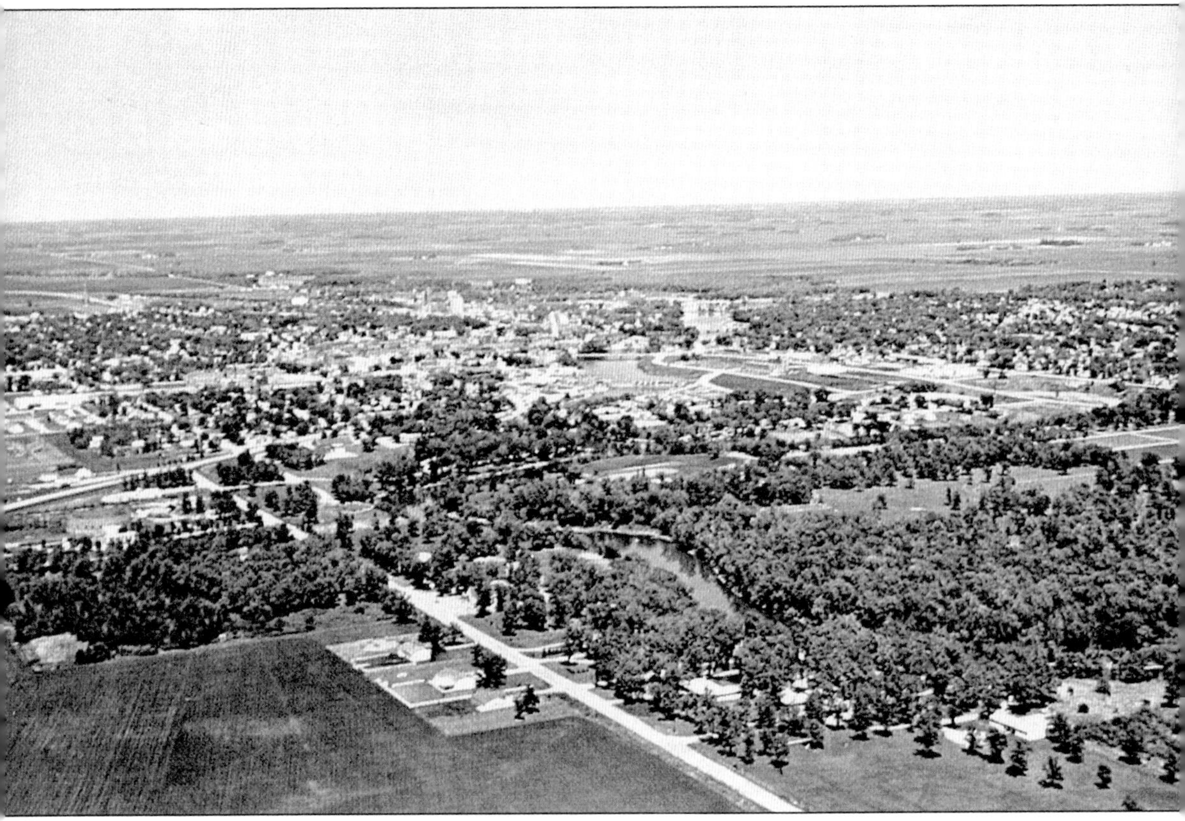

THIEF RIVER FALLS AERIAL VIEW, LOOKING NORTHEAST. Oakland Park Road runs along the west side of the Red Lake River in this view. The circular building on the left, below Highway 32, is the city sewage treatment plant which, when abandoned, became a part of the Peder Engelstad Pioneer Village.

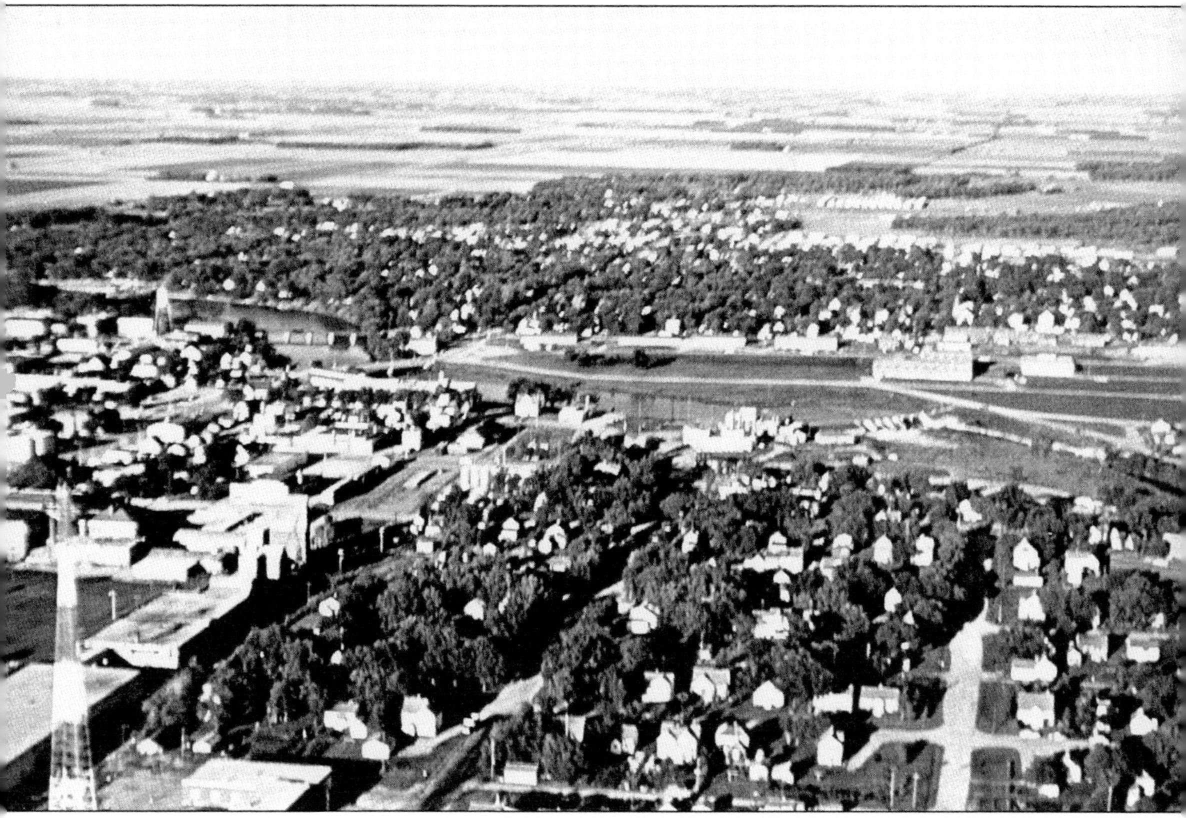

THIEF RIVER FALLS AERIAL VIEW. In this picture looking northeast from the State Highway Patrol Tower, the Hartz Warehouse complex crosses Arnold Avenue and is next to the Great Northern Railroad tracks. The football field, Lincoln High School, and Washington Elementary School are on the left. The Farmers Grain and Seed Elevator is on South Knight Avenue.

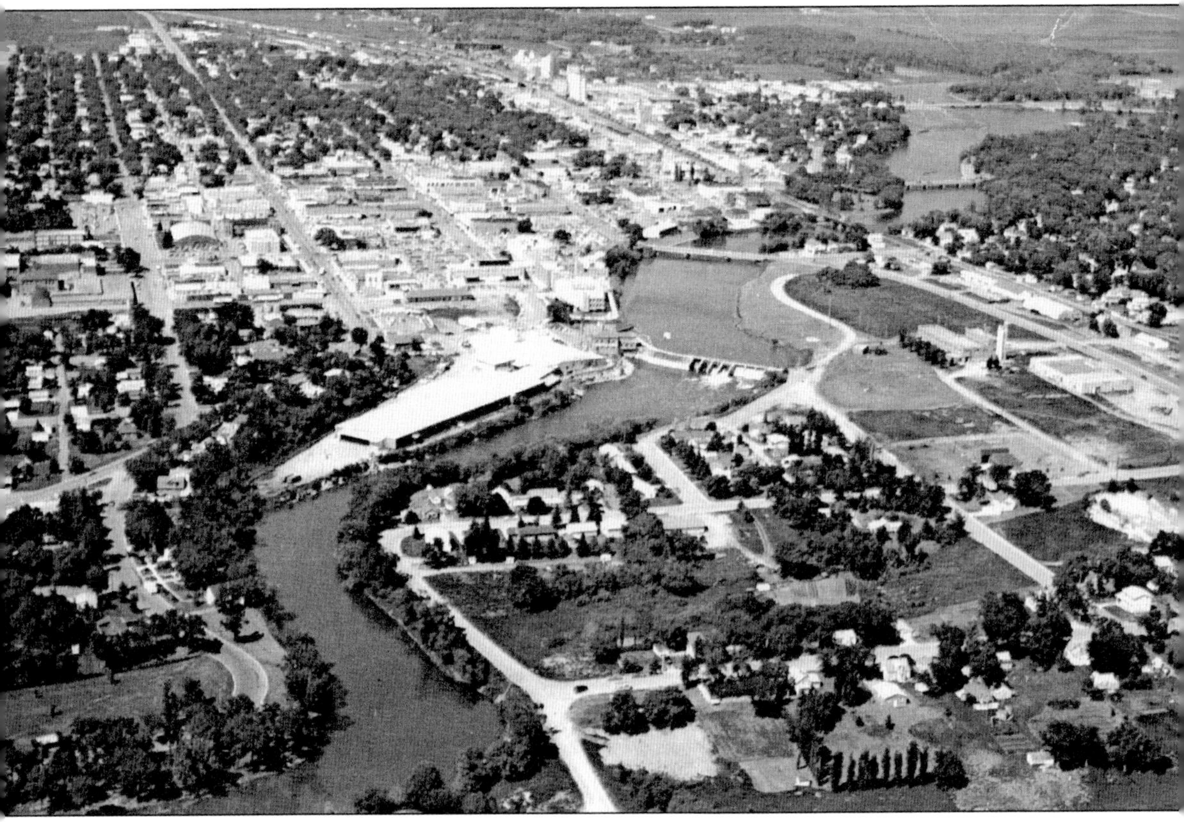

THIEF RIVER FALLS AERIAL VIEW SHOWING RED LAKE RIVER. In this north-northeast view, the dam and the First Street, Soo Line Railroad, Third, and Eighth Street Bridges cross over the Red Lake River. The large white-roofed building was the original site of the Arctic Cat (Polar) Manufacturing Plant located below the dam.

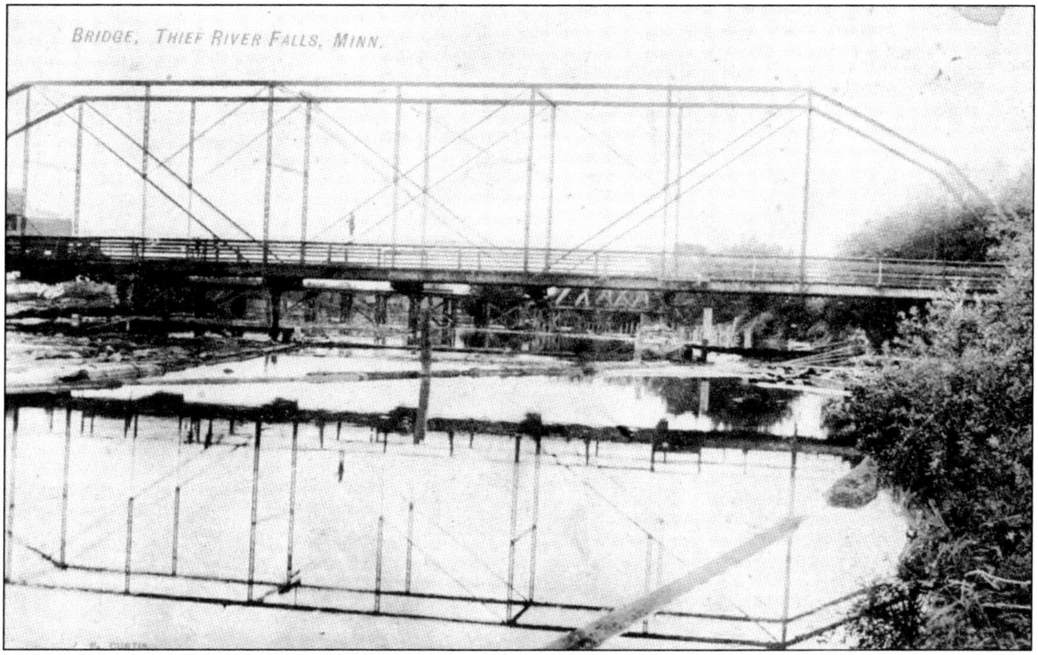

THIEF RIVER FALLS STEEL BRIDGE. In this view looking south, the first steel bridge crossed the Red Lake River and was built in 1891 on Bridge Street (First Street). The railroad bridge viewed in the background under the bridge was the Great Northern Bridge crossing to the lumber mill on the east side of the river.

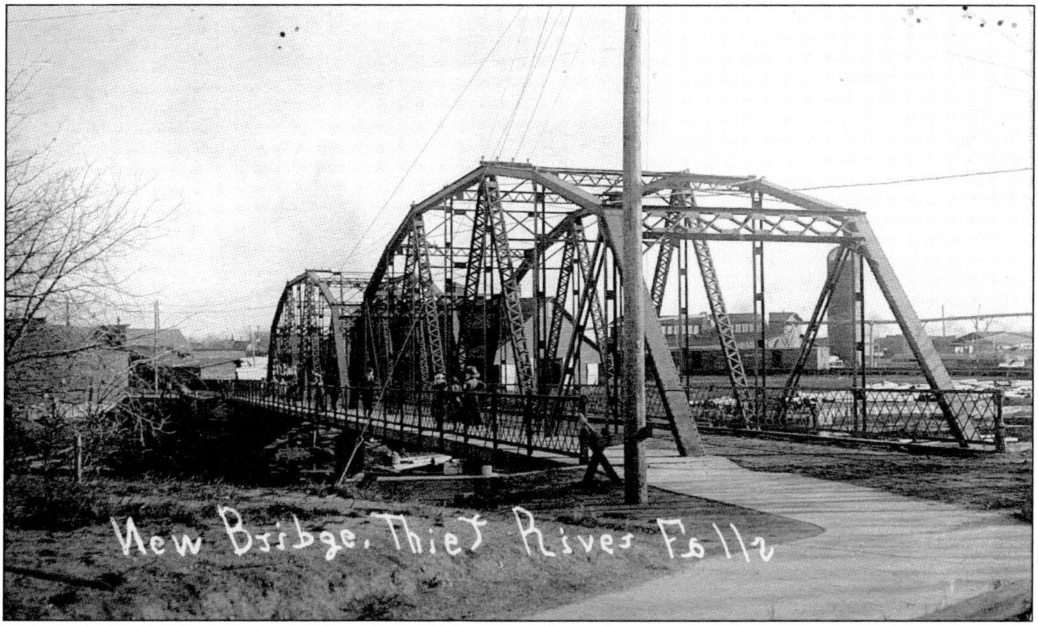

THIEF RIVER FALLS NEW STEEL BRIDGE, EAST VIEW. In this view looking east from the west side of the river, the new steel bridge crossed the river on Bridge Street. Construction began in 1907 and was completed in 1908. The lumber mill and livery are shown in the background. This card is postmarked 1912.

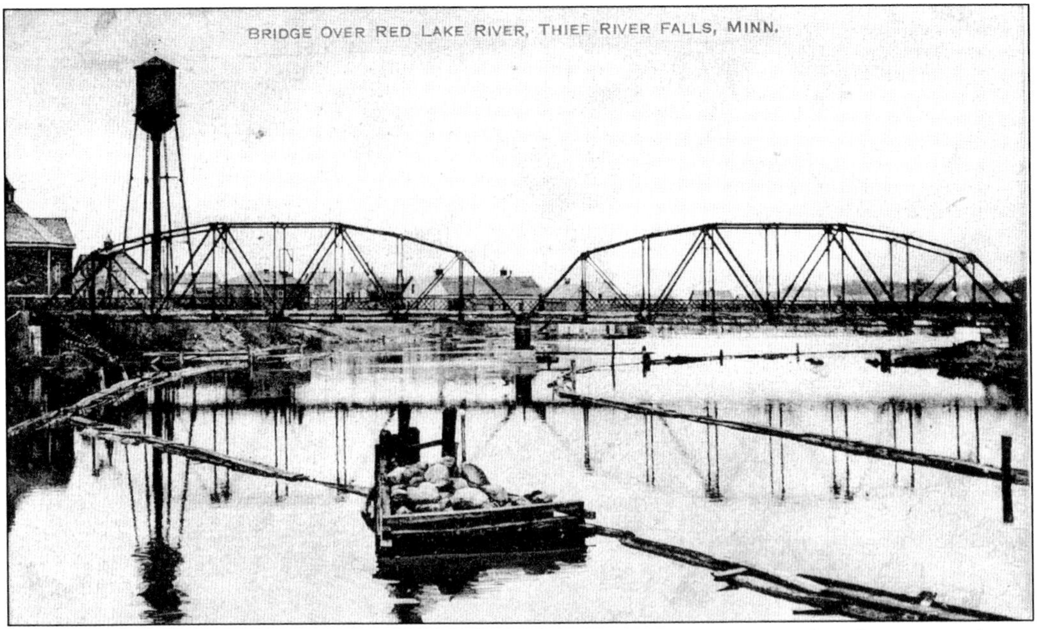

THIEF RIVER FALLS NEW STEEL BRIDGE, NORTH VIEW. Looking north, a later view shows the edge of the Presbyterian church and the city water tower on the east side of the river. This card is also postmarked 1912.

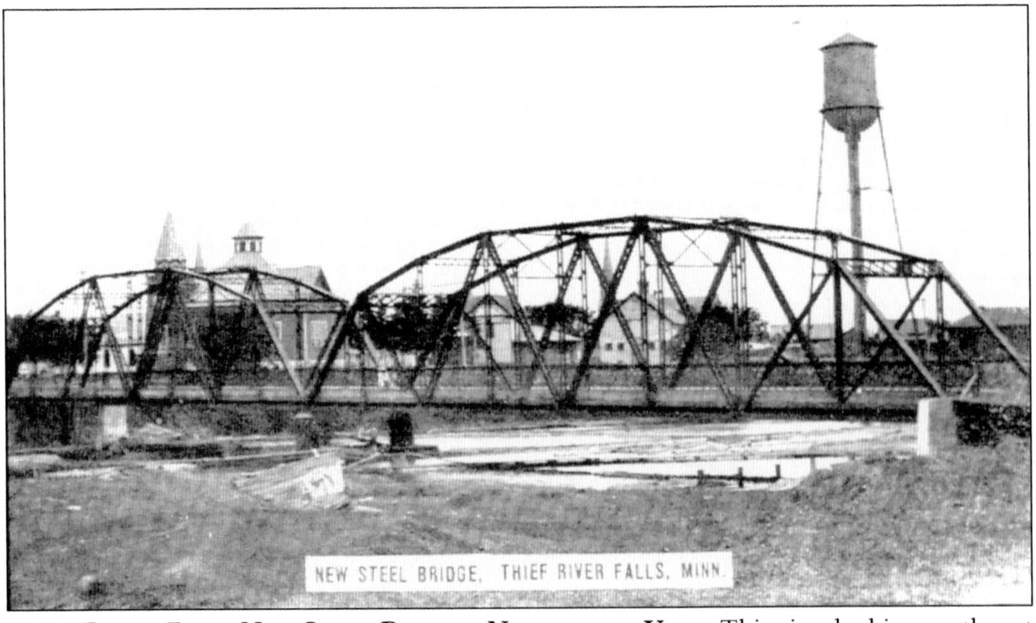

THIEF RIVER FALLS NEW STEEL BRIDGE, NORTHWEST VIEW. This view looking northwest from the east side of the river shows another later view of the bridge. The Presbyterian church, Scandinavian Evangelical church, and city water tower are across the river.

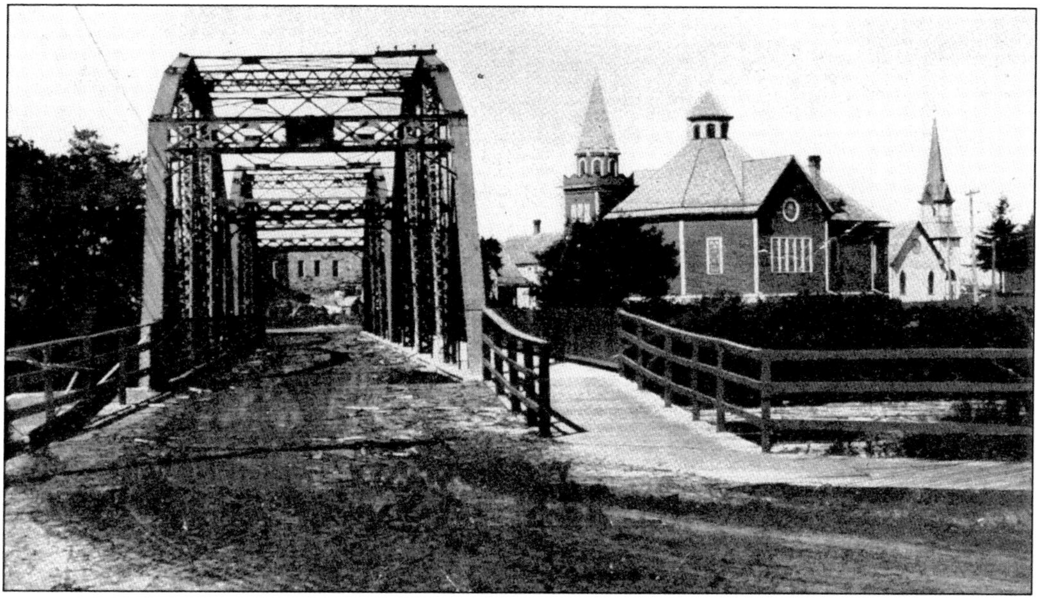

THIEF RIVER FALLS NEW STEEL BRIDGE, POSTMARKED 1913. Looking northwest, this view shows the Presbyterian church and Scandinavian Evangelical church.

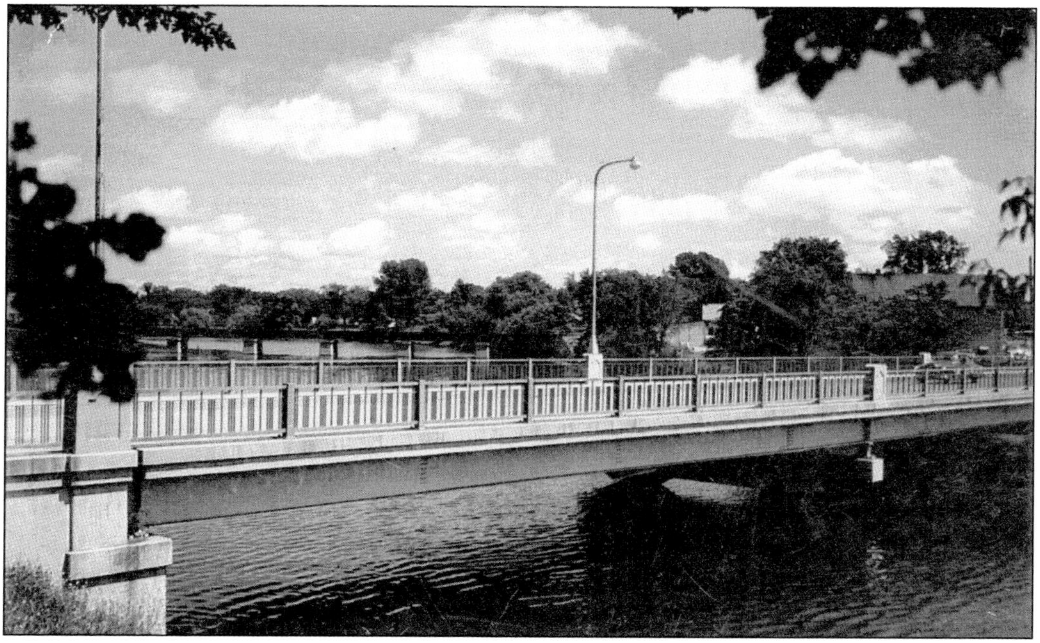

THIEF RIVER FALLS FIRST STREET BRIDGE. In this view looking northeast, the concrete and steel bridge across the Red Lake River at First Street is viewed from the west side of the river. The Soo Line Railroad Bridge is in the background.

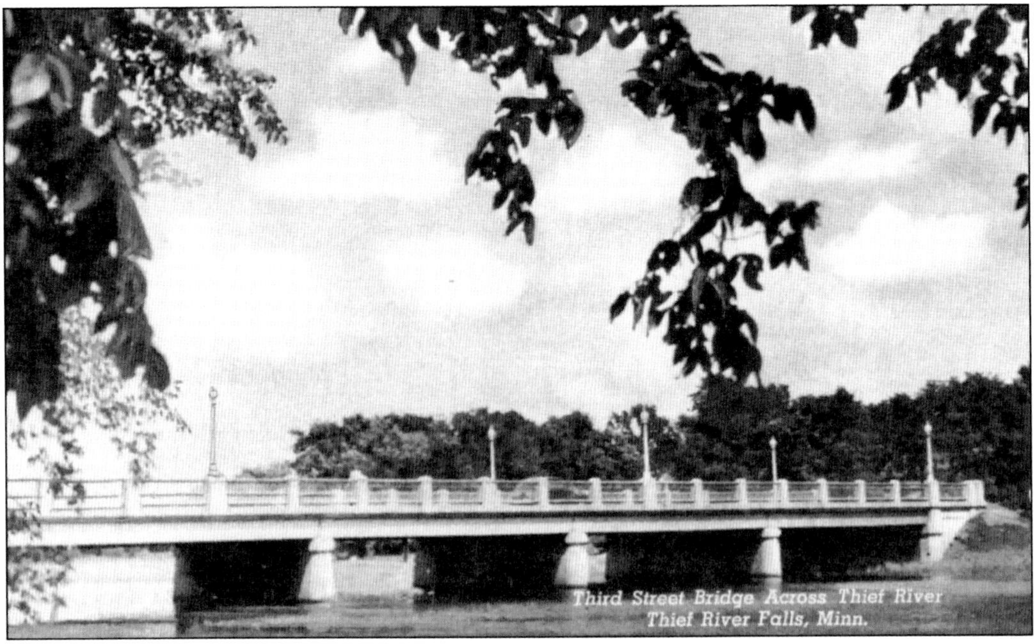

THIEF RIVER FALLS THIRD STREET BRIDGE. Looking northeast across the Red Lake River at Third Street in the 1950s, this view of the bridge was originally labeled such that the bridge was over the Thief River, which is a frequent error in identification.

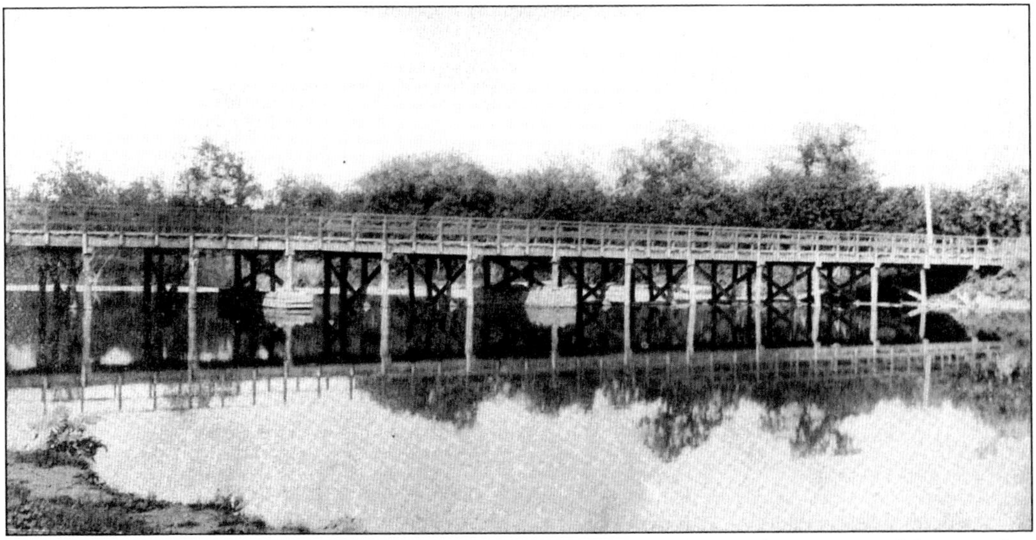

THIEF RIVER FALLS EIGHTH STREET BRIDGE. Looking northeast, this view is of the wooden bridge across the Thief River at Eighth Street in the early 1900s.

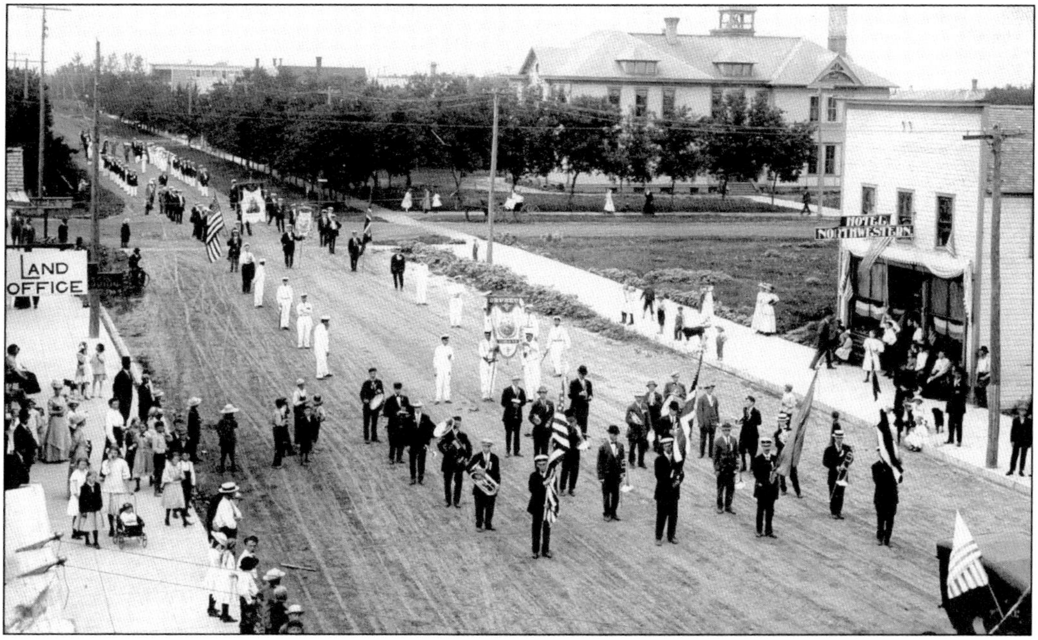

Thief River Falls La Bree Avenue, Northeast View. From Third Street, in a view looking northeast, a parade stretches past Fourth Street. The Hotel Northwestern was at 316 La Bree Avenue North and is seen on the right. Central School, also on the right, stood at 209 Fourth Street East in the early 1900s.

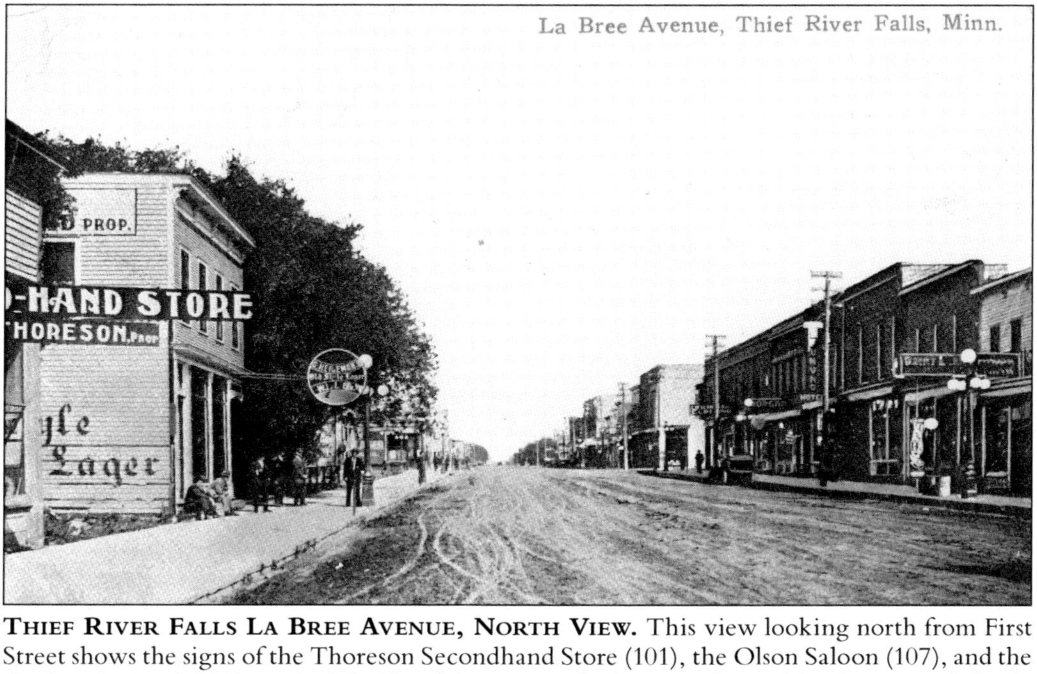

Thief River Falls La Bree Avenue, North View. This view looking north from First Street shows the signs of the Thoreson Secondhand Store (101), the Olson Saloon (107), and the Ogahmah Hotel (109) on the left side of the street. The Brumund Hotel (116), Morgan's (118), and Lieberman's (120) are on the right.

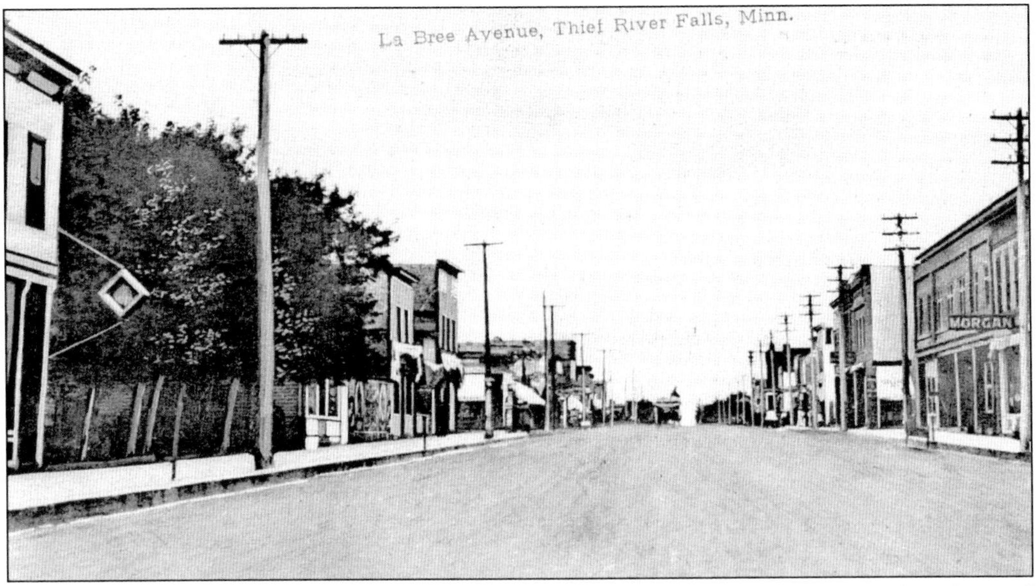

LA BREE AVENUE, C. 1910. In this view looking north from First Street, the Ogahmah Hotel (109) is behind the trees on the left, and Morgans (118) and the Odd Fellows building (202) are on the right.

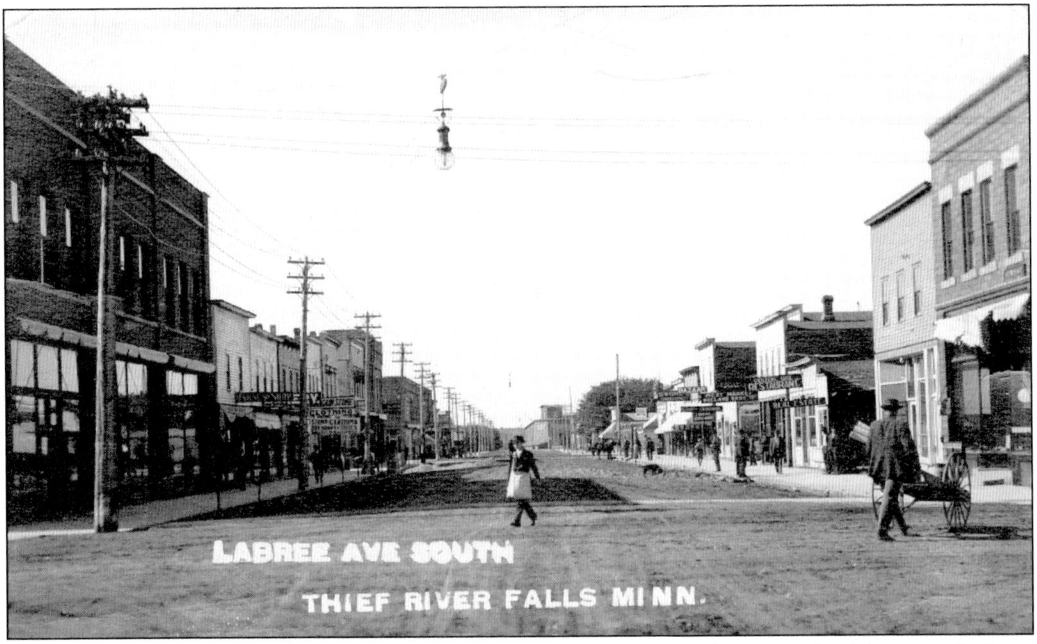

THIEF RIVER FALLS LA BREE AVENUE, SOUTH VIEW. In this view looking south from Third Street, the Oen Mercantile (224), Froseth Harness (218), Roth Bakery (216), and Giller Clothing (214) are on the left. Across the street are the McGinn Hardware (223), the Papberg Lunch Room and Roark Saloon (221), Stockholm Saloon (219), Johnson Restaurant (217), Porter's Saloon (215), the City Meat Market (213), Ellingson Restaurant (211), Mulry's Bazaar (209), and Swore's Confectionery (207).

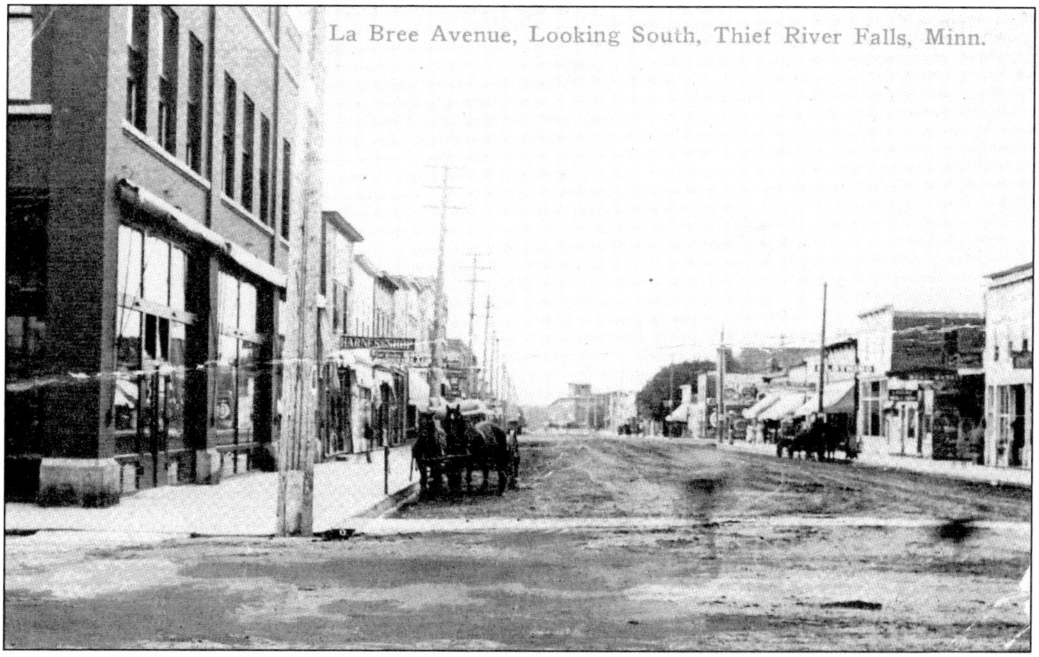

THIEF RIVER FALLS LA BREE AVENUE, POSTMARKED 1912. In this view looking south from Third Street, the dirt street in the rain leads all the way to the Hanson Barzen Elevator at the foot of the avenue.

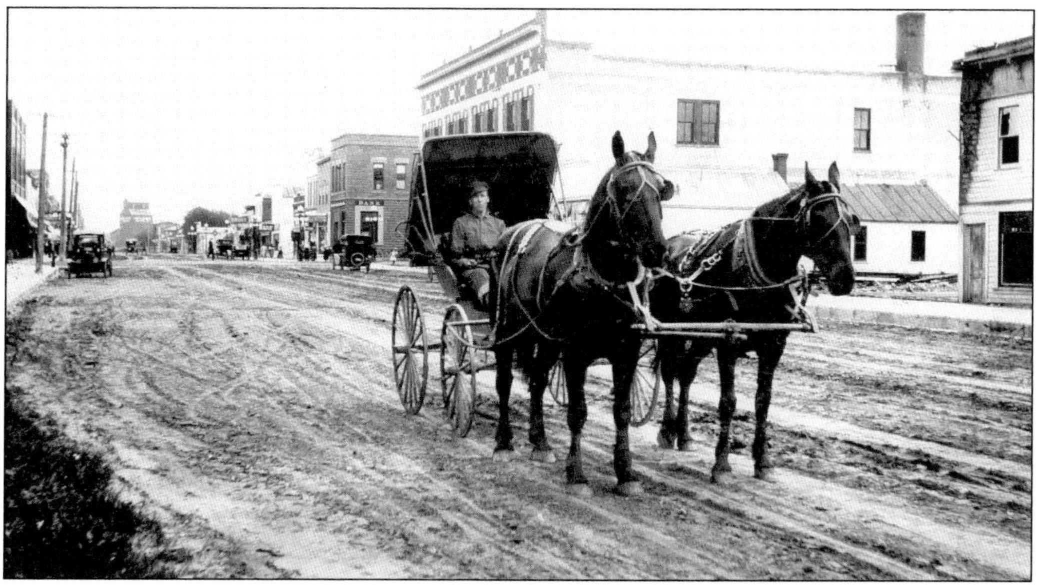

THIEF RIVER FALLS LA BREE AVENUE, EDWIN HANSON. In this view looking south from Fourth Street, Edwin Hanson is driving the buggy. The building on the right is at the northwest corner of Third Street and is currently the Elks building. The bank across the street is currently where Lori's Hallmark is located. Edwin and his wife, Valborg (née Engelstad), had five children.

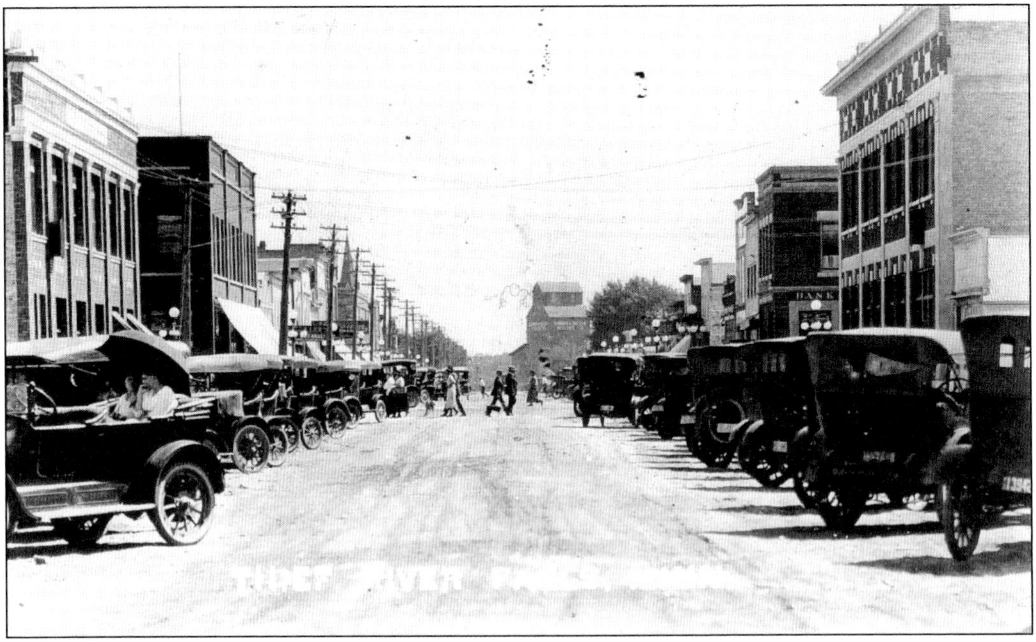

THIEF RIVER FALLS LA BREE AVENUE, *C.* 1910. In this view looking south from the corner of Third Street, the street is busy with the commerce of the day in the second decade of the 20th century. The elevator at the far right is the Hanson Barzen Milling Company.

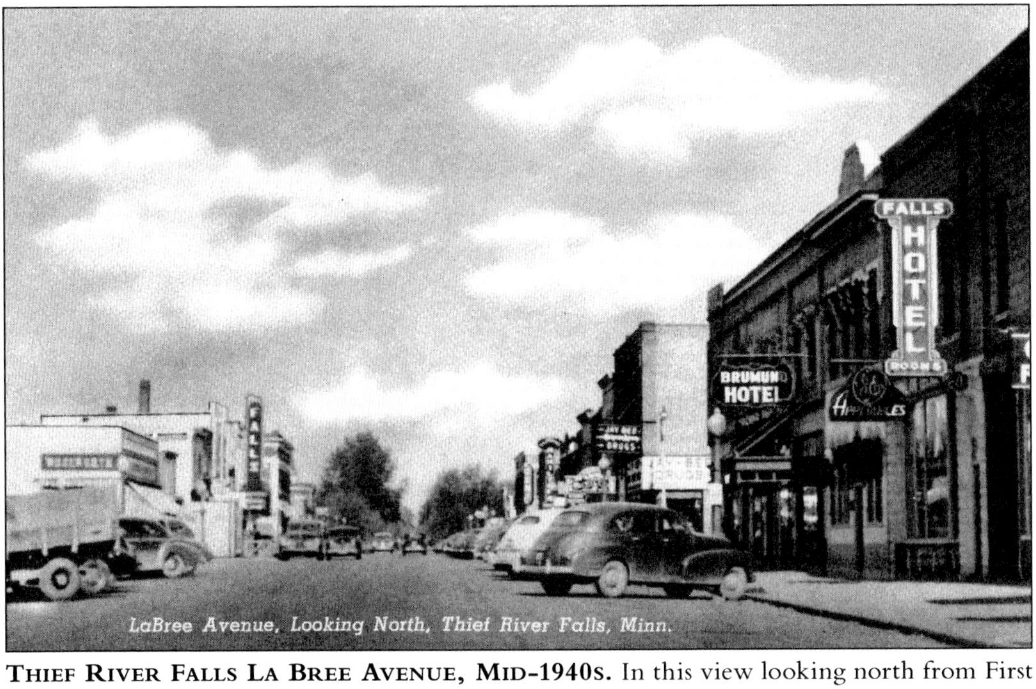

THIEF RIVER FALLS LA BREE AVENUE, MID-1940S. In this view looking north from First Street, Woolworth's (221) and the Falls Theatre (213–215) are on the left. The Falls Hotel (114), Brumund Hotel (118), Jay Bee Drugs (202), Hamilton's Clothing (216), and Oens Mercantile (224) are on the right in the mid-1940s.

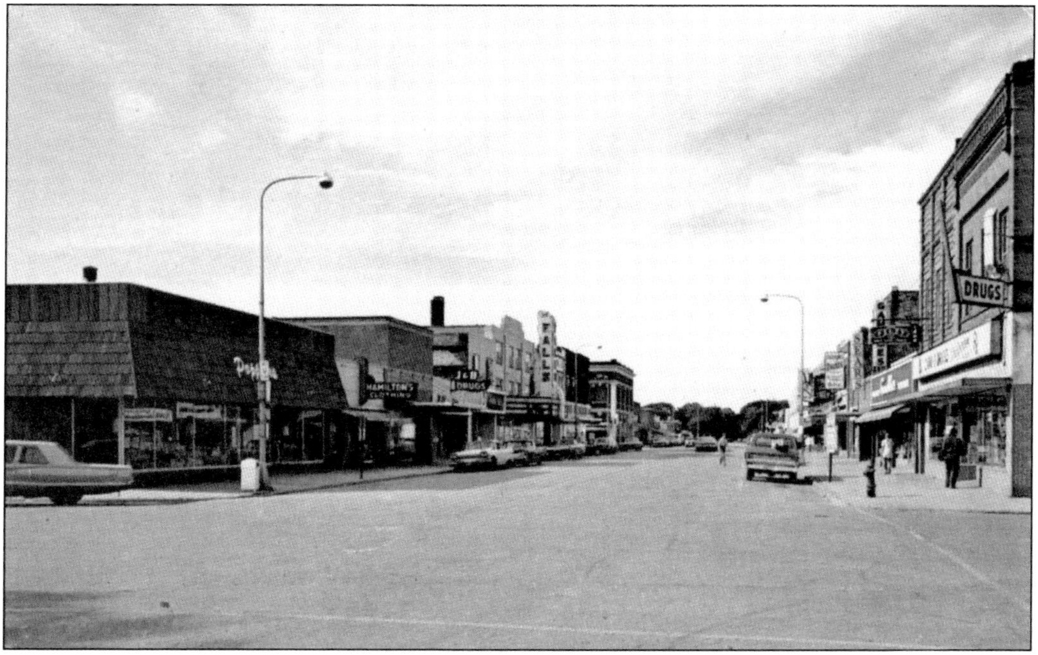

THIEF RIVER FALLS LA BREE AVENUE, MID-1970S. In this view looking north from Second Street in the mid-1970s, Popplers (201), Hamiltons Clothing (205), Bjorkman's (207), J&B Drug Store (209), the Falls Theatre (213), and the Ben Franklin (219) are on the left. The Corner Drug (202), the Odd Fellows Hall (202½), Gamble's (208), Sears (210), Parkin's Drug (212), and the Rex Café (218) are on the right.

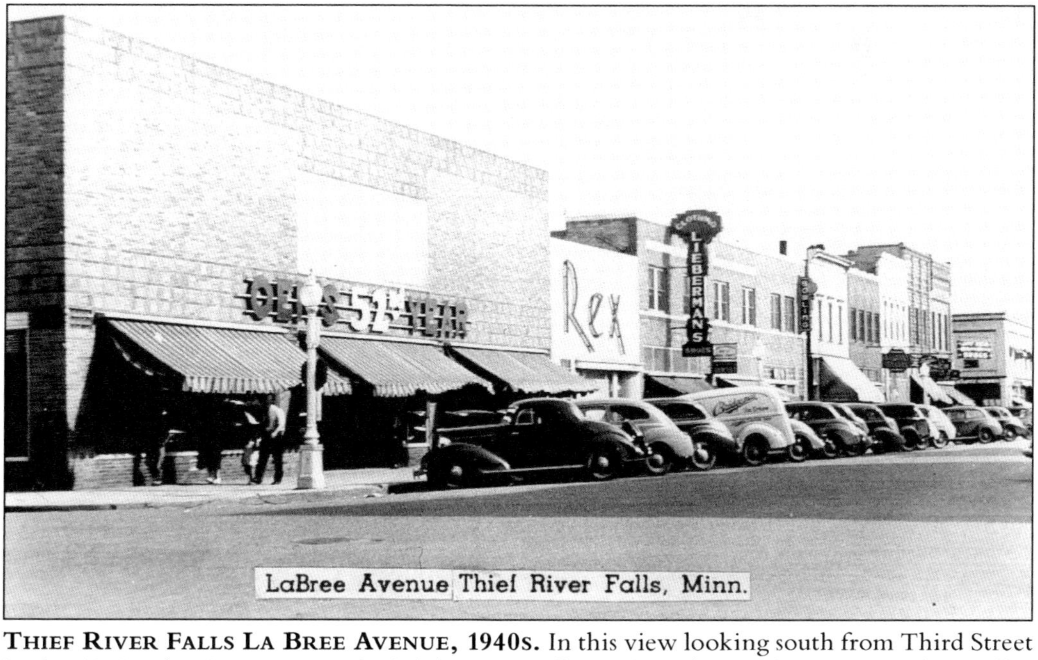

THIEF RIVER FALLS LA BREE AVENUE, 1940S. In this view looking south from Third Street in the 1940s, the Oen Mercantile (224), Rex Café (218), Lieberman's (216), Bowling Alley (212½), The Mint (212), and Jay Bee Drug (202) line the east side of the street.

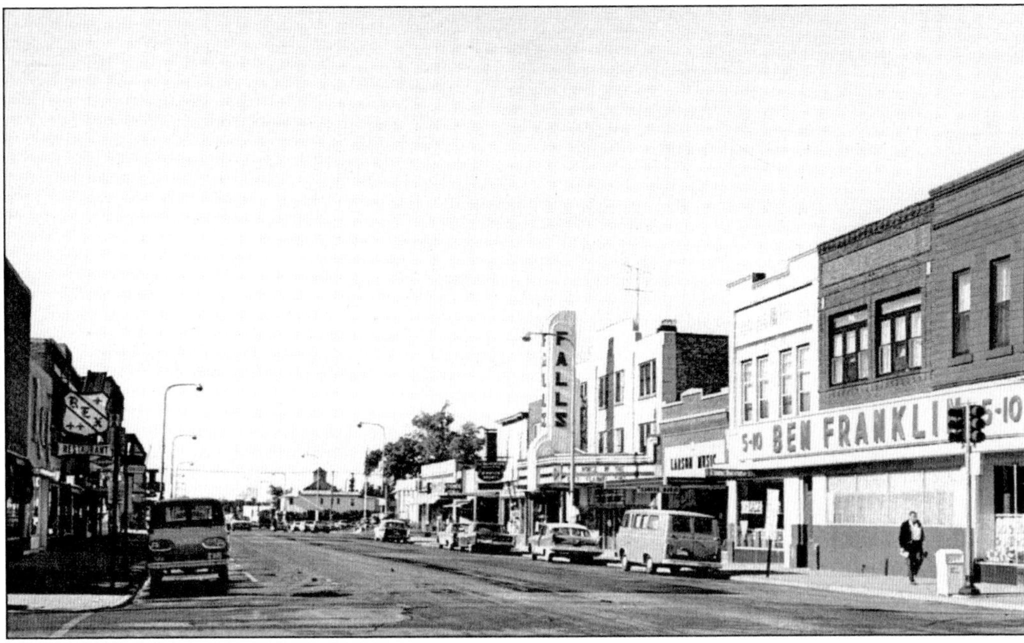

THIEF RIVER FALLS LA BREE AVENUE, 1960S. In this view looking south from Third Street, Ben Franklin (219), Larson Music (217), and Falls Theatre (213) are on the on right in the 1960s.

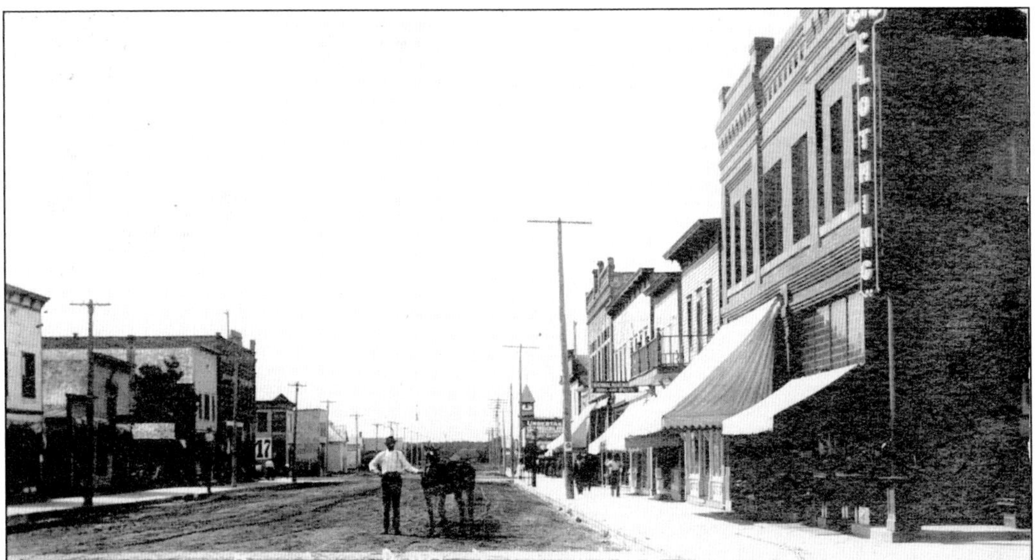

THIEF RIVER FALLS MAIN AVENUE. In this view looking south from Third Street in the early 1900s, E&E Clothing Company (223), Voss and Vigness Meat Market (215), Stebbin's (209), and Hick's Furniture (201–205) are on the right. The city hall tower can be seen just above the Hick's Undertaking sign at the end of the block.

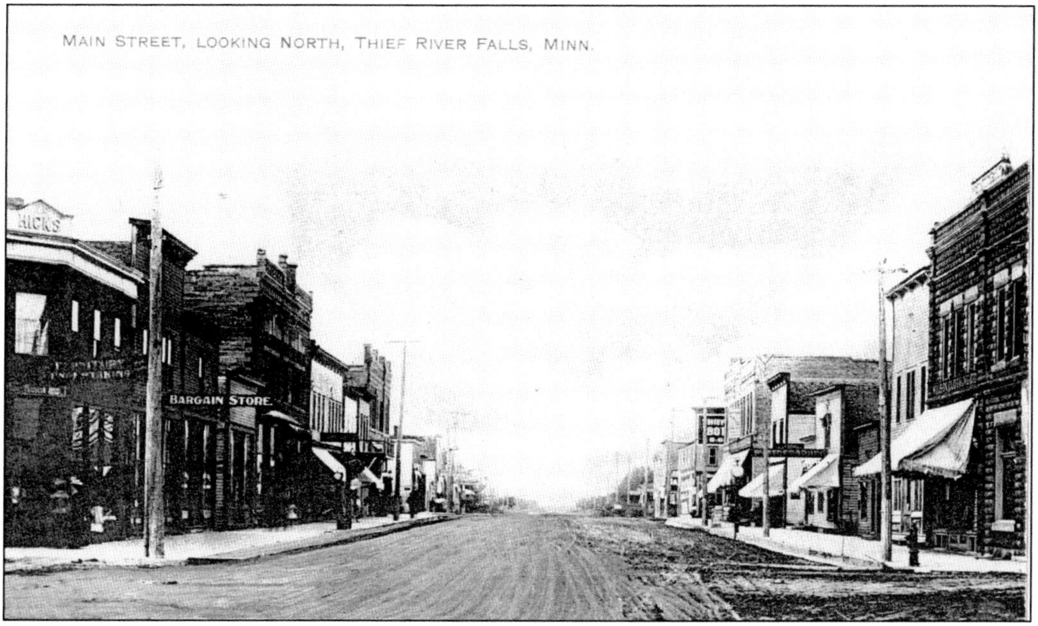

THIEF RIVER FALLS MAIN AVENUE, EARLY 1900S. In this view looking north from Second Street, Hicks Furniture (201–205) is the first building on the left. The Dobner-Meehan building, housing the First State Bank, is on the right. Jacob Borry Photography (214) was in the middle of the block, and the Thief River Bottling Company was at the corner of Third Street in the early 1900s.

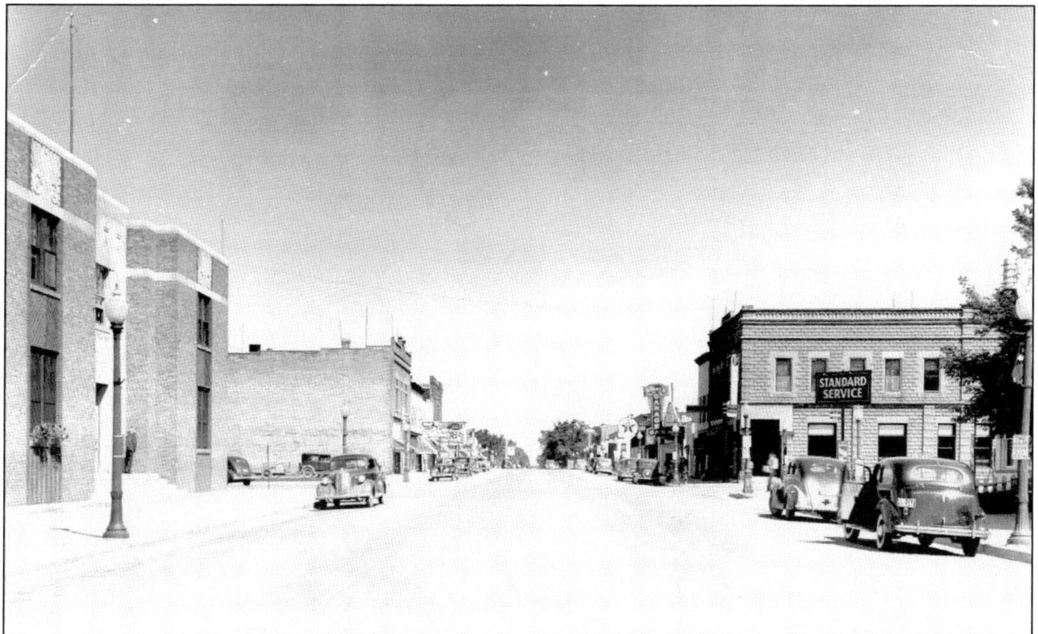

THIEF RIVER FALLS MAIN AVENUE, EARLY 1940S. In a view looking north from between First and Second Streets, the city auditorium is on the left corner. Across the avenue, Mave's Standard Station is on the corner. Across Second Street, the Dobner-Meehan building (burned in 1997) is on the corner, and Borry's Garage (210–214) is further down the street in the early 1940s.

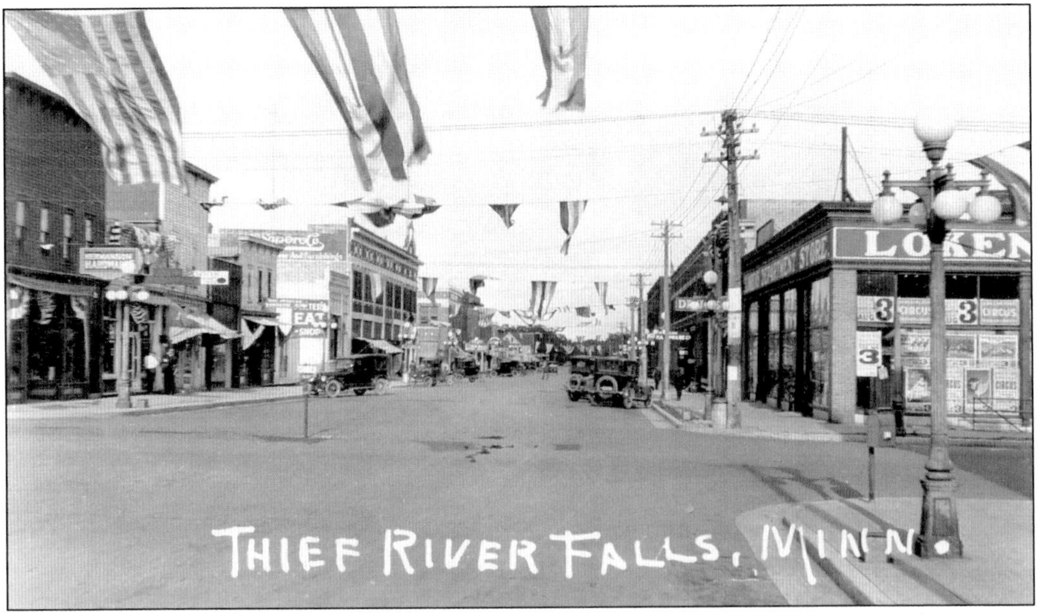

THIEF RIVER FALLS THIRD STREET, EARLY 1920S. In this view looking east from Main Avenue, Hermanson's Hardware (101), the Peoples Cooperative Store (109), and the Sapero Company (115-117) are on the left. Loken Brothers (104), Lambert's Drug (108), and Bottem Hardware (116) are on the right in the early 1920s.

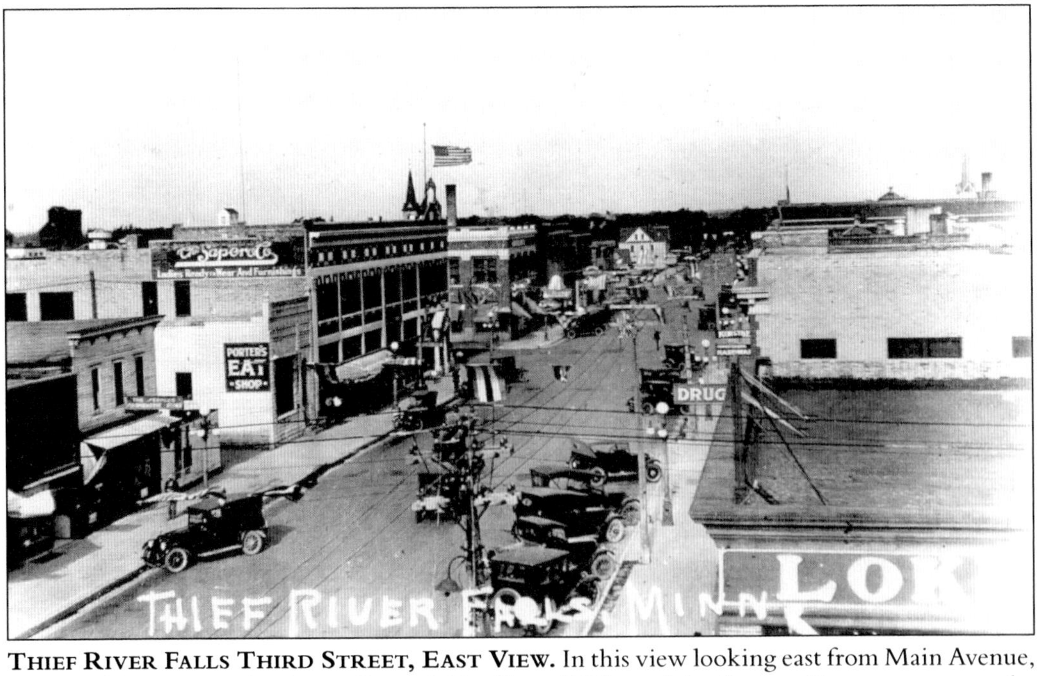

THIEF RIVER FALLS THIRD STREET, EAST VIEW. In this view looking east from Main Avenue, the People's Cooperative Store, Porter's Eat Shop (113), and the Sapero Company are on the left. Loken Brothers, Lambert's Drug, and the Christenson Hardware (116) are on the right. The Sapero sign can still be seen on the west side of the Elks building.

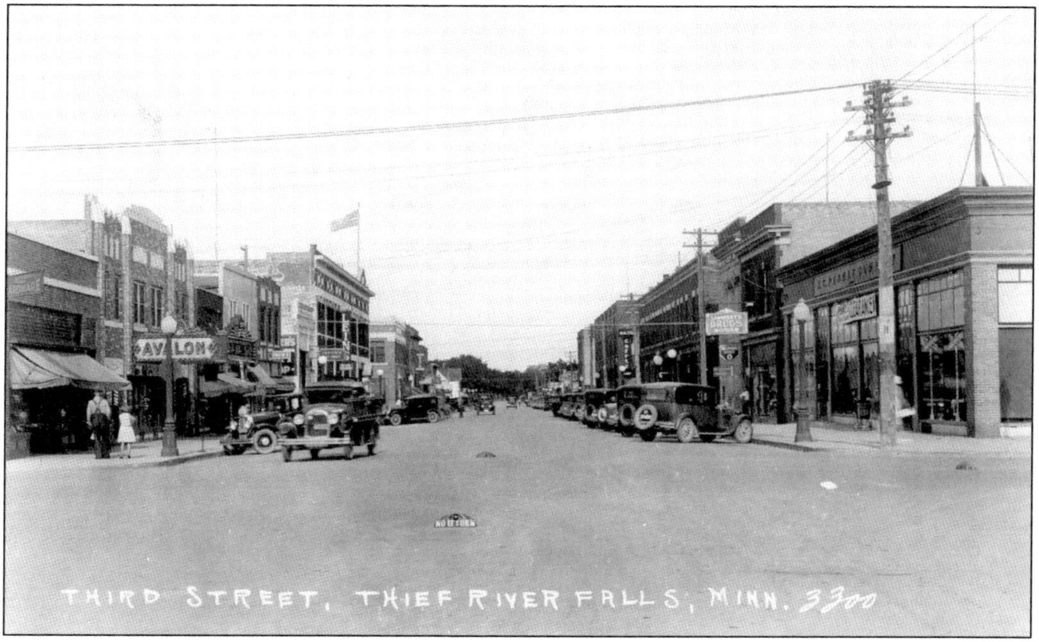

THIEF RIVER FALLS THIRD STREET, EARLY 1930S. In this view looking east from Main Avenue, Kelly Hardware (101), Avalon Theatre (103), Porter's Eat Shop (113), and Lien's (117) are on the left. J. C. Penney (102–103), Lambert's, and the Union State Bank (108½) are on the right, with Wold's Coffee Shop on the corner in the Dudley Building (118) in the early 1930s.

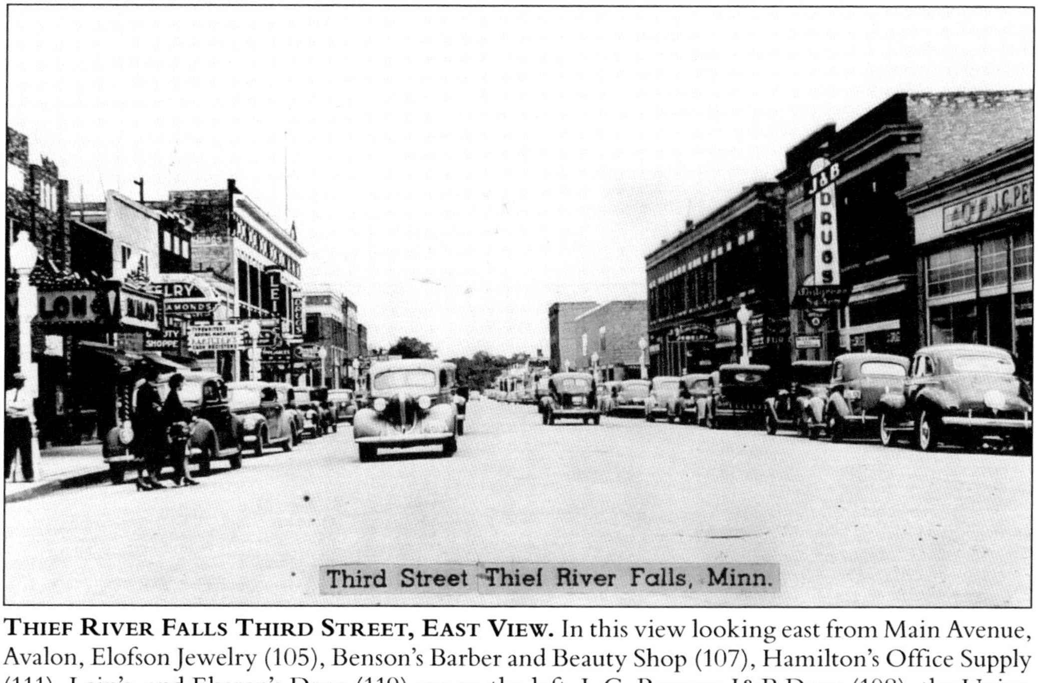

THIEF RIVER FALLS THIRD STREET, EAST VIEW. In this view looking east from Main Avenue, Avalon, Elofson Jewelry (105), Benson's Barber and Beauty Shop (107), Hamilton's Office Supply (111), Lein's, and Ekeren's Drug (119) are on the left. J. C. Penney, J&B Drug (108), the Union State Bank, and Wangenstein's Jewelry (114) are on the right in the early 1940s.

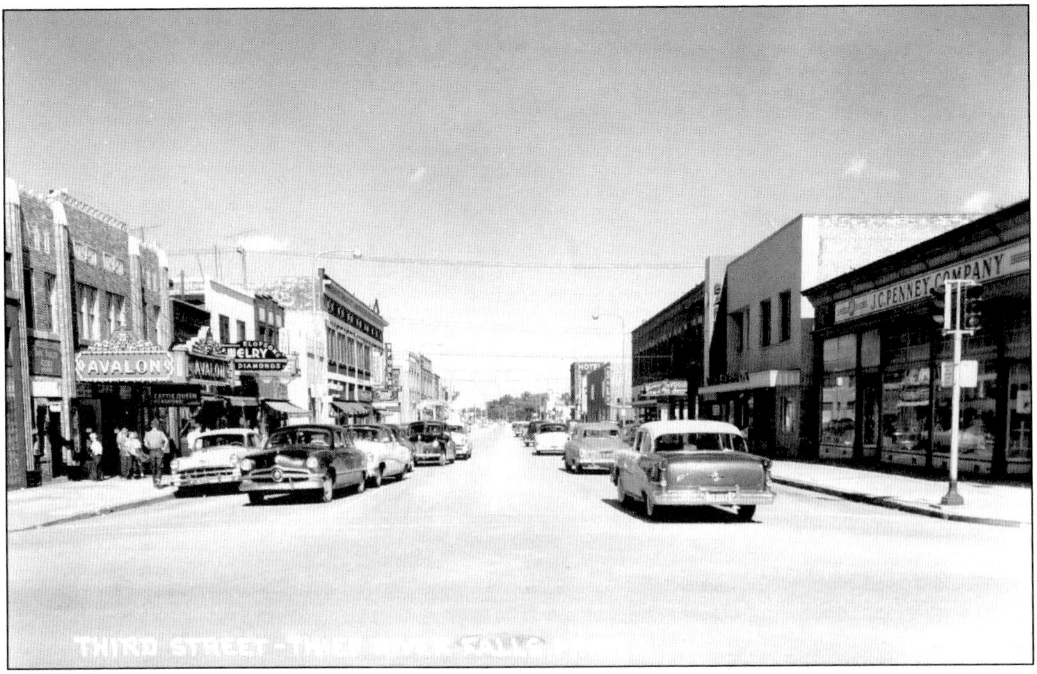

Thief River Falls Third Street, 1950s. In this view looking east from Main Avenue, Avalon, Elofson's, Junior Shop (115), Lein's, Ekeren's, and the Elks Building are on the left. J. C. Penney, Union State Bank, Vogue (112), Wangenstein's, S & L, and Pennington Hotel are on the right in the 1950s.

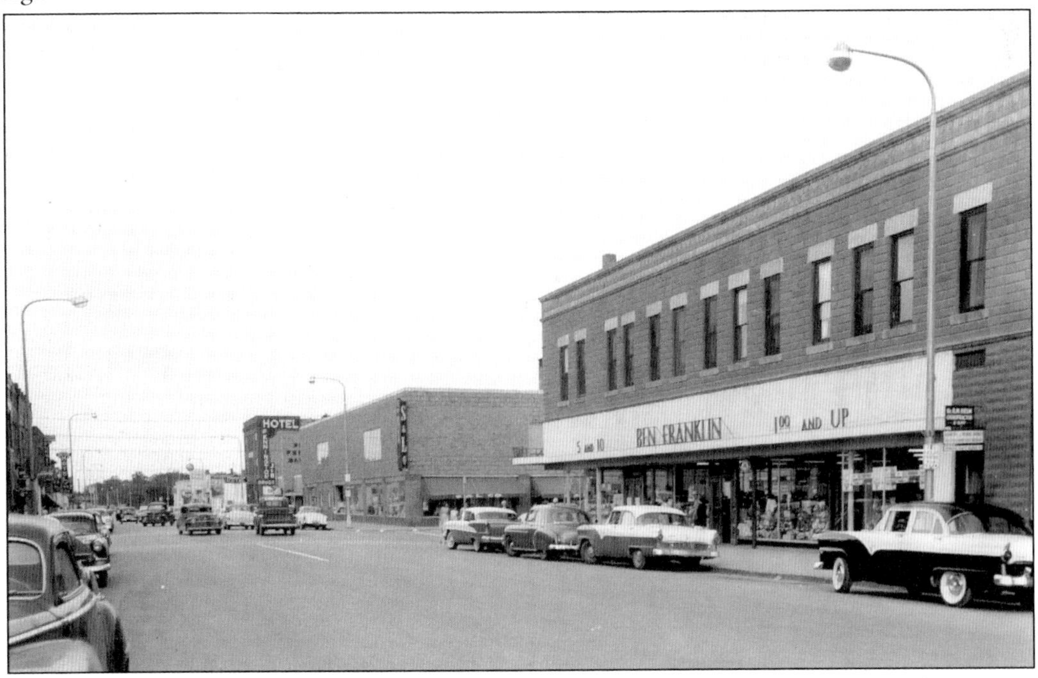

Third Street, Looking East from Main Avenue. In this view looking east from Main Avenue on Third Street, Ben Franklin (122), S & L, First Federal (214), J&B Drugs (216), and Pennington Hotel (224) are on the right in the 1950s.

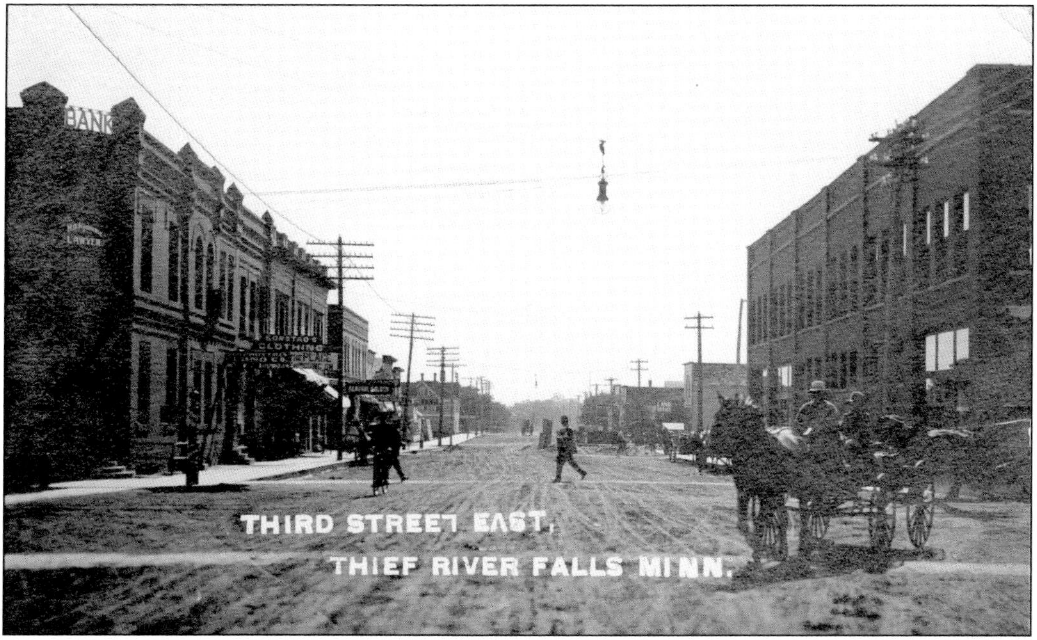

THIEF RIVER FALLS THIRD STREET EAST. Looking east from La Bree Avenue, the First National Bank, Korstad Brothers (205), Central Saloon (213), Soo Café (223), and the Park Hotel are on the left. The Oen Mercantile is on the right in the early 1900s.

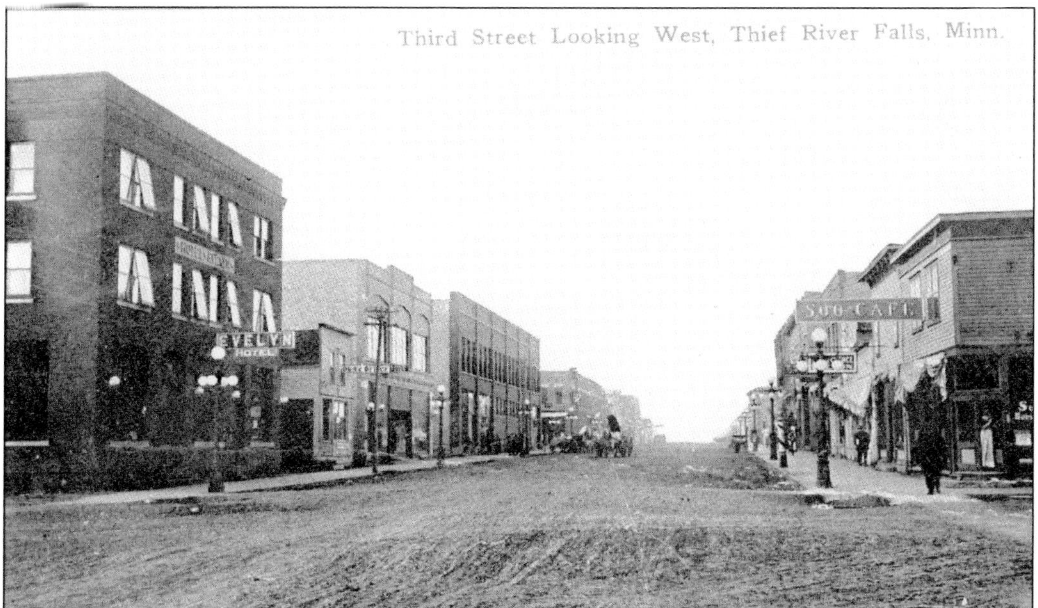

THIEF RIVER FALLS THIRD STREET LOOKING WEST. In this view looking west from Horace Avenue, the Hotel Evelyn (222–224), O'Hara Dray (218), Union Block (214–216), and Oen Mercantile are on the left. The Soo Café (223) and the First and Last Chance Saloon (221) are on the right in the second decade of the 20th century.

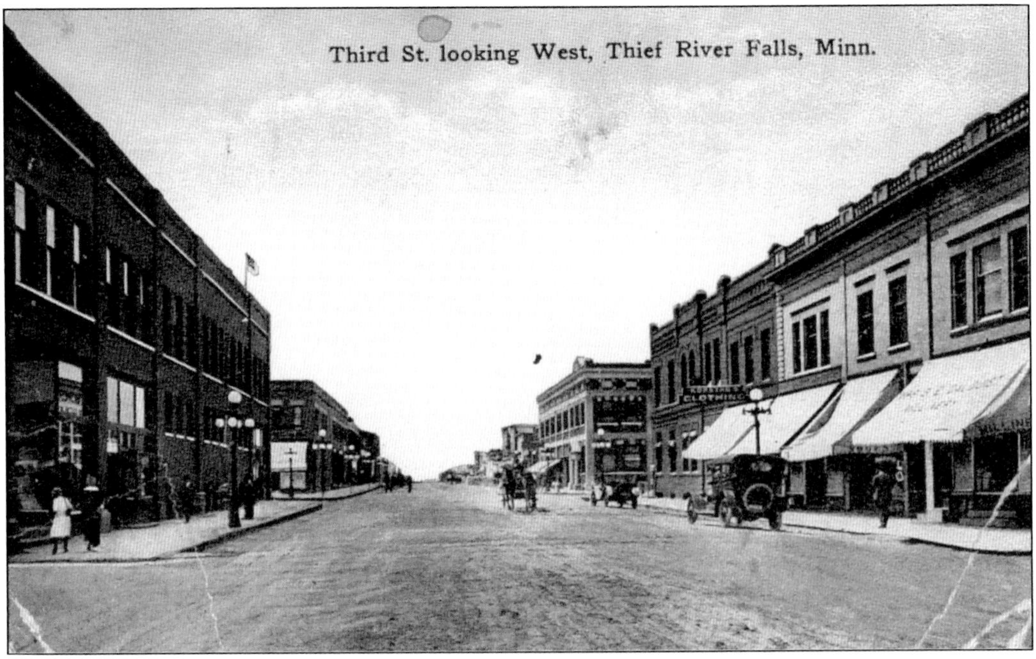

THIRD STREET, LOOKING WEST. In this view looking west from Horace Avenue, the Oen Mercantile is on the left and Mrs. B. E. Dalquist Milliners (211), Langseth's (209), Korstad Brothers (205), and the First National Bank (203) are on the right in the second decade of the 20th century.

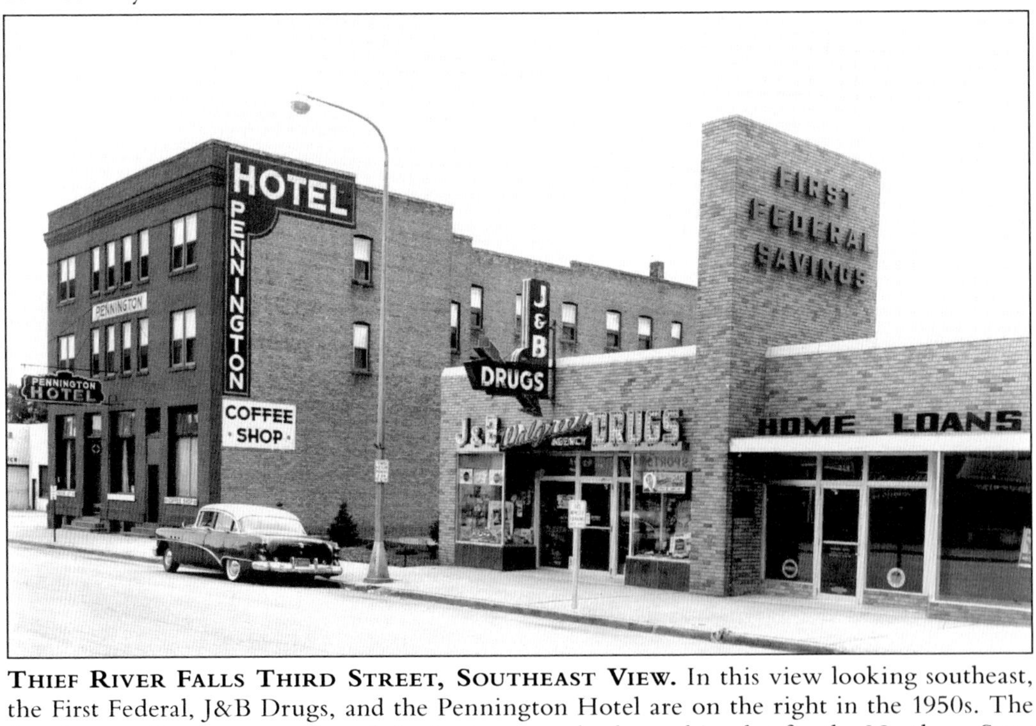

THIEF RIVER FALLS THIRD STREET, SOUTHEAST VIEW. In this view looking southeast, the First Federal, J&B Drugs, and the Pennington Hotel are on the right in the 1950s. The Pennington Hotel was razed, and the lot is currently the parking lot for the Northern State Bank drive-through.

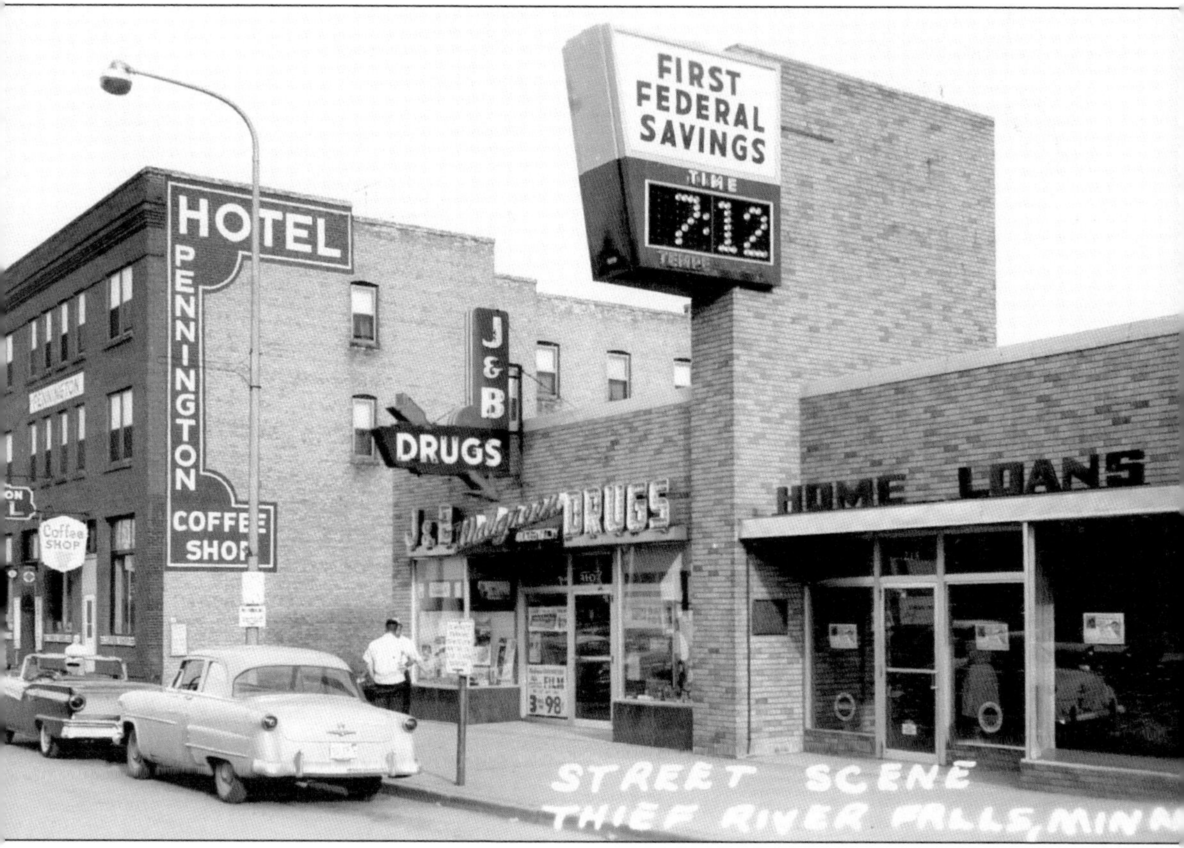

THIEF RIVER FALLS THIRD STREET, WITH SIGNS BY EMMET MOUSLEY. In this view looking southeast, the J&B Drugs and the Pennington Hotel had signs by Emmet Mousley. The Emmet Mousley Sign Company on North Main Avenue constructed and painted most of the signs in the city from the 1940s until the 1980s.

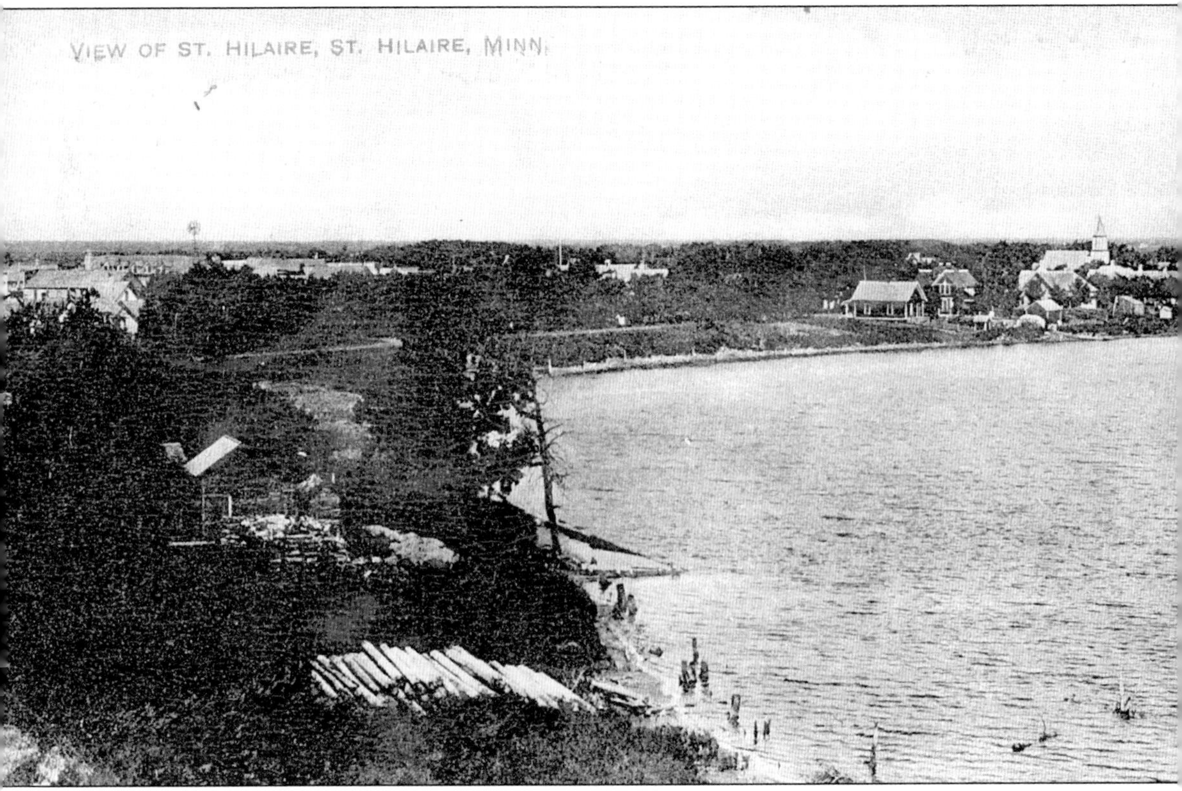

St. Hilaire, Postmarked 1909. In this view looking northwest over the southeast corner of town, the windmill belonged to the Markham Hotel, and the homes were along Water Avenue. The message on this card, postmarked 1909, stated that the church on the right was the United Lutheran Church. The writer noted that the minister had returned with his bride last Wednesday.

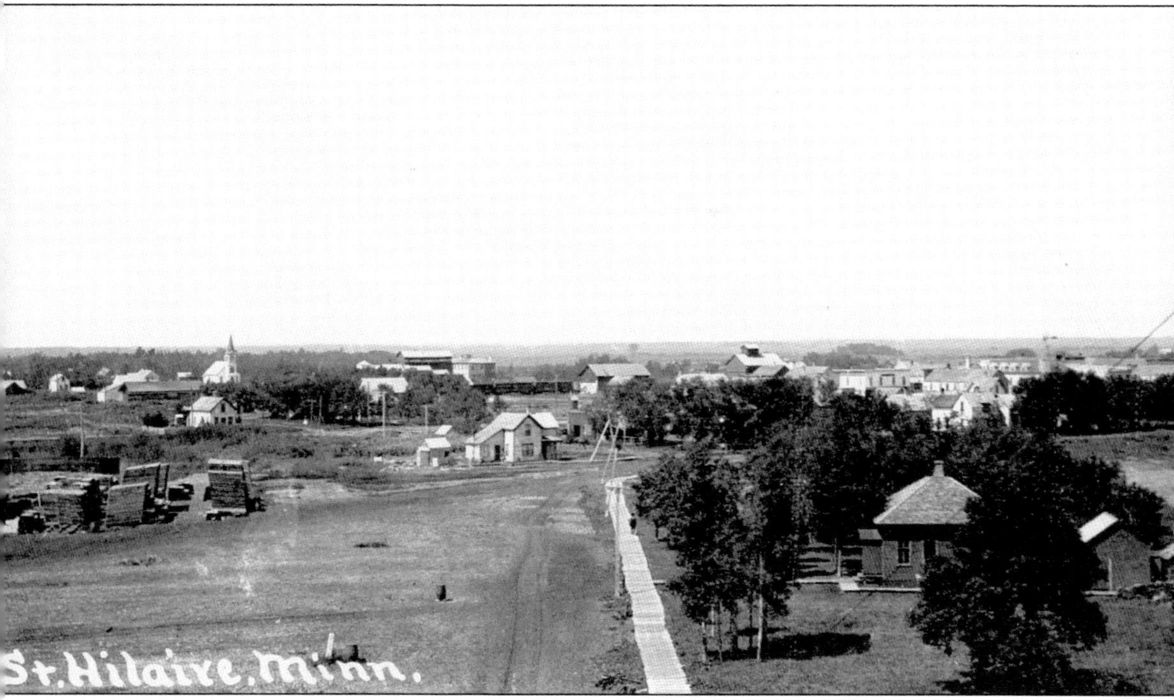

ST. HILAIRE, NORTHWEST VIEW. In this view looking northwest, the lumberyard, the Norwegian Lutheran Church, Mike Fricker's House, and the wooden school are on the left of the boardwalk. The creamery is straight out from the end of the boardwalk, and the elevator, Soderburgs, and the Markham Hotel with its windmill are on the right of the boardwalk. The stone structure on the right foreground is the office for the sawmill.

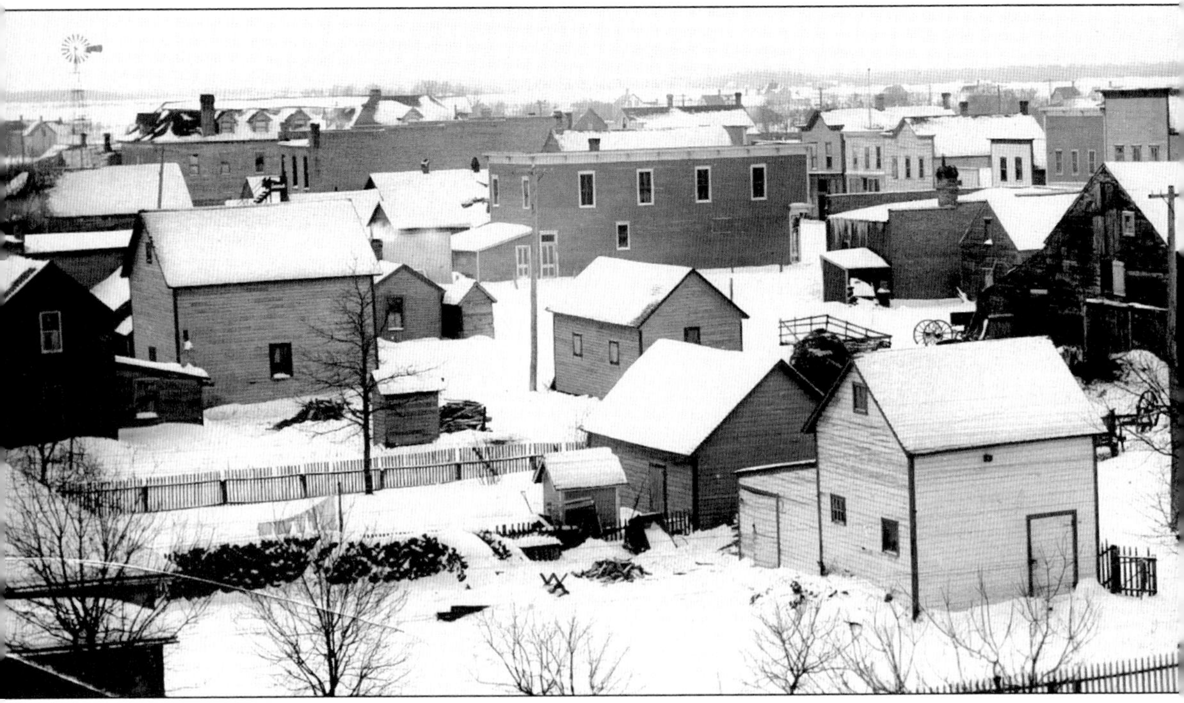

St. Hilaire, Southwest View. In this view looking southwest, the Markham Hotel and windmill, dance hall, bank, shoe repair, and livery stable line the backside of Broadway in the winter. The small building in the center of this view is the telephone office.

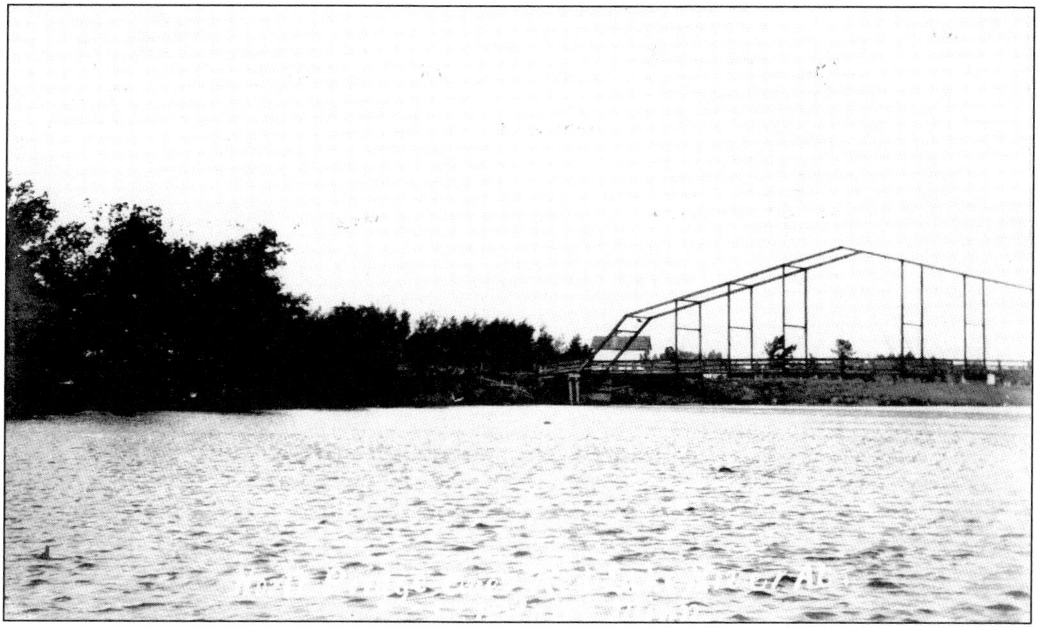

St. Hilaire North Bridge over Red Lake River. The house at the left end of the bridge over the Red Lake River belonged to Anna Olson, mother of Rufus Olson. A second bridge with two spans was built in 1929 just south of the first bridge. The pier for the second bridge is still in the river.

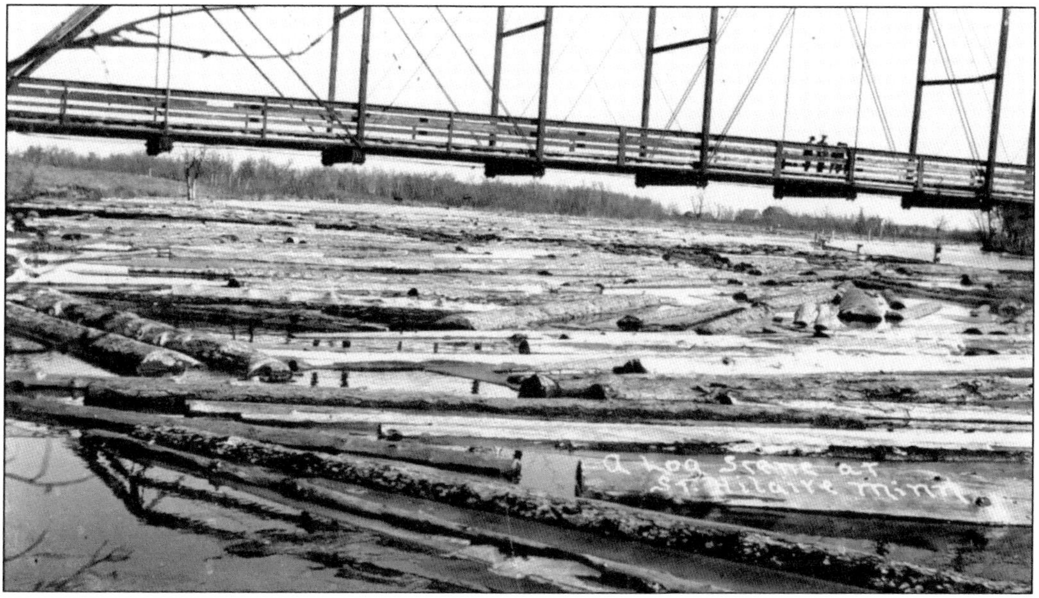

Logs on the Way to the Mill. Logs fill the Red Lake River under the first North Bridge on their way to the sawmill.

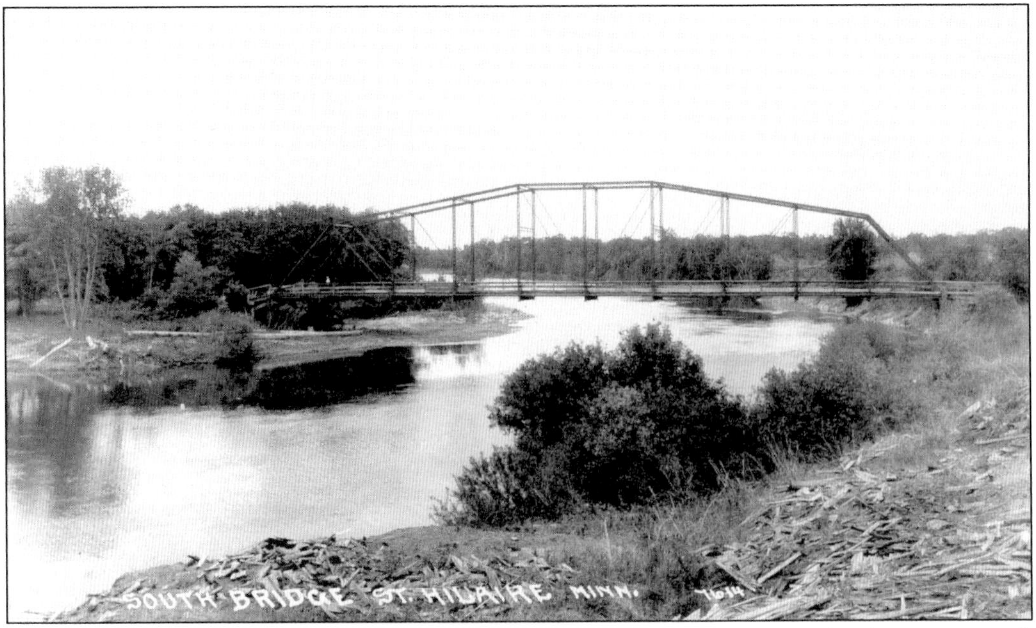

St. Hilaire South Bridge. This bridge was further south over the Red Lake River. Both shores were strewn with pieces of lumber.

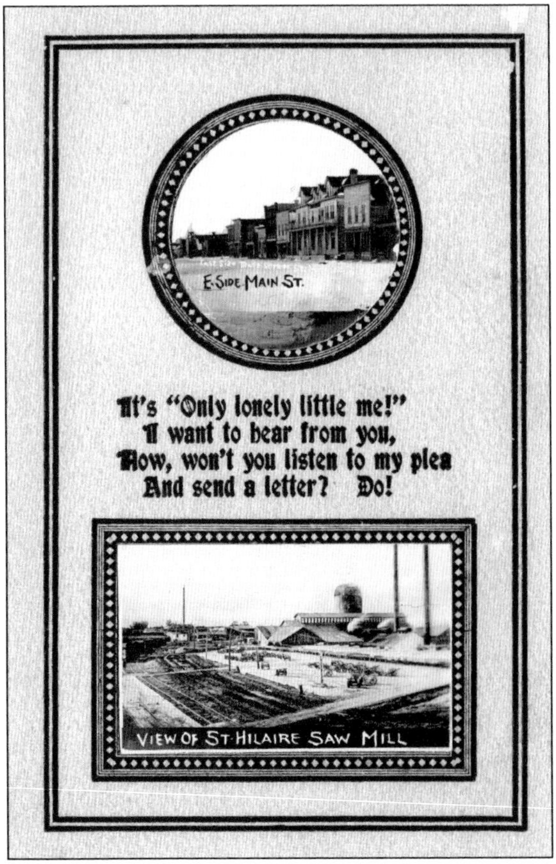

St. Hilaire Popular Greeting. The "East Side of Main Street" was actually the east side of Broadway. The use of the word Main to describe a city's busiest street was common on cards. The sawmill and railroad tracks were on the lower view of this popular greeting of the era.

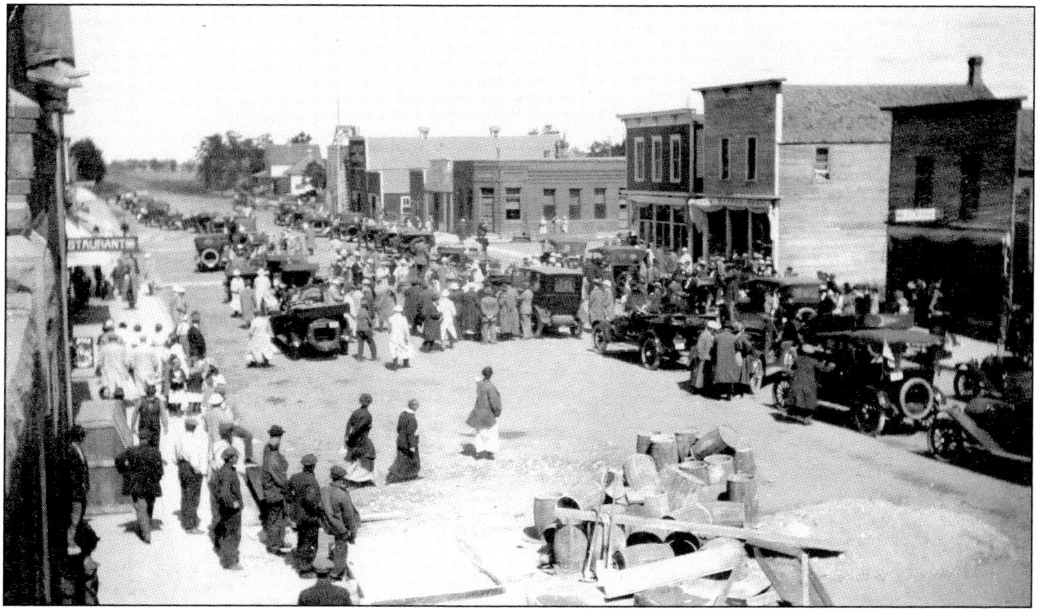

ST. HILAIRE BROADWAY, POSTMARKED 1915. Looking north, J. A. Hanson photographed the right side of Broadway. The Meat Market, Sande's Restaurant (later Pickard's), and the gas and auto store with the dance hall upstairs are before Third Street. The bank on the next corner had a well outside for public use, and the city jail, livery stable, and town hall are further down the street on this card postmarked 1915.

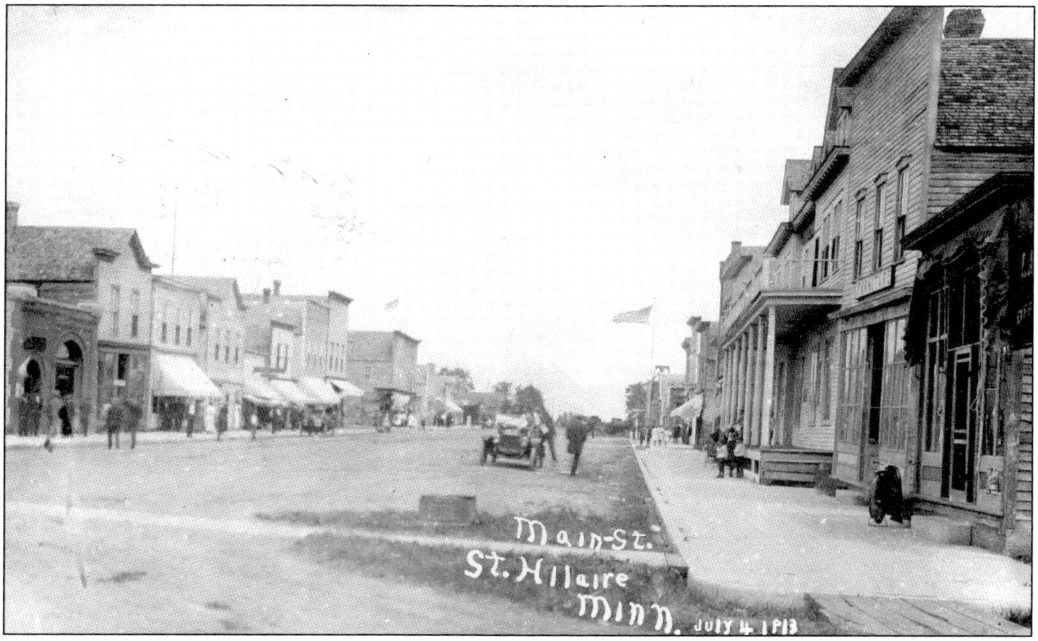

ST. HILAIRE BROADWAY, 1913. In this view looking north in 1913, the drug store, pool hall, hair salon, card room, Jackson Store, general store, hardware store, and Mike Highland's gas station are on the left. The first door on the right is to the *Spectator* office, followed by a furniture store, the Markham Hotel, livery stable, city hall, and the fire hall.

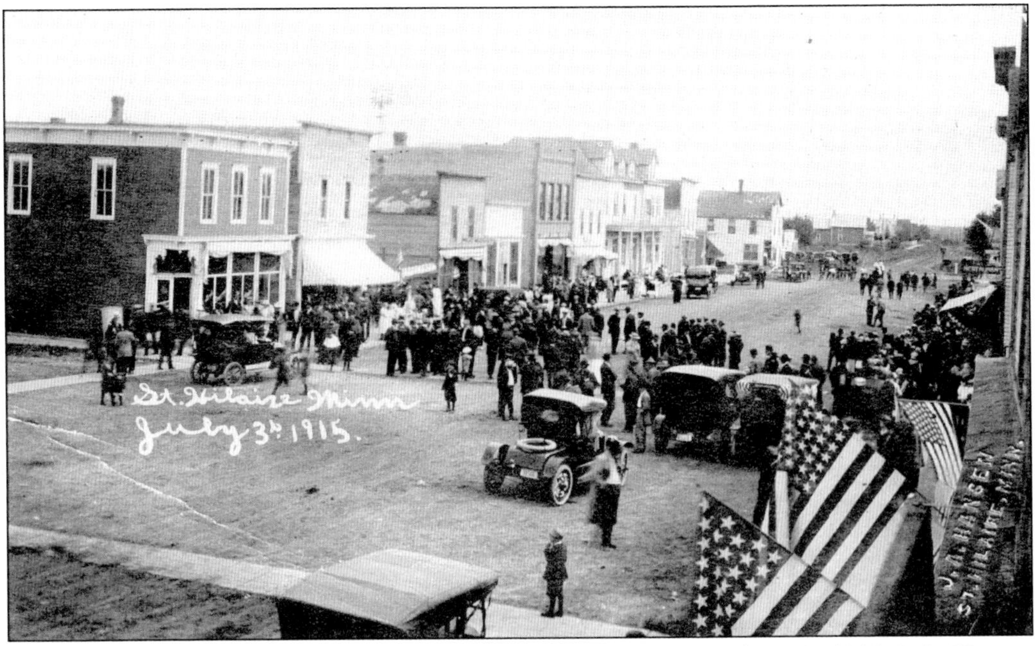

ST. HILAIRE BROADWAY, SOUTHEAST VIEW, 1915. Looking southeast in 1915, J. A. Hansen photographed Broadway from Third Street. The auto supply and gas station, restaurant, meat market, *Spectator* office, the Jackson Store and opera house, the general store, Markham Hotel, furniture store, boardinghouse, and auto repair are on the left.

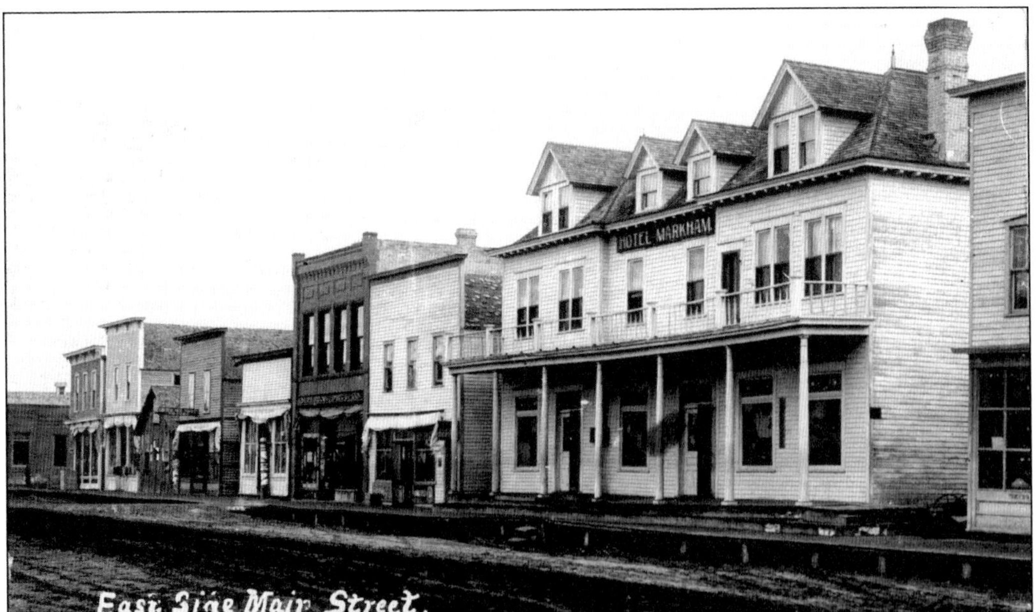

ST. HILAIRE BROADWAY, POSTMARKED 1909. In this view looking northeast from Third Street, the auto supply and gas station with a dance hall upstairs, the restaurant, meat market, *Spectator* office, Jackson Store and opera house, general store, and the Hotel Markham line the street.

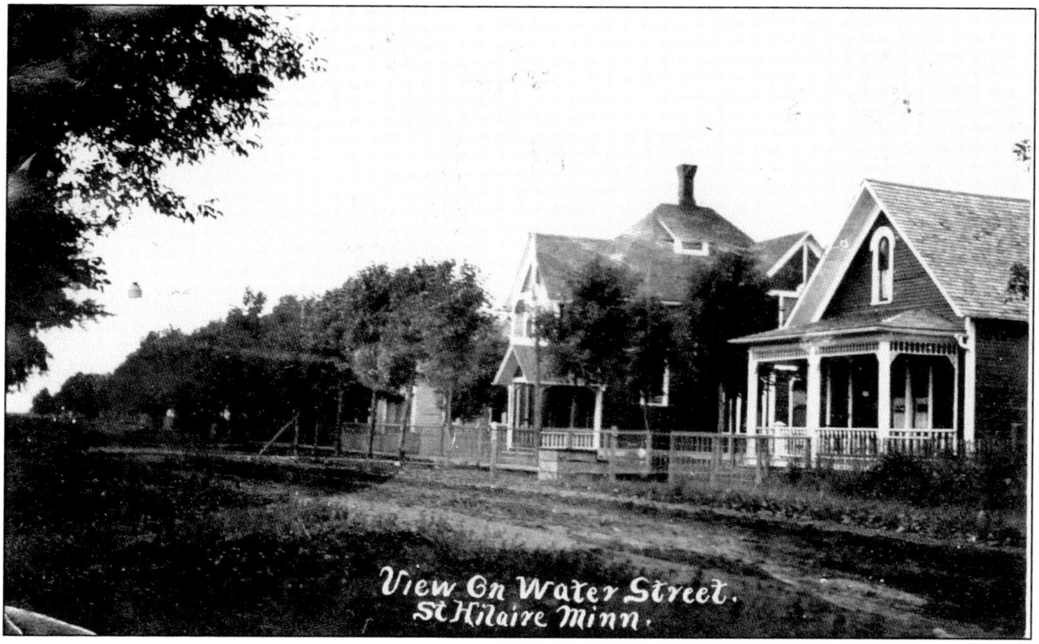

St. Hilaire Water Avenue, Northeast View. In this view looking northeast from Third Street, this card postmarked in 1909 displays the homes along the wooded avenue that bordered Lake St. Hilaire. The tallest house with the chimney still stands at the end of the avenue. The house on the far right is also still standing, but without the porch.

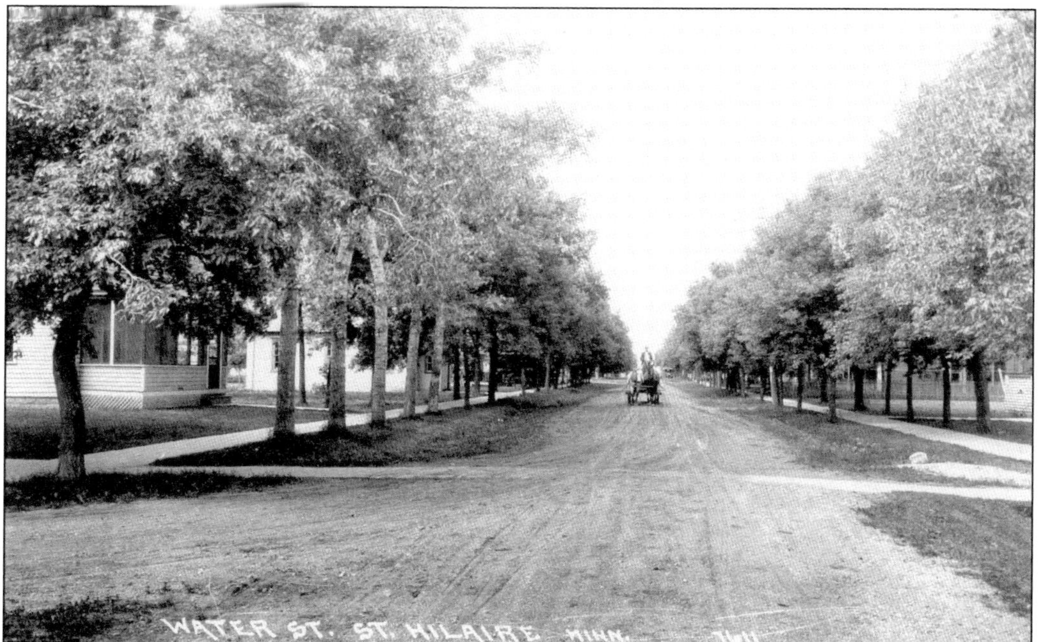

St. Hilaire Water Avenue, North View. In this view looking north, abundant trees and white wood-frame houses line the avenue. In the past, Water Avenue was most frequently called Water Street, and most property titles reflected that usage. The signs on the avenue were changed to Water Avenue in the recent past.

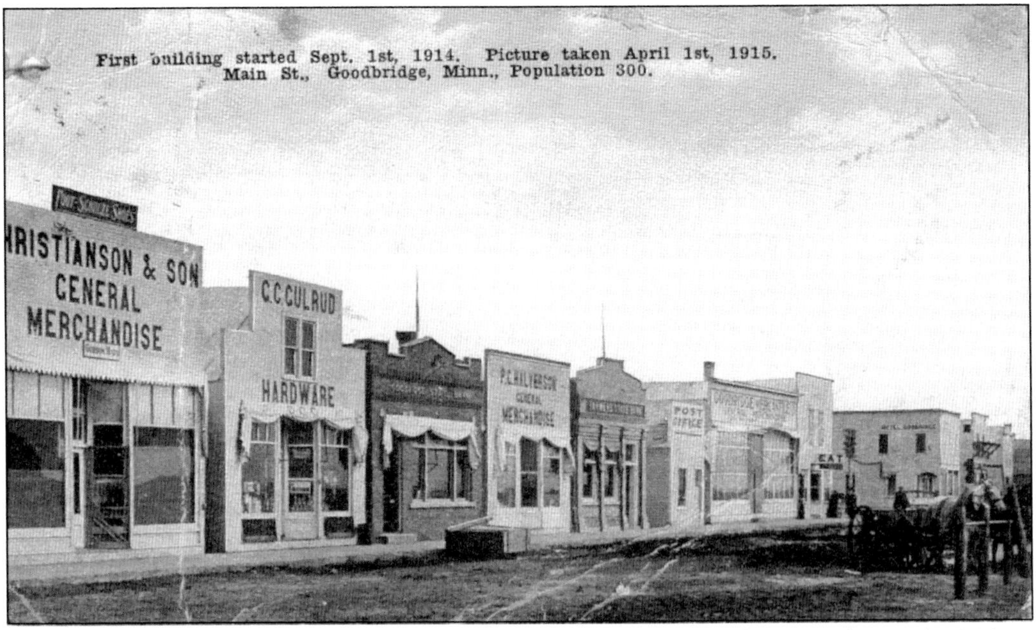

Goodridge Main Street, Northeast View. In this view looking northeast, the Halvor Christianson and Son General Merchandise, Gilbert Gulrud Hardware, Goodridge State Bank, Halverson Merchandise, Farmers State Bank, post office, Goodridge Mercantile, O. K. Restaurant, Hotel Goodridge, an unidentified building, and the Goodridge Hall and *Eleven Towns* Print Shop line the main street in 1915.

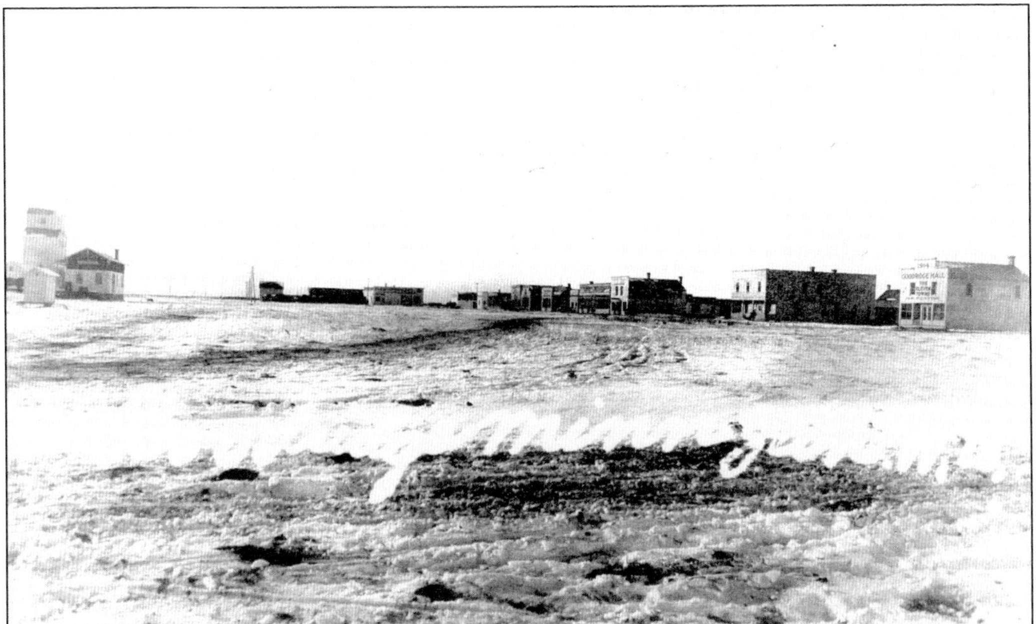

Goodridge Main Street, Northwest View. In this view looking northwest, the Hanson Barzen Milling Company and the depot for the Minnesota Northwestern Electric Railway are on the left January 11, 1915. The depot was moved to Grygla later. The area surrounding the town was opened to homesteading in 1904. Goodridge was incorporated in 1916.

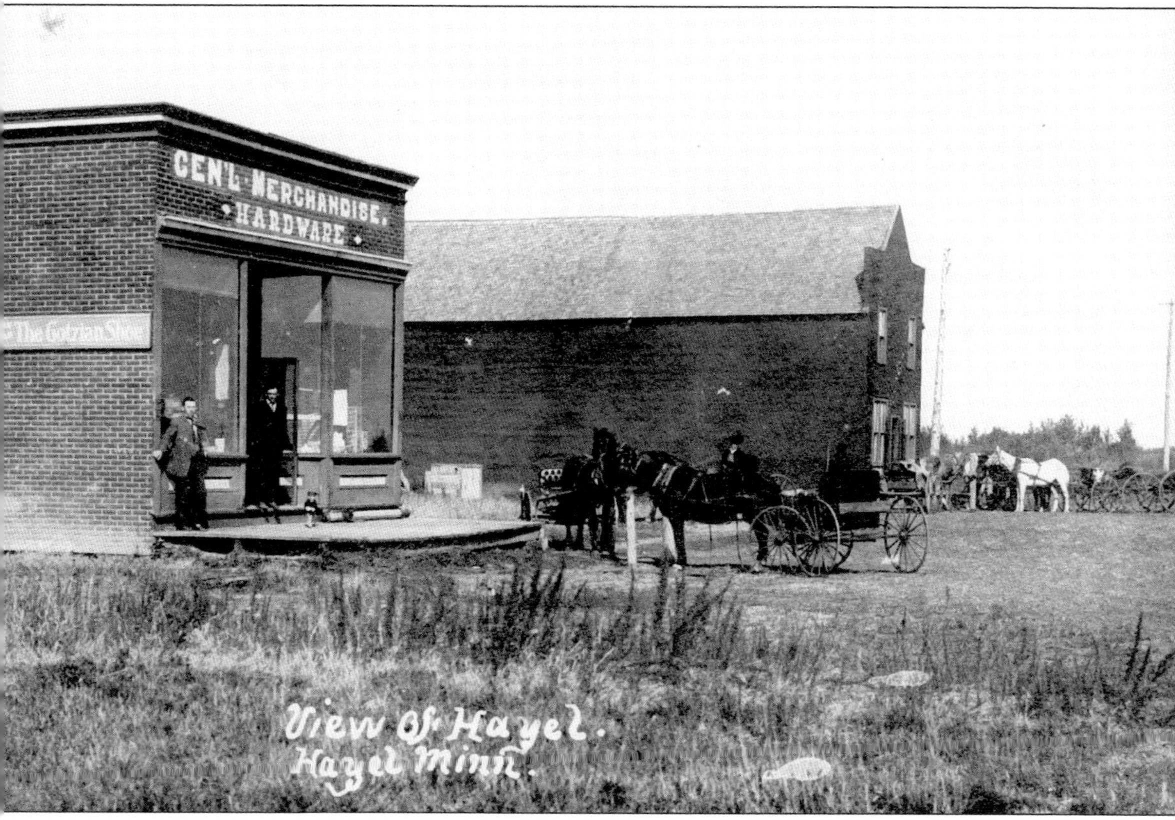

HAZEL. In this view looking southeast, the general merchandise and hardware and the Magnuson Store and Hall were located in Hazel in River Falls Township.

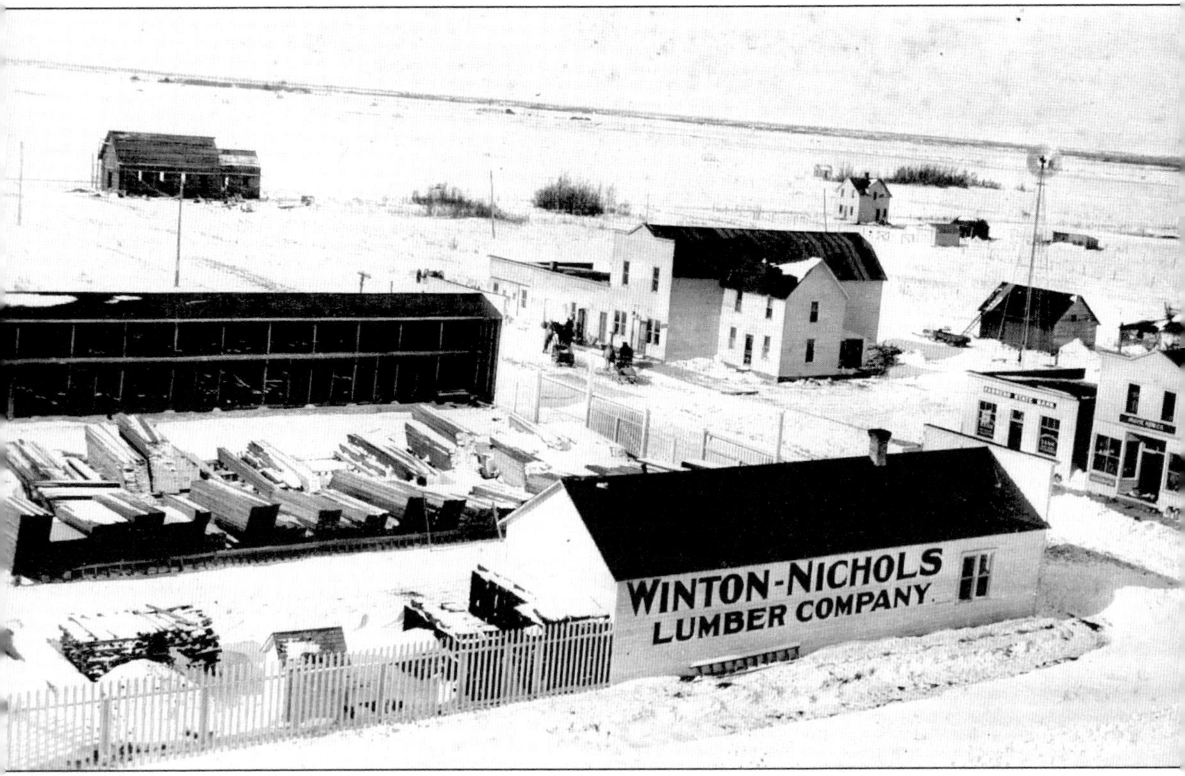

Mavie. In this view looking northwest, the Winton Nichols Lumber Company is on the left, across Nelson Street from the Mavie Hardware Company, Farmers State Bank, and city hall. Mavie was in Cloverleaf Township.

Three

Churches, Schools, and Hospitals

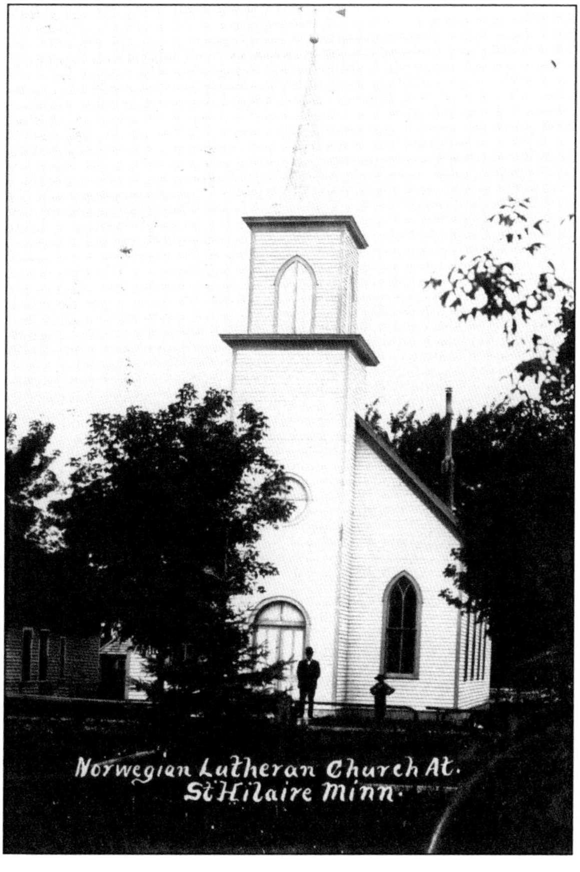

St. Hilaire Norwegian Lutheran Church. In this view looking west, this church is still standing at Fourth Street and Water Avenue. Many changes and additions have been made to the building, and the current name of it is the Calvary Lutheran Church.

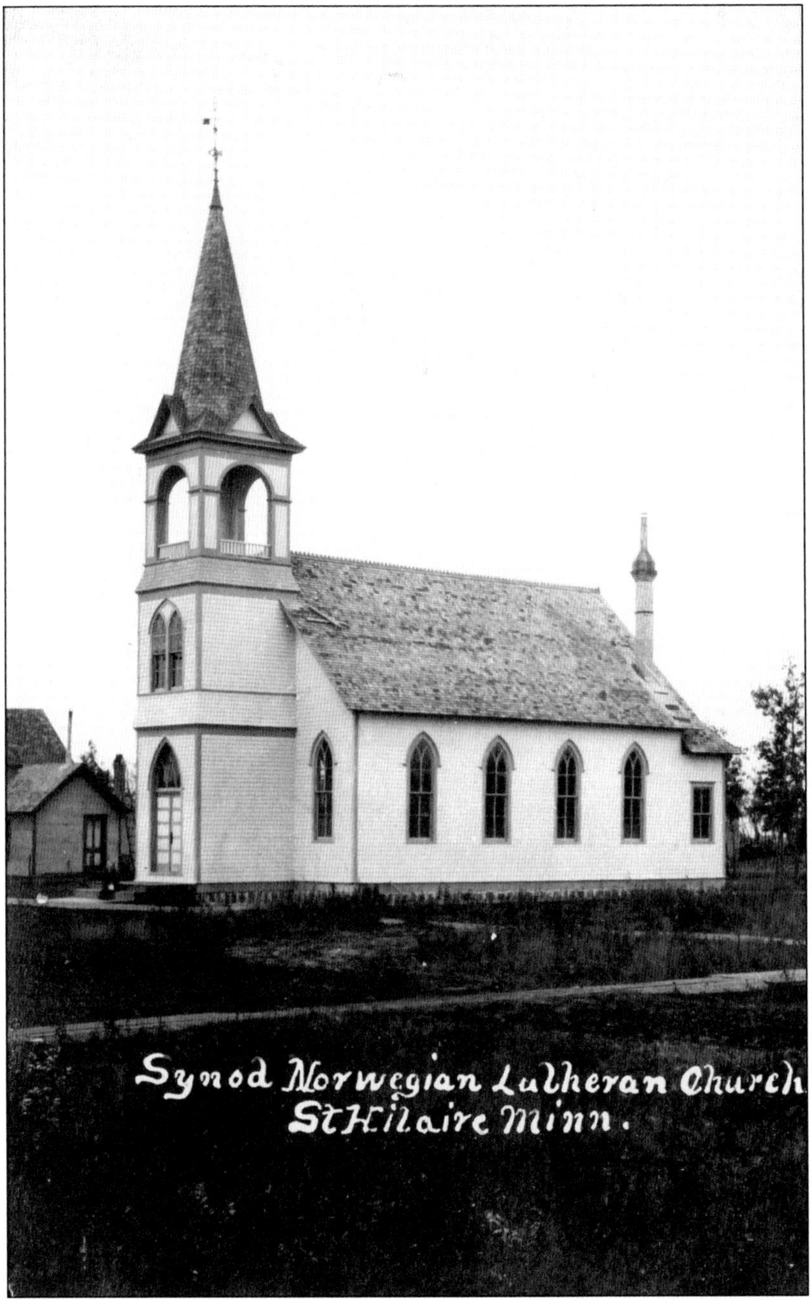

St. Hilaire Synod Norwegian Lutheran Church. This church was located on the west side of the railroad tracks and was built in 1899. Early records indicate that the town had six churches, and among them were two Norwegian and one Swedish Lutheran Church. The photograph taken of this church in 1909 was labeled as the Norwegian Lutheran Church.

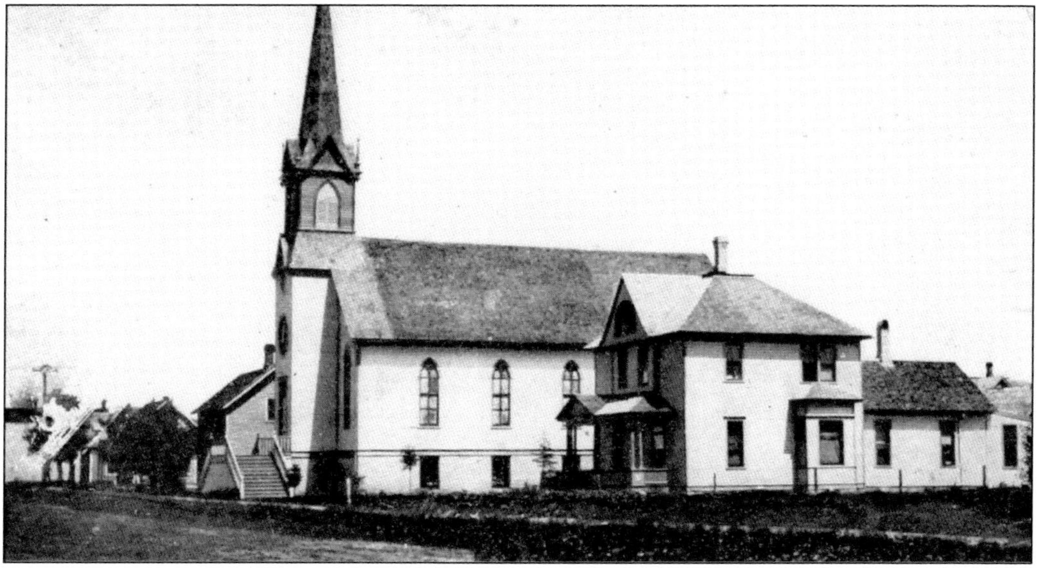

Thief River Falls Trinity Lutheran Church, Postmarked 1912. The congregation was organized in 1893 as the Scandinavian Evangelical Lutheran Church, and the building was built in 1893 at 218 Horace Avenue North. This card labeled it as the "Norvigan Synod Church" and was postmarked 1912. The parsonage stood next to the church at 214 Horace Avenue North and is still standing.

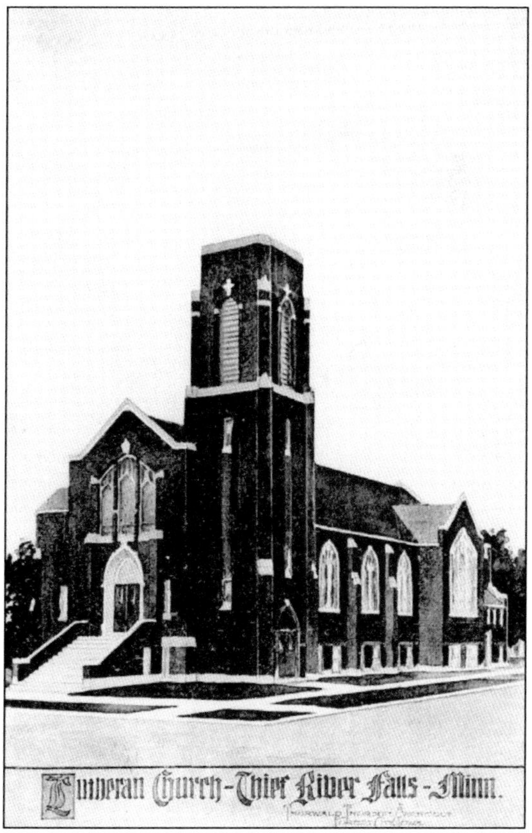

Thief River Falls Trinity Lutheran Church. In 1919, three Norwegian churches (Scandinavian Evangelical, Our Saviours, and the Trinity Lutheran of the Hauge Synod) merged, and the name of Trinity Lutheran Church was adopted. In 1926, the building was erected on the foundation of the former Our Saviours Church at 325 Horace Avenue North.

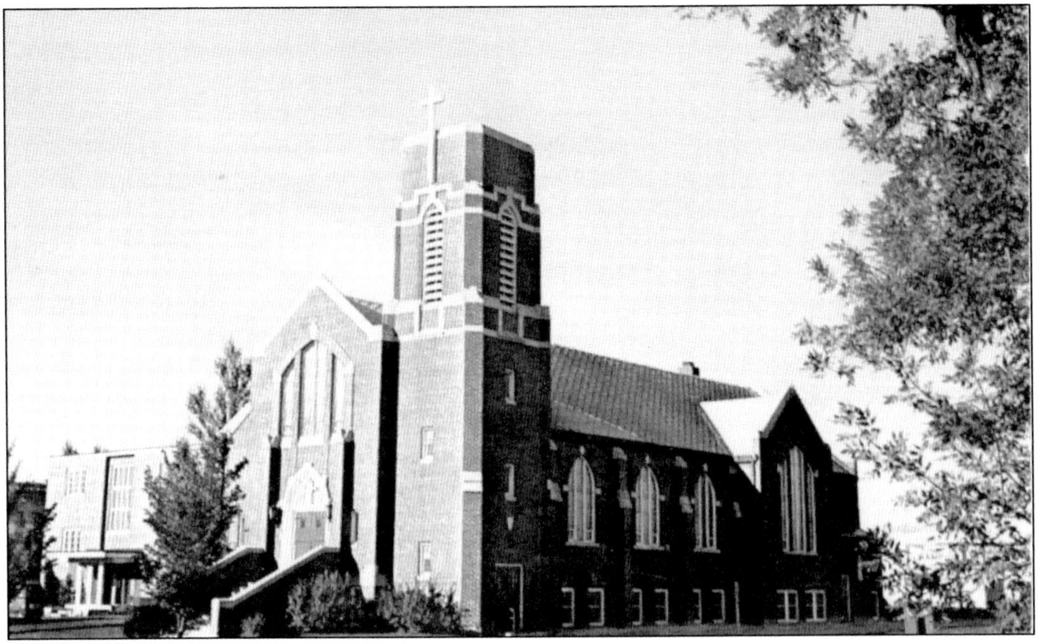

THIEF RIVER FALLS TRINITY LUTHERAN CHURCH, SOUTHWEST VIEW. In this view looking southwest from the corner of Fourth Street and Horace Avenue, the Trinity Lutheran Church building includes the education building that was completed in 1952. The front steps were later removed from the building.

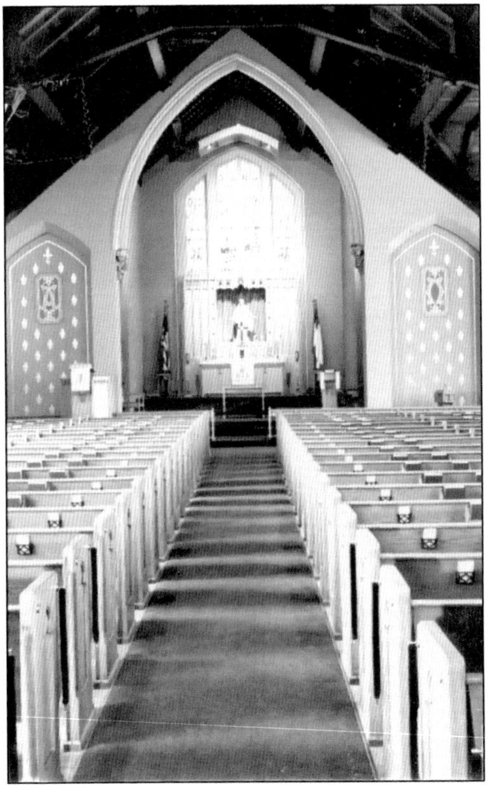

TRINITY LUTHERAN CHURCH SANCTUARY. The sanctuary was completely remodeled and painted in 1957. The chancel was remodeled, and the organ was moved to the balcony, which became the choir loft. The furniture was refinished, and a new altar, pulpit, flooring and light fixtures were installed.

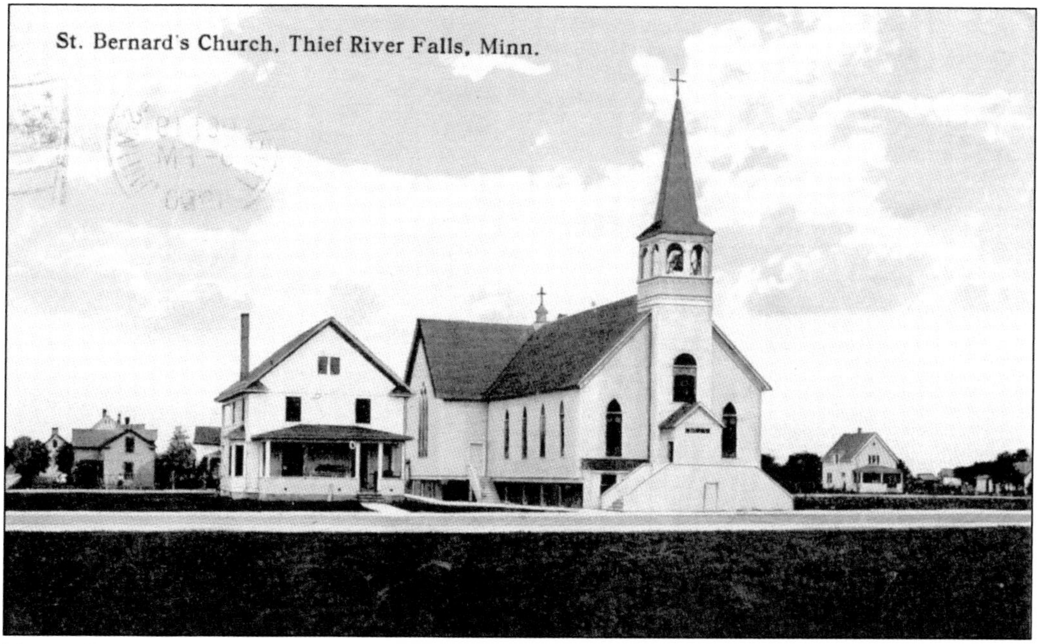

Thief River Falls St. Bernard's Church. In this view looking west from between First and Second Streets on North Knight Avenue, the first Catholic Church was built of wood at 303 Duluth Avenue South and moved to this site in 1914. The rectory was added in 1914 and later moved to Dewey Avenue. The church added to the sanctuary after a fire in 1915.

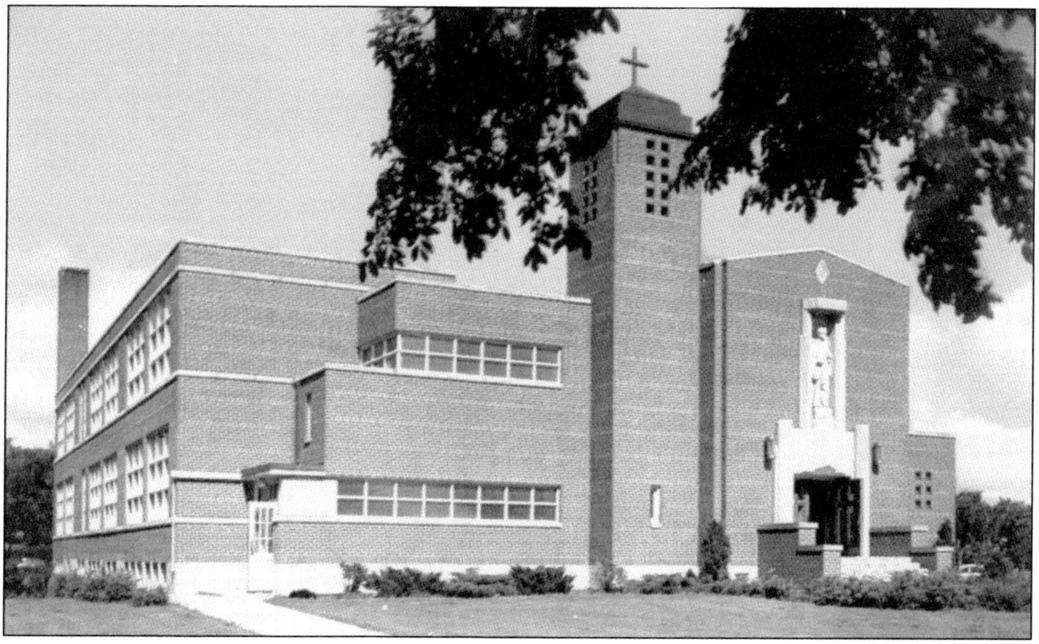

Thief River Falls St. Bernard's Church and School. In this view looking northwest on Knight Avenue North, the current St. Bernard's Catholic Church and School building was dedicated in 1949. The rectory was added in 1966 and houses the offices, classrooms, library, and sanctuary.

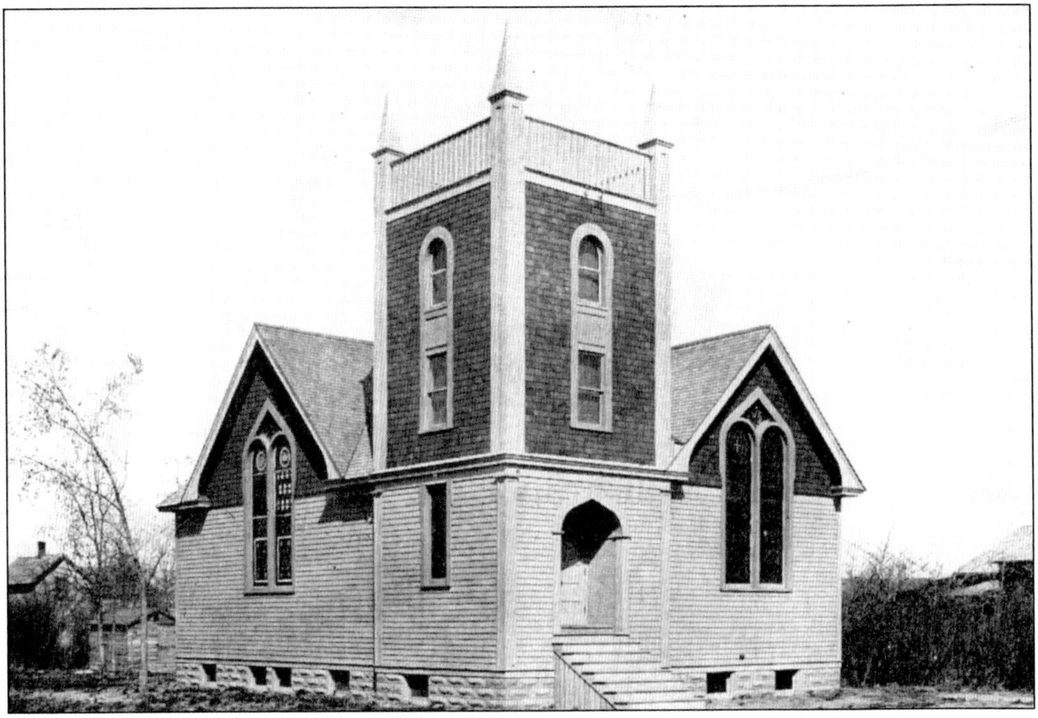

THIEF RIVER FALLS SWEDISH BAPTIST CHURCH. In this view looking northwest, the church was built at 223 South Markley Avenue. The congregation was originally organized in St. Hilaire in 1886. This building's address was first listed in the city directory in 1911. The building burned on November 13, 1948. The congregation was later reorganized as the First Baptist Church and is currently located at 414 Horace Avenue North.

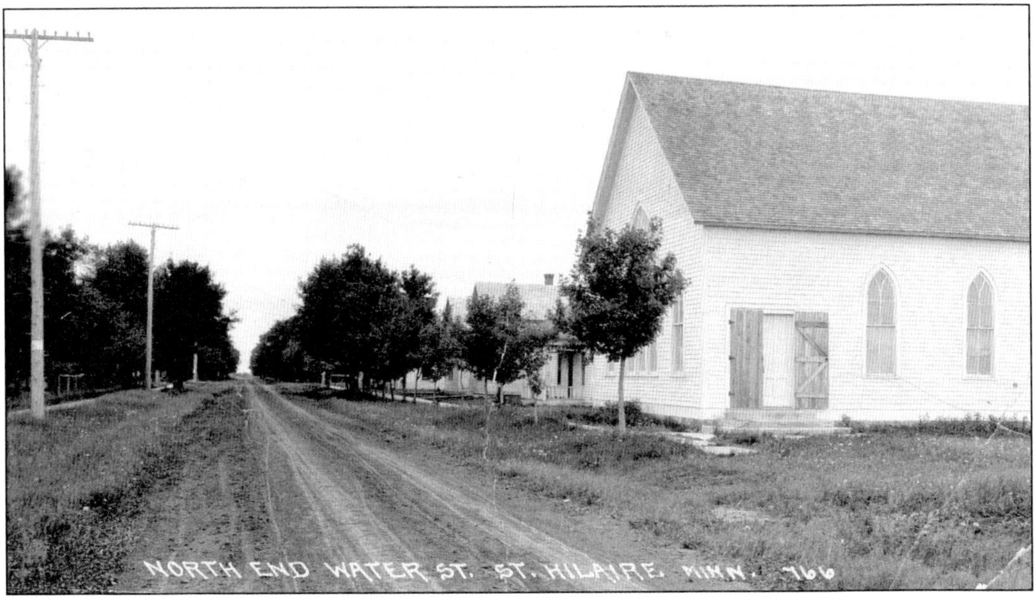

ST. HILAIRE TARNA SWEDISH CHURCH. Shown in this view looking south from Sixth Street on Water Avenue North, the building later burned down. This card is postmarked 1920.

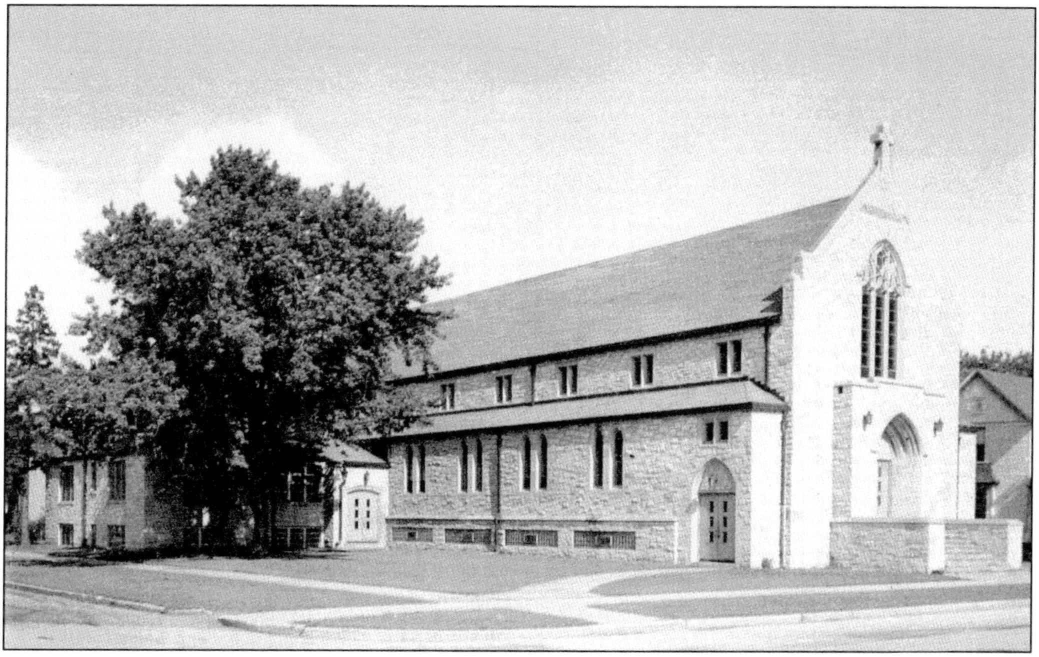

THIEF RIVER FALLS ZION LUTHERAN CHURCH, NORTHWEST VIEW. Shown in this view looking northwest from Main Avenue North and Fifth Street, the current Zion Lutheran Church was reincorporated from the Lutheran Free Church of Scandinavian ancestry, and the first building was completed in 1903 at Horace Avenue and Second Street. The building on the far right edge was removed to make the current parking lot.

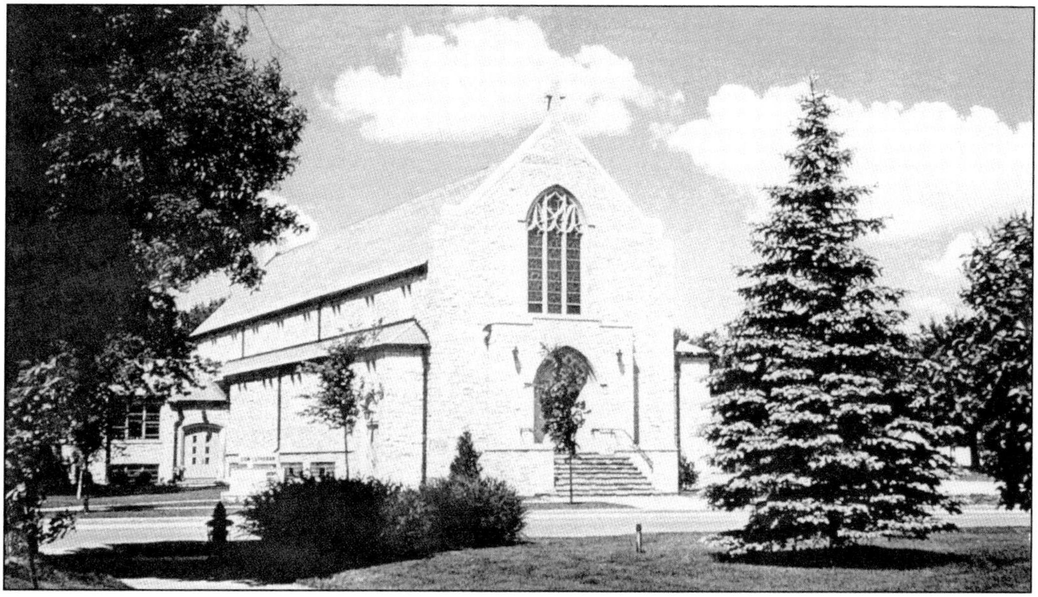

ZION LUTHERAN CHURCH. The Froseth-Larson property was purchased for the new building in 1945, the cornerstone was laid in 1949, the first service in the completed sanctuary was held in 1950, and the building was dedicated in 1954. Ground was broken for the education unit in 1979. The main entrance was moved, the narthex enlarged, and a library, kitchen, and classrooms were added along with other improvements.

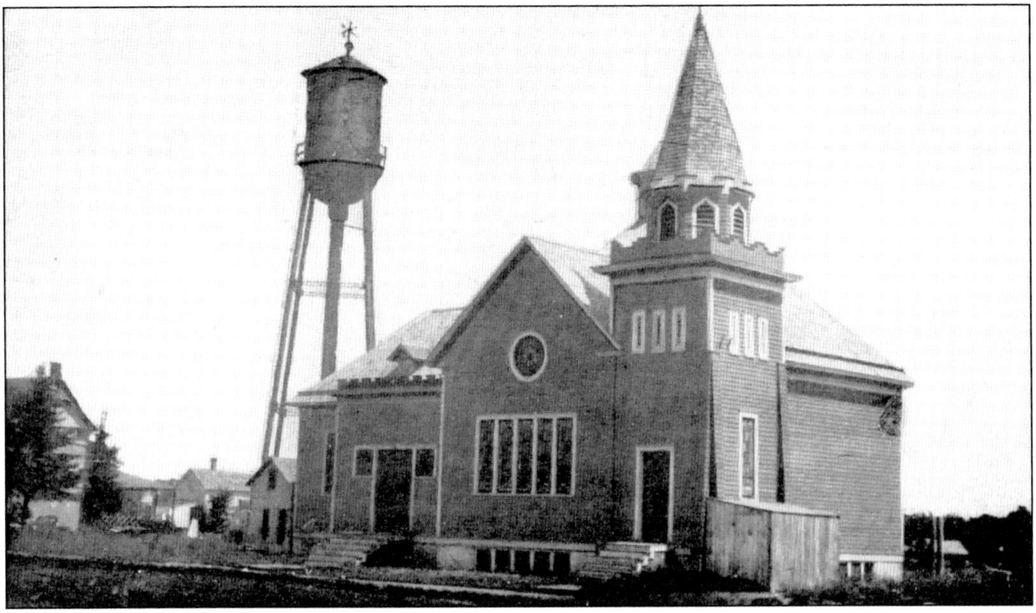

Thief River Falls Presbyterian Church. Shown in a picture looking northeast on Horace Avenue at the west end of the bridge, the church held the first known religious service in the territory in 1844. The congregation organized in 1900, and the building was dedicated in 1903. In 1927, the congregation merged with the Methodist Episcopal Church from across the bridge. The congregations chose the name Community Church and retained the Presbyterian Manse at 518 Main Avenue North.

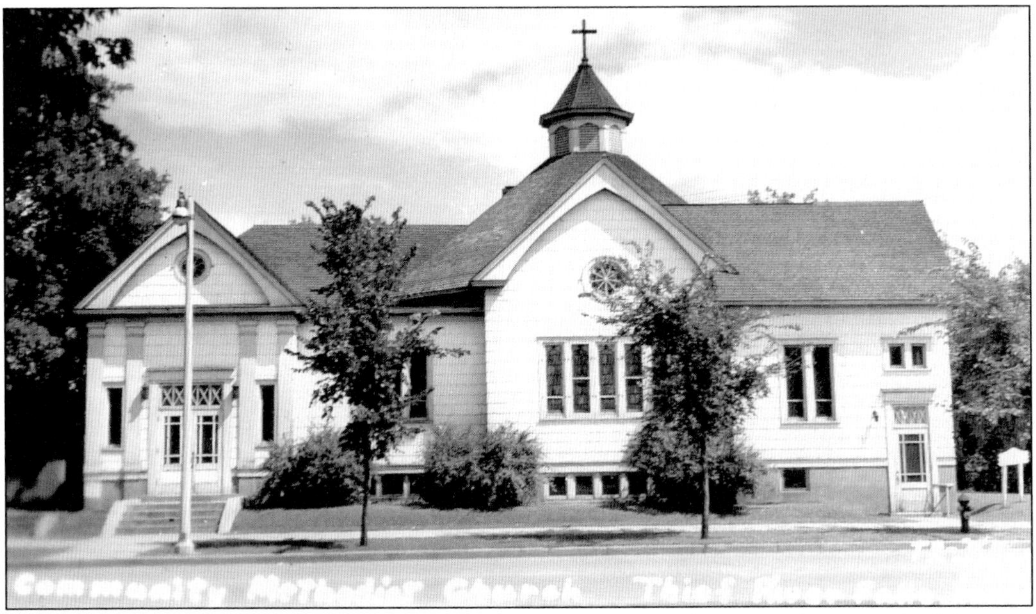

Thief River Falls Community Methodist Church. Shown in this view looking east on Horace Avenue, the Presbyterian building had the steeple that had no bell removed, and additions were made at both ends of the building in 1940. The new building was dedicated in 1941. The combined congregations of the Methodist Episcopal and Presbyterian churches became the United Methodist Church in 1968.

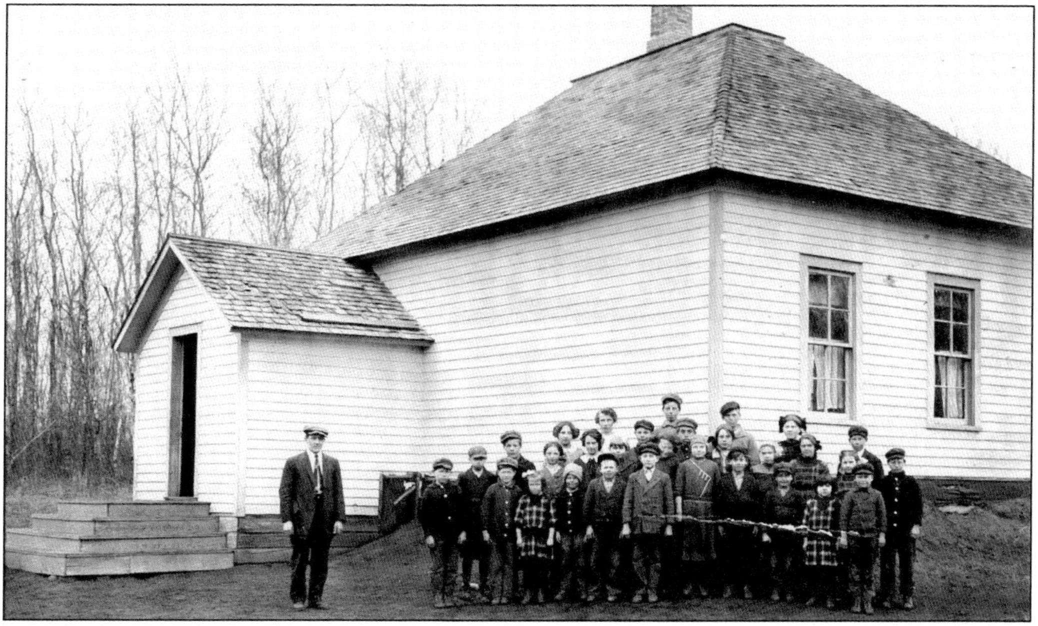

River Falls Township. The Erickson or East Side Country School was located in Section 23, near St. Hilaire. Myles Jackson, who later owned a store in St. Hilaire, was the teacher of the school from 1913 to 1914.

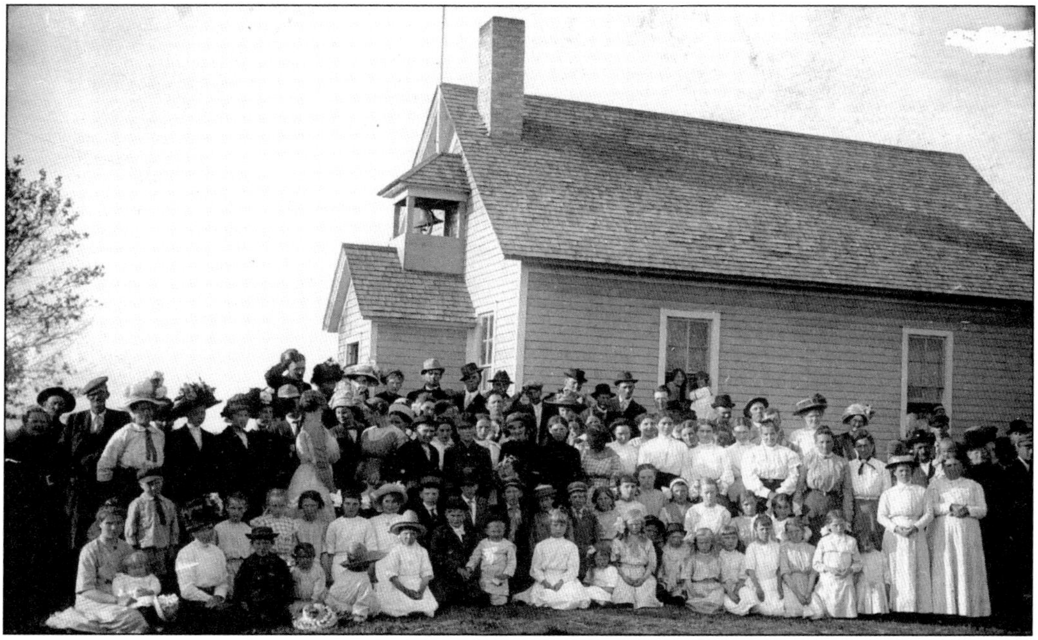

Rocksbury Township. The Riverside or Aubol Country School was located in Section 29, near the Red Lake River. The first year that the school was at this site was 1890, and the teacher was Louisa Johnson. The building was later moved to Thief River Falls and became the restaurant currently named Dee's on North Atlantic.

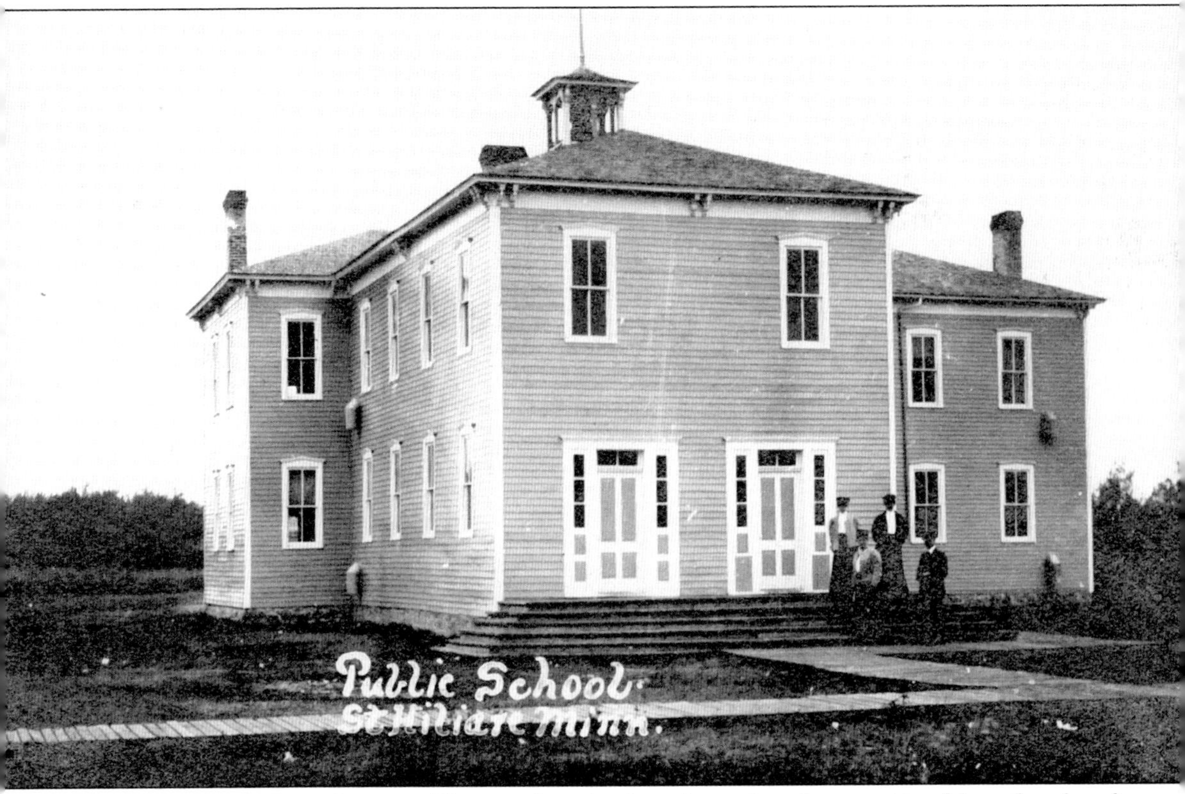

ST. HILAIRE PUBLIC SCHOOL. The wooden school was located on the west side of the railroad tracks and across the creek, between Third and Fourth Streets on Minnesota Avenue. A boardwalk ran from Broadway to the school with a walking bridge over the creek. The school closed in 1919.

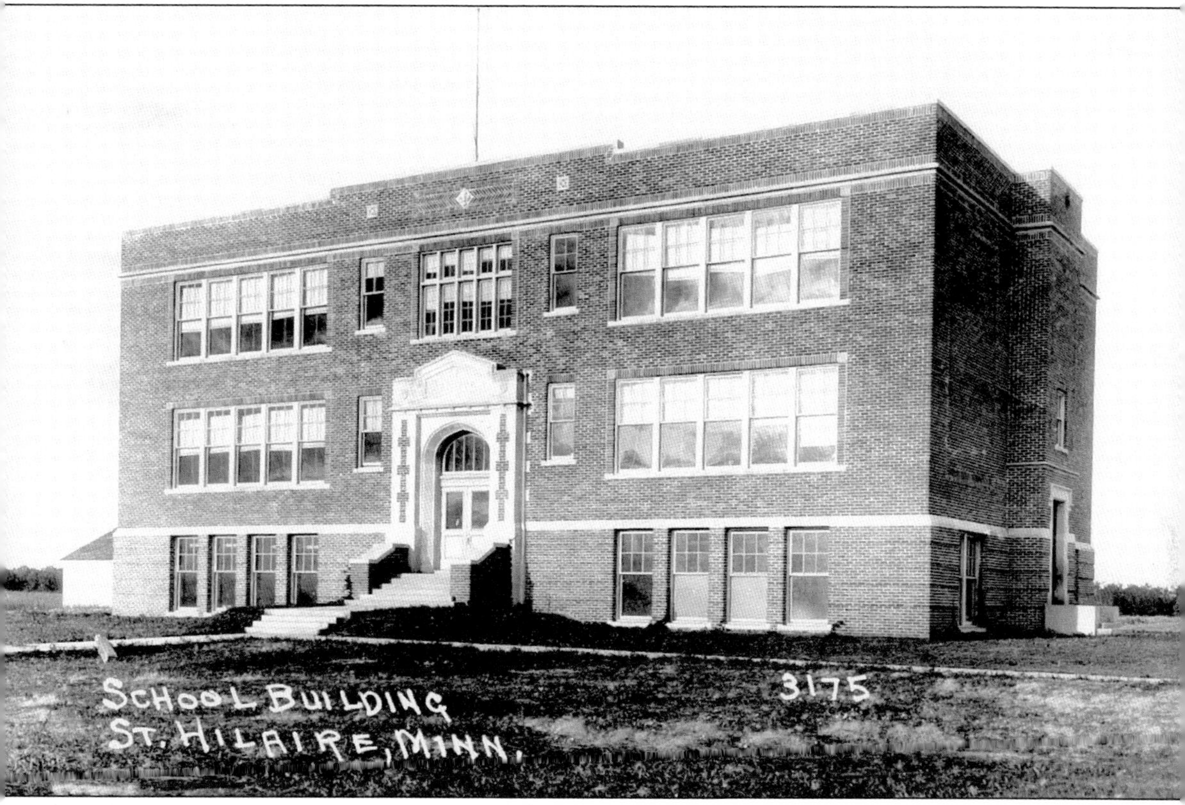

ST. HILAIRE HIGH SCHOOL. In this view looking northeast, the high school was on the east side of Highway 32 between Seventh and Eighth Streets. Opened in 1920, the last graduating class was in 1943, the last classes met in the building in 1981, and the building was demolished in 1999.

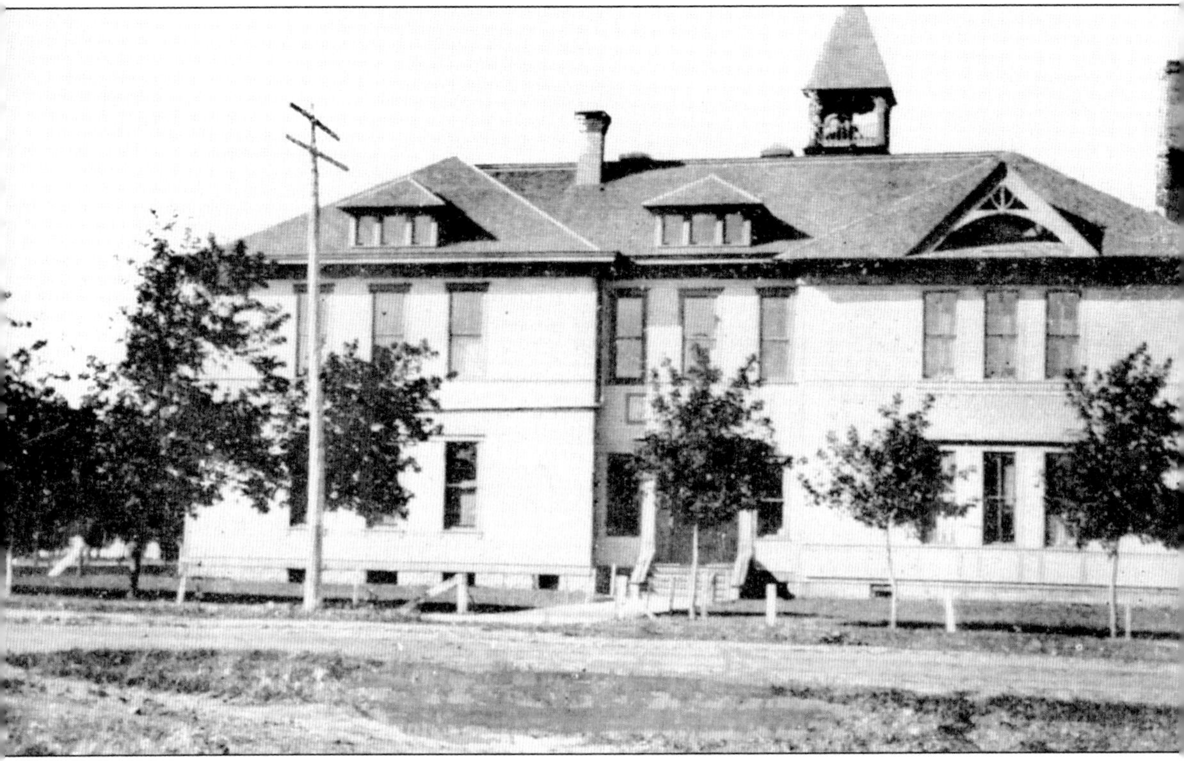

THIEF RIVER FALLS CENTRAL SCHOOL. Shown in this picture looking north, the school was at 209 Fourth Street. Built in 1893 with eight classrooms, the east wing of the building was added in 1906.

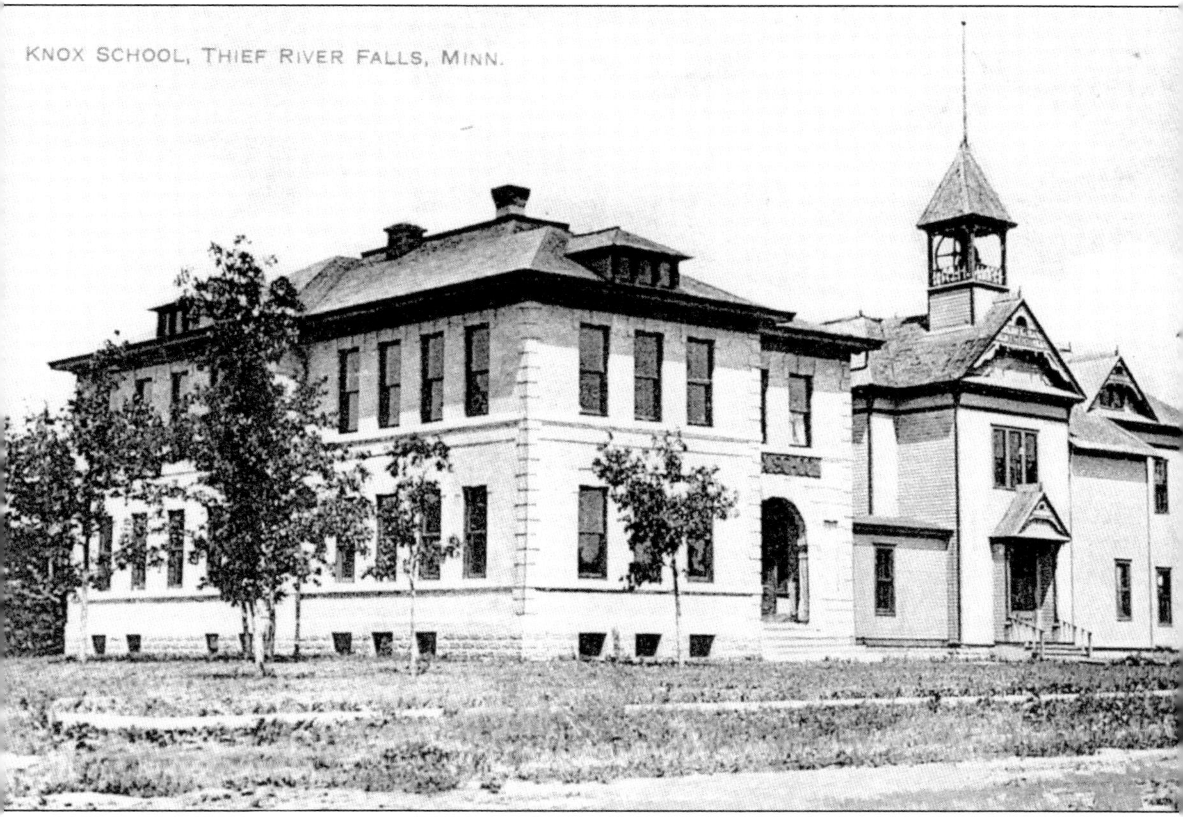

THIEF RIVER FALLS NEW AND OLD KNOX SCHOOL. In this view looking northeast, the school was at 310 Markley Avenue South. The first Knox School (on the right) was made of wood and was later sold to the Catholic church. The building sank through the river ice while being moved and had to be razed before the move was completed. The New Knox School (on the left) was built in 1906 and closed in 1994.

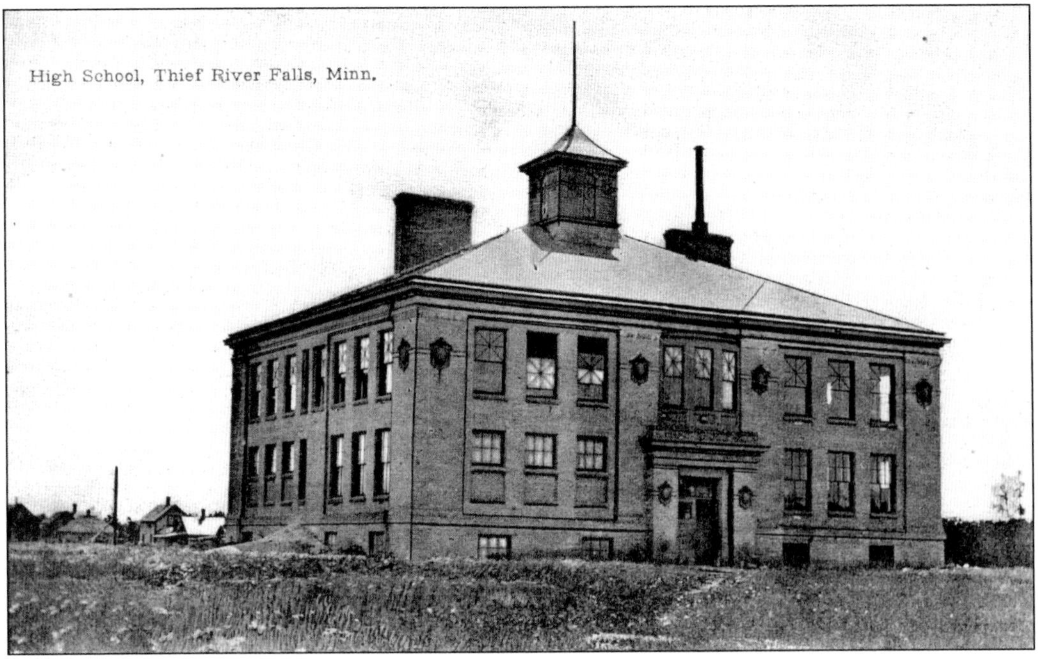

THIEF RIVER FALLS HIGH SCHOOL. Shown in this view looking southwest from the corner of First Street and Knight Avenue, the building was listed as the high school in the 1908–1909 city directory. The land sale of 1904 was held on the steps of the school, and it became Washington Elementary School in 1911.

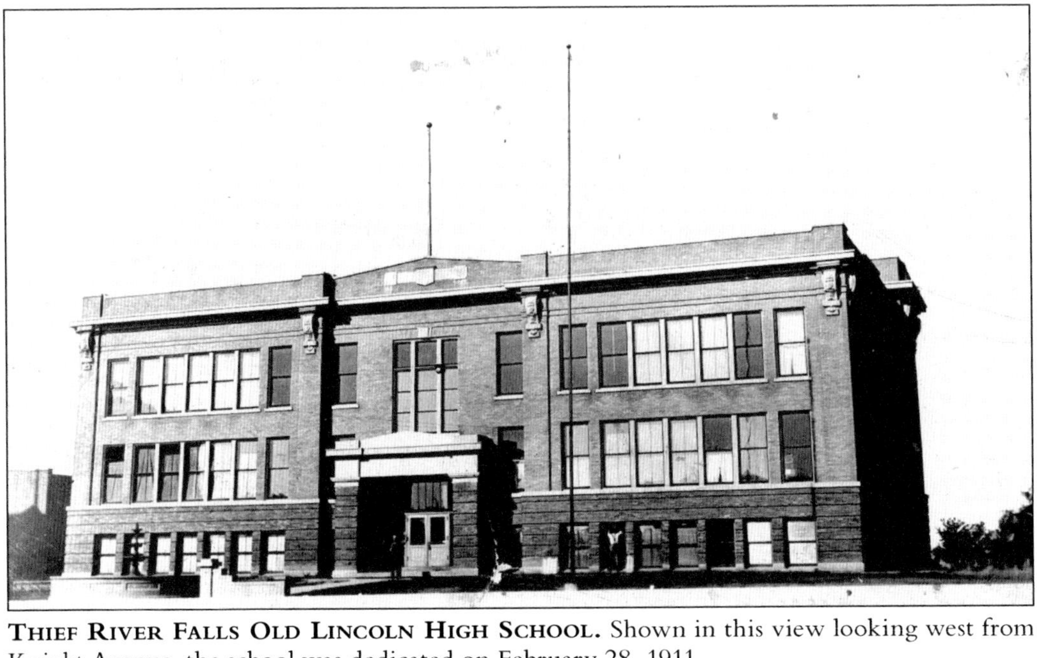

THIEF RIVER FALLS OLD LINCOLN HIGH SCHOOL. Shown in this view looking west from Knight Avenue, the school was dedicated on February 28, 1911.

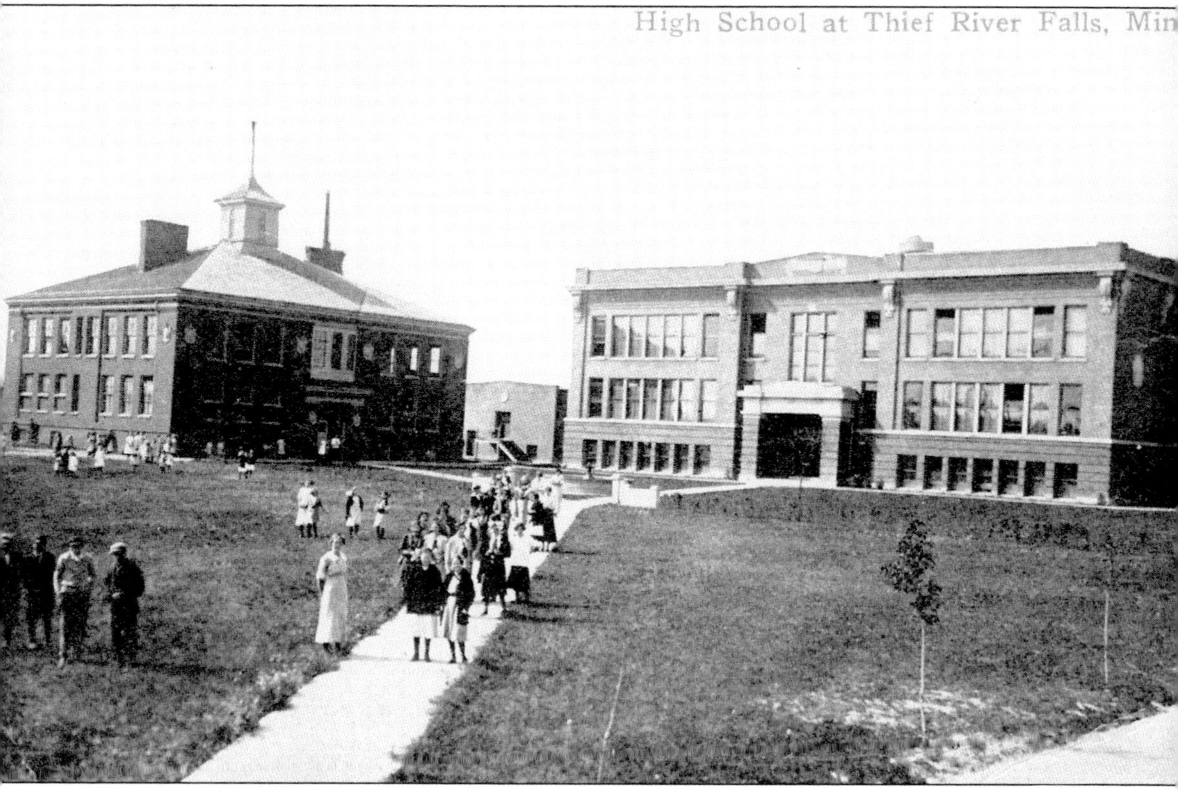

THIEF RIVER FALLS LINCOLN HIGH SCHOOL AND WASHINGTON ELEMENTARY. Looking from the corner of First Street and Knight Avenue, the views of both of the first high schools are included on this card. The two girls at the front on the sidewalk are Jeanette Oftedahl (left) and Clara Oen who graduated in 1918.

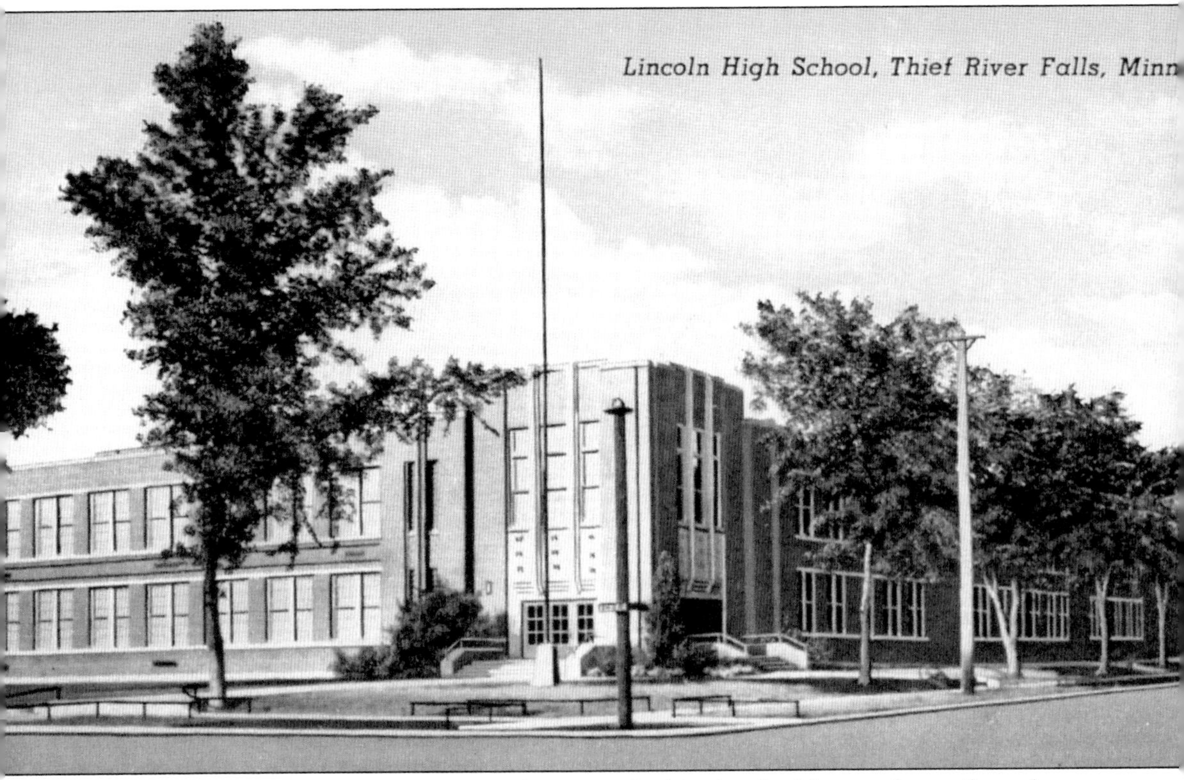

THIEF RIVER FALLS LINCOLN HIGH SCHOOL. In this view looking southwest from the corner of First Street and Knight Avenue, the high school is an amalgam of the past buildings and additions. The ground for the original building was broken in 1938.

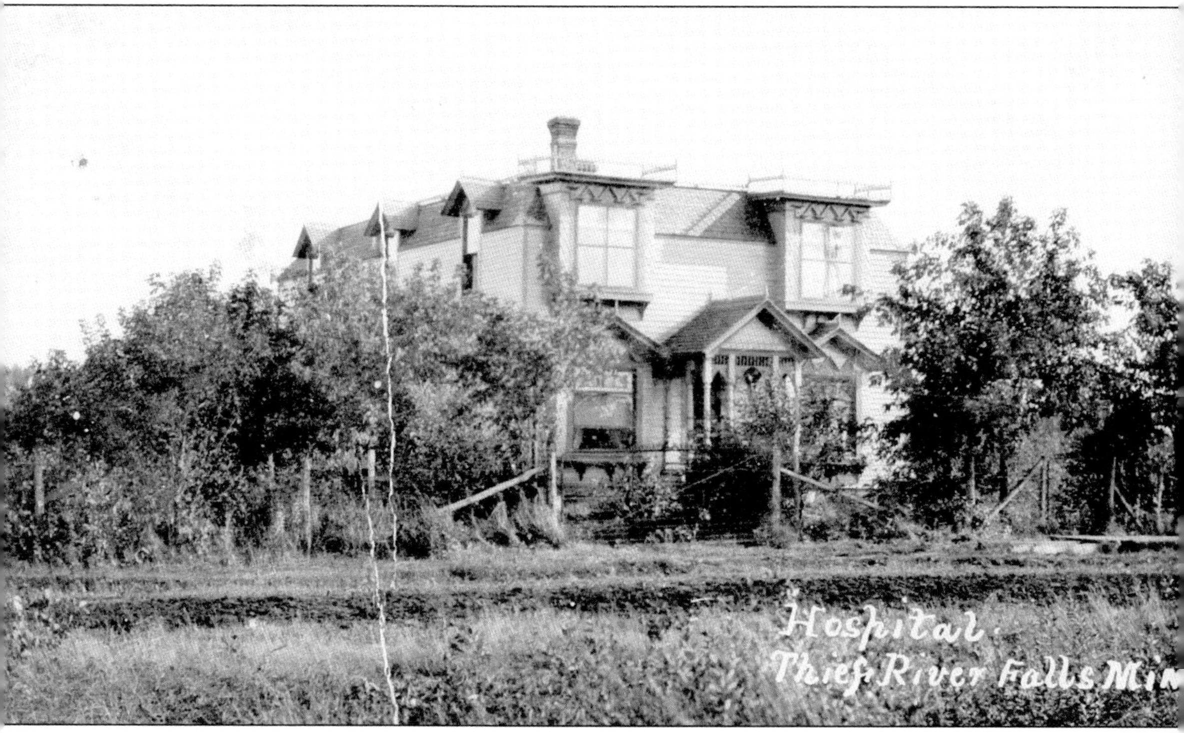

THIEF RIVER FALLS BETHANY HOSPITAL. In this view looking southeast, the first hospital was at 522 Red Lake Boulevard. The hospital was organized by Inga Boen and Marie Vistaunet in 1903, at the site of Dr. Paul L. Vistaunet's clinic. The hospital had eight beds, and Inga Boen was both the superintendent and the nursing staff.

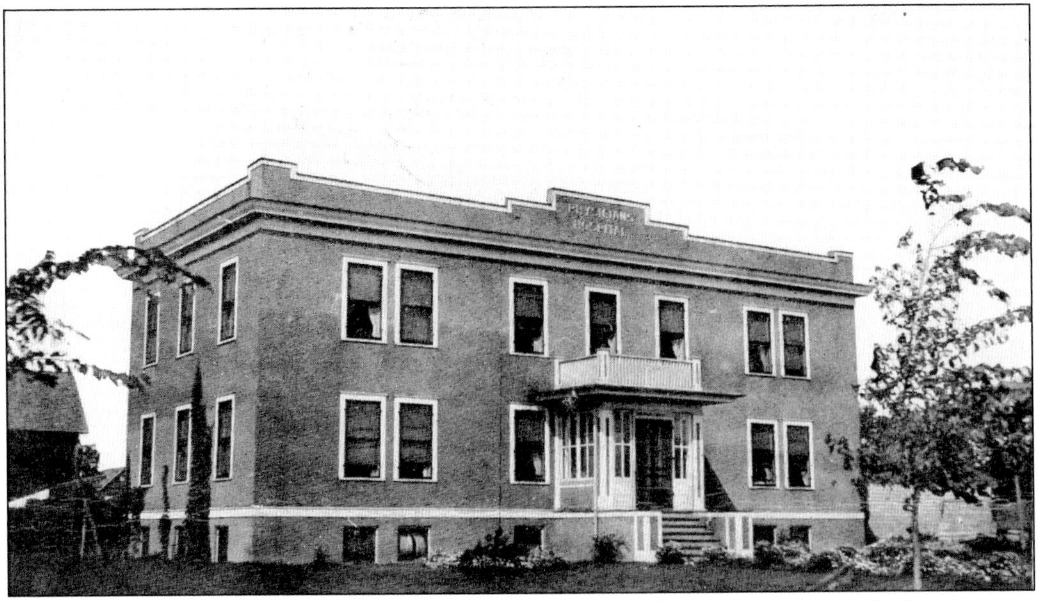

THIEF RIVER FALLS PHYSICIANS HOSPITAL. In this view looking northeast, the hospital is at 219 Fifth Street West. The hospital opened in 1915 at a total cost of $20,000, held 25 patients, and had an operating room on the northwest corner of the second floor.

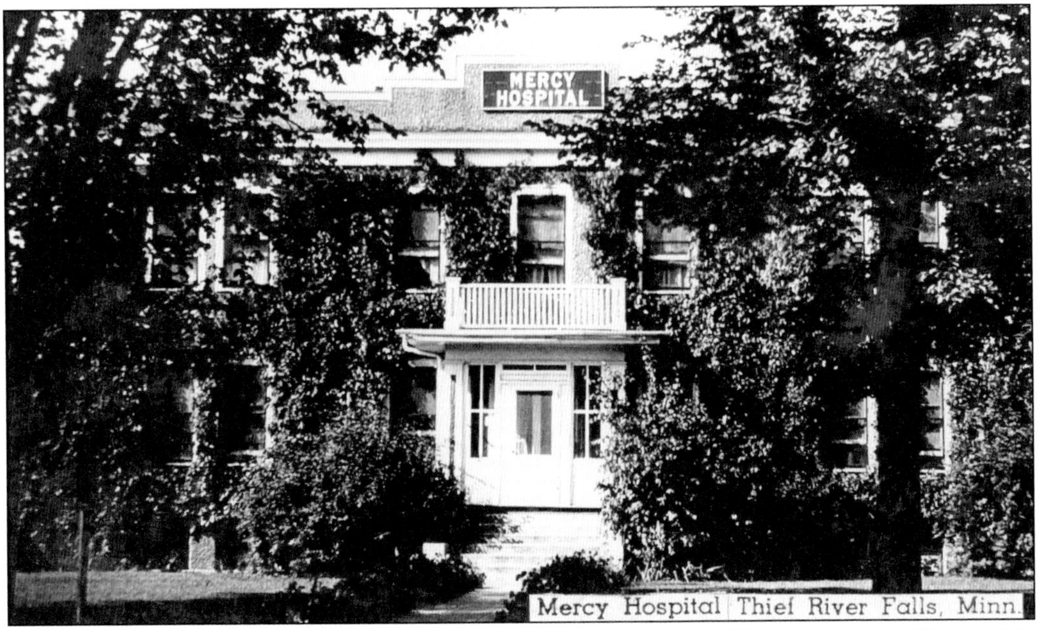

THIEF RIVER FALLS MERCY HOSPITAL. The Physicians Hospital became Mercy Hospital in 1938. A Quonset-type addition was built behind the hospital in 1947 to accommodate 20 beds. The second floor was vacated in 1951, and the building became the Masonic hall in 1954.

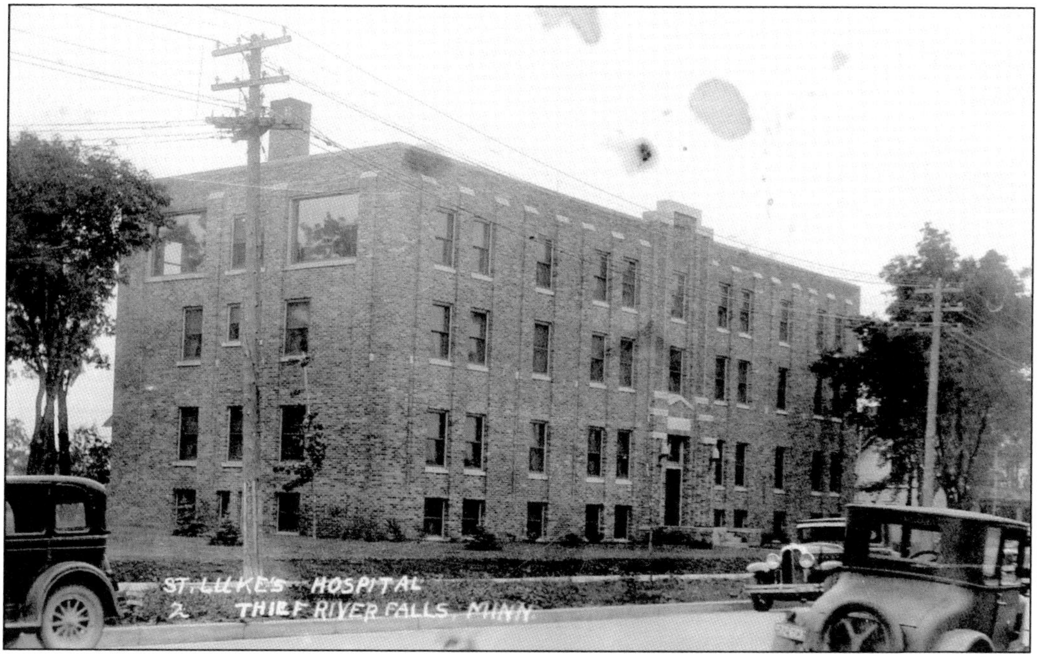

THIEF RIVER FALLS ST. LUKE'S HOSPITAL, DEDICATED 1931. In this view looking southeast, the hospital was at 120–124 South La Bree Avenue and was dedicated in 1931. The Bratrud Clinic was housed on the first floor of the hospital when it opened but moved west across the street in 1947. The building is currently in about the middle of the Northwest Medical Center Complex.

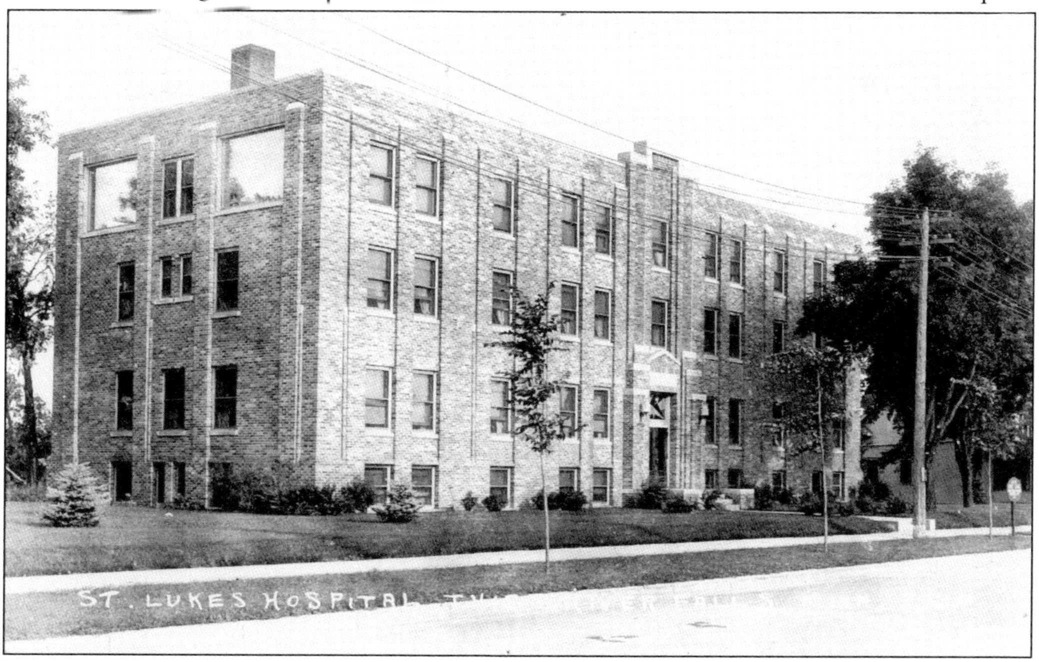

ST. LUKE'S HOSPITAL. An addition to the hospital was completed in 1954. The new wing included two 32-bed wards, new surgical suites, outpatient, x-ray, and physical therapy departments, a new kitchen, and a new heating system. Later, the name of the hospital was changed to Northwestern Hospital.

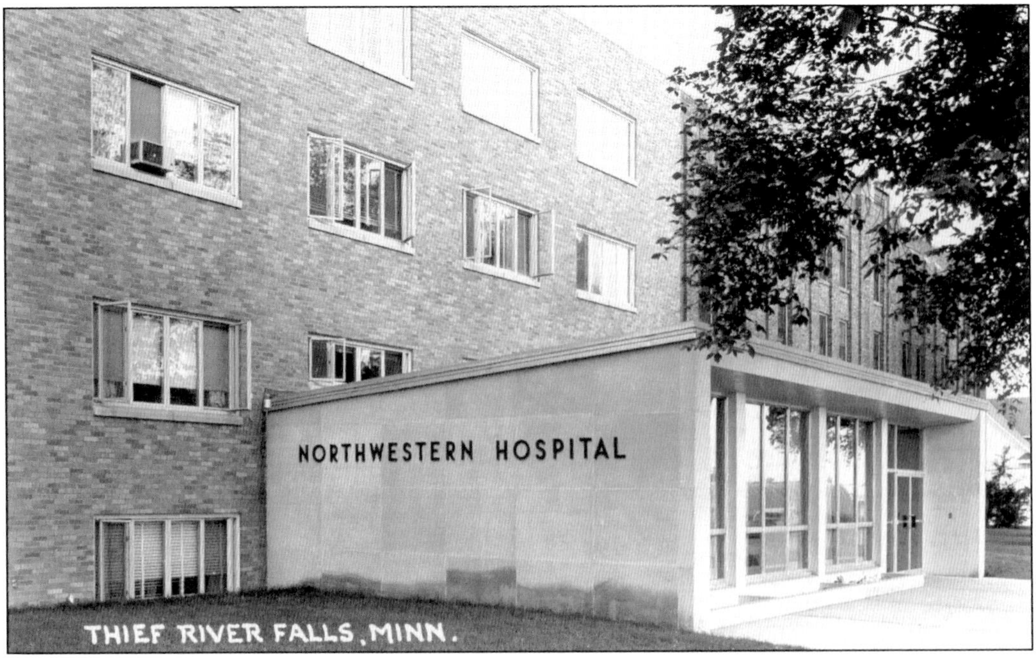

THIEF RIVER FALLS NORTHWESTERN HOSPITAL. This view looking southeast shows the hospital that was again expanded in 1964 to include a rehabilitation center of 36 beds for physical medicine, occupational therapy, radiology, and additional intensive care beds.

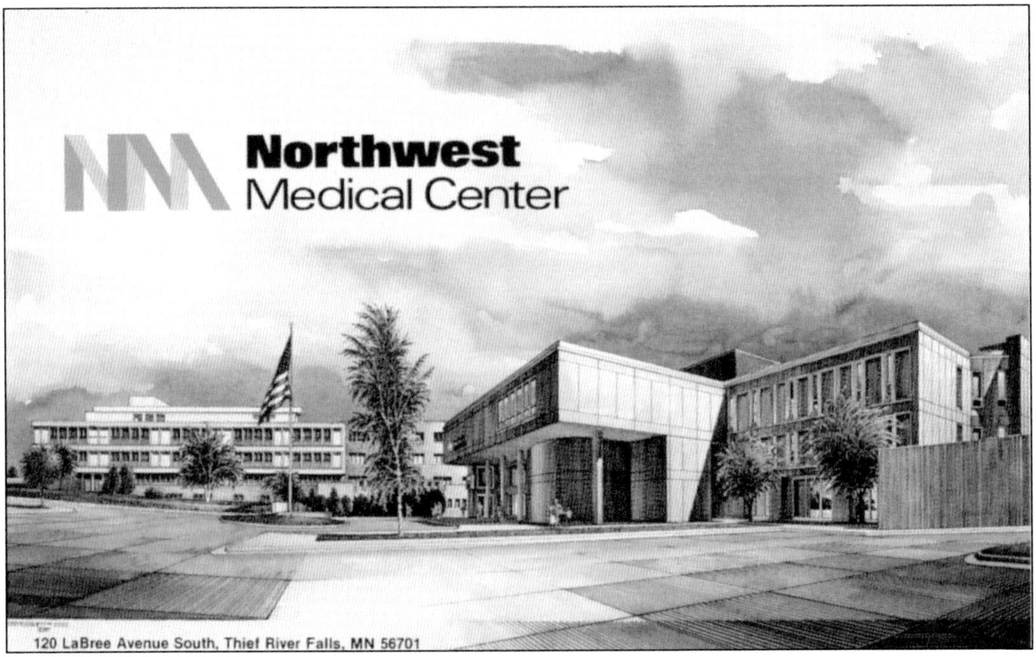

THIEF RIVER FALLS NORTHWEST MEDICAL CENTER. A 90-bed long-term care unit was added just south of the hospital in 1968. Also added were a psychiatric unit and department of physical medicine and rehabilitation, which were opened in 1969 and 1970. The name was changed again in 1985 to the current name. The hospital complex image is used with the permission of the artist Marv Espe.

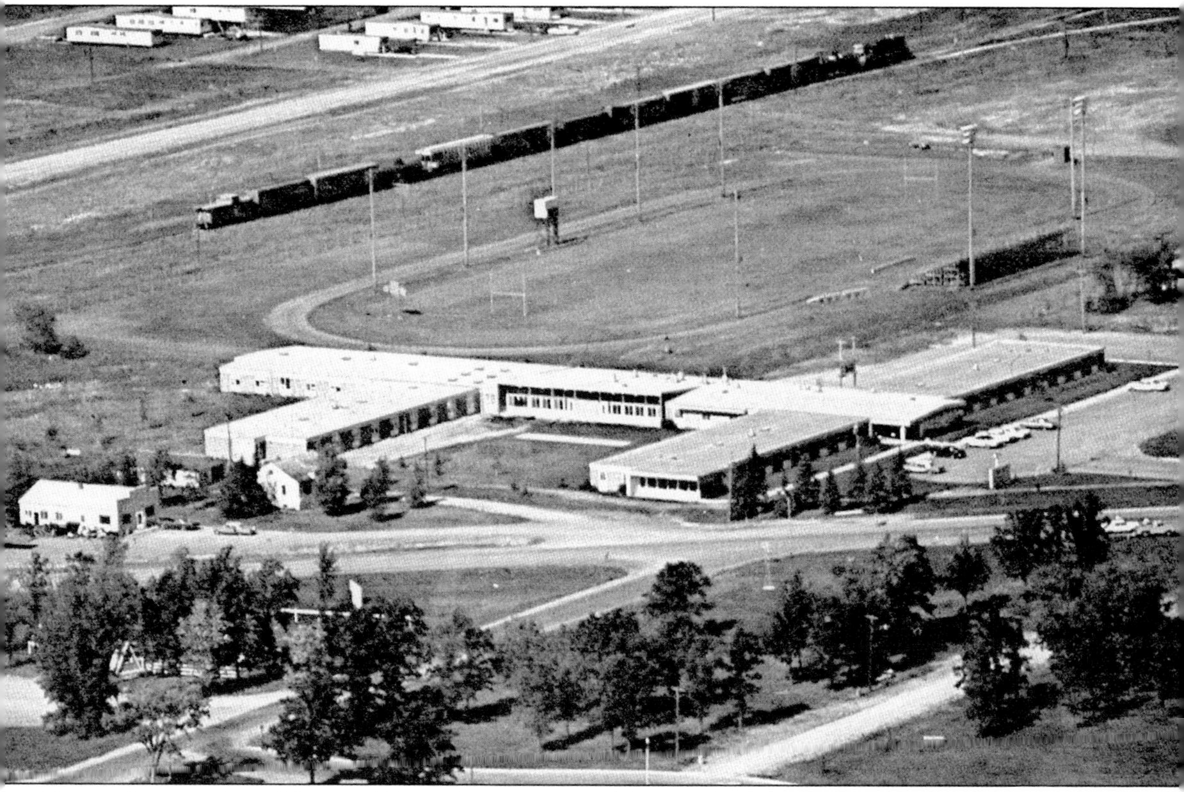

THIEF RIVER FALLS VALLEY HOME SOCIETY. Looking northwest, this housing for the elderly is located on the northwest edge of Highway 32 and Arnold Avenue North. The Red River Valley Home for the aged was located in the Central Hotel at the corner of Horace Avenue and Fourth Street in 1946. The Valley Home Society was formed in 1956. A new facility was built in the 1960s and expanded in 1968 and 2005.

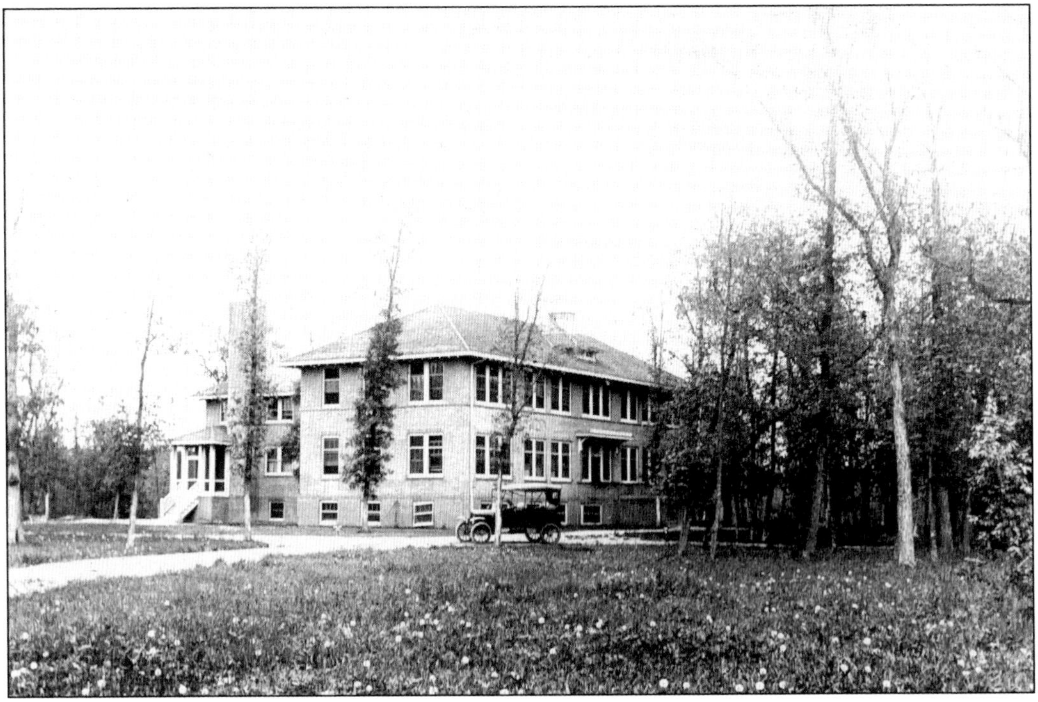

THIEF RIVER FALLS OAKLAND PARK SANATORIUM. Looking northeast, the sanatorium and nurses' residence were southwest of the city off Oakland Park Road. The tuberculosis sanatorium was built in 1916 by Pennington, Marshall, and Roseau Counties. Red Lake County joined the ownership in 1922. The facility was enlarged in 1938 to provide care for 50 patients.

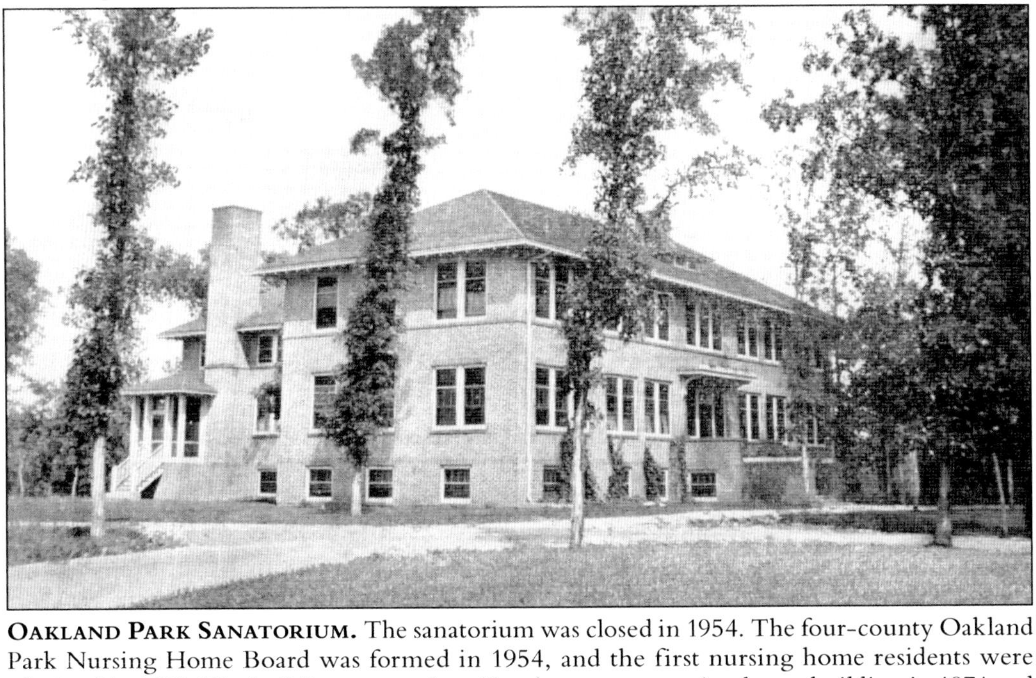

OAKLAND PARK SANATORIUM. The sanatorium was closed in 1954. The four-county Oakland Park Nursing Home Board was formed in 1954, and the first nursing home residents were admitted in 1955. The building was replaced by the current nursing home building in 1974 and was demolished in 1999.

Four

Government, Banks, and Business

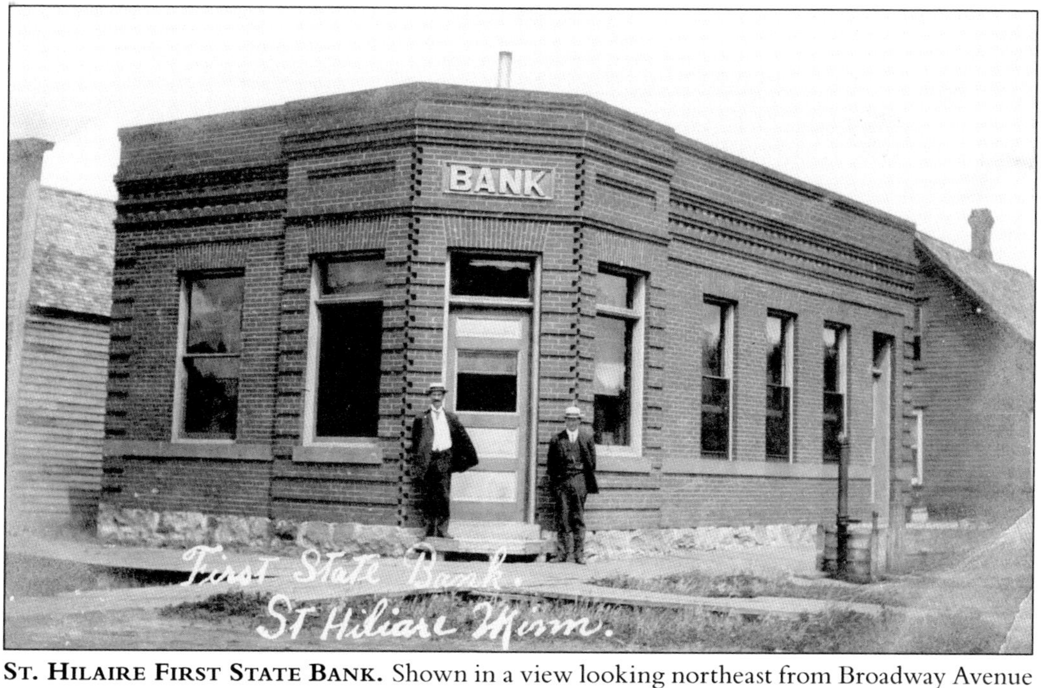

St. Hilaire First State Bank. Shown in a view looking northeast from Broadway Avenue and Third Street, this bank failed, and the building became the city post office. The flowing well and the telephone building were on the right. The building was later torn down, and a new post office, which still stands on the corner, was built.

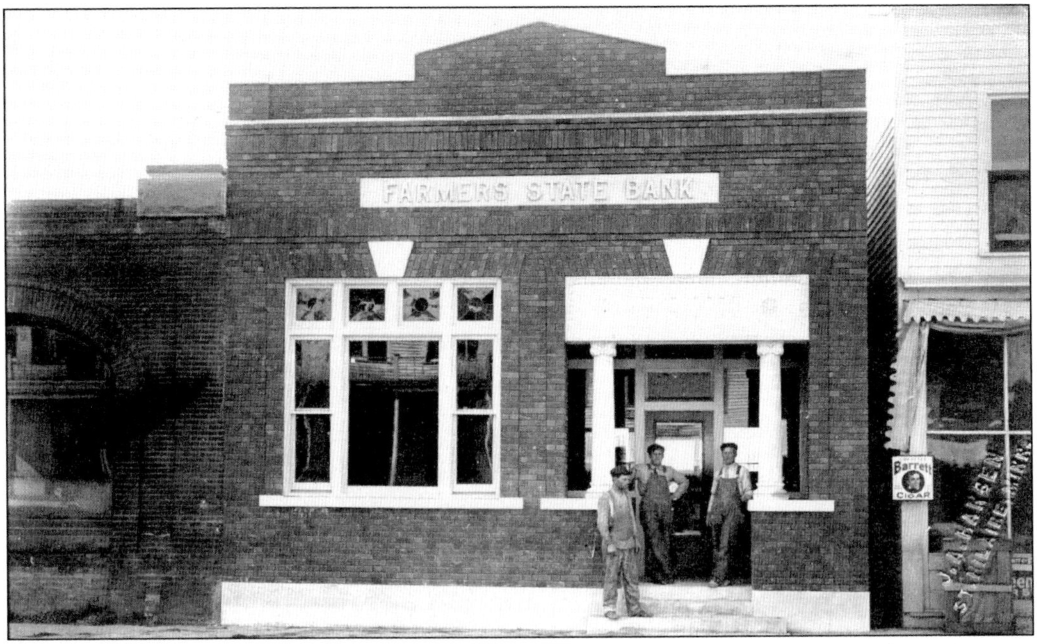

St. Hilaire Farmers State Bank. Shown in a view looking west on Broadway Avenue, this bank was opened to the public on September 19, 1915. Knute Gigstad was the president of the bank, and Olaf Aaberg was the cashier.

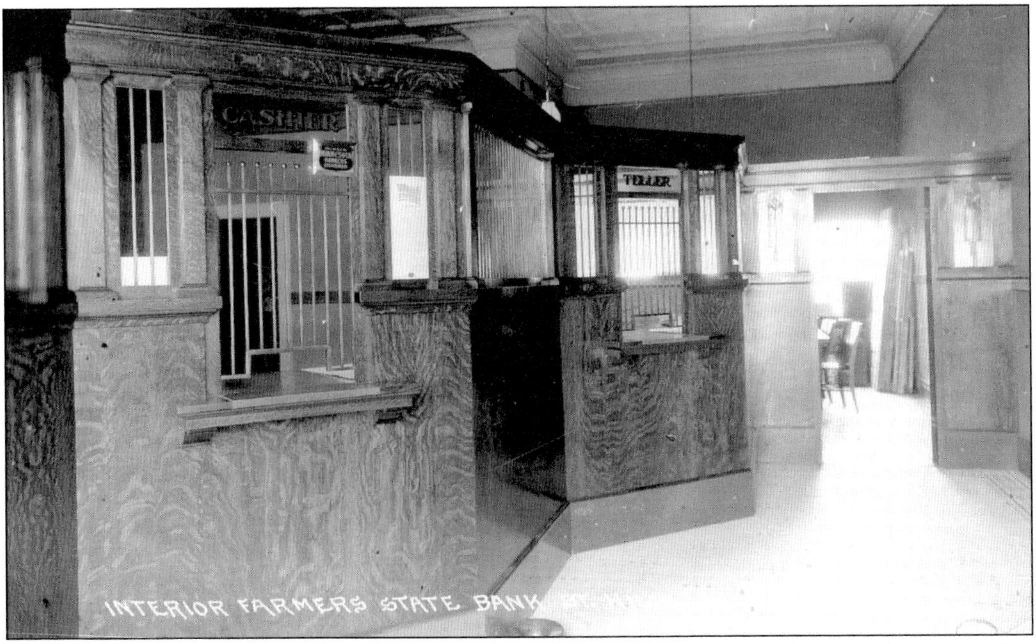

St. Hilaire Farmers State Bank, Interior. The interior of the bank is shown on this card postmarked 1921. The bank closed in 1925.

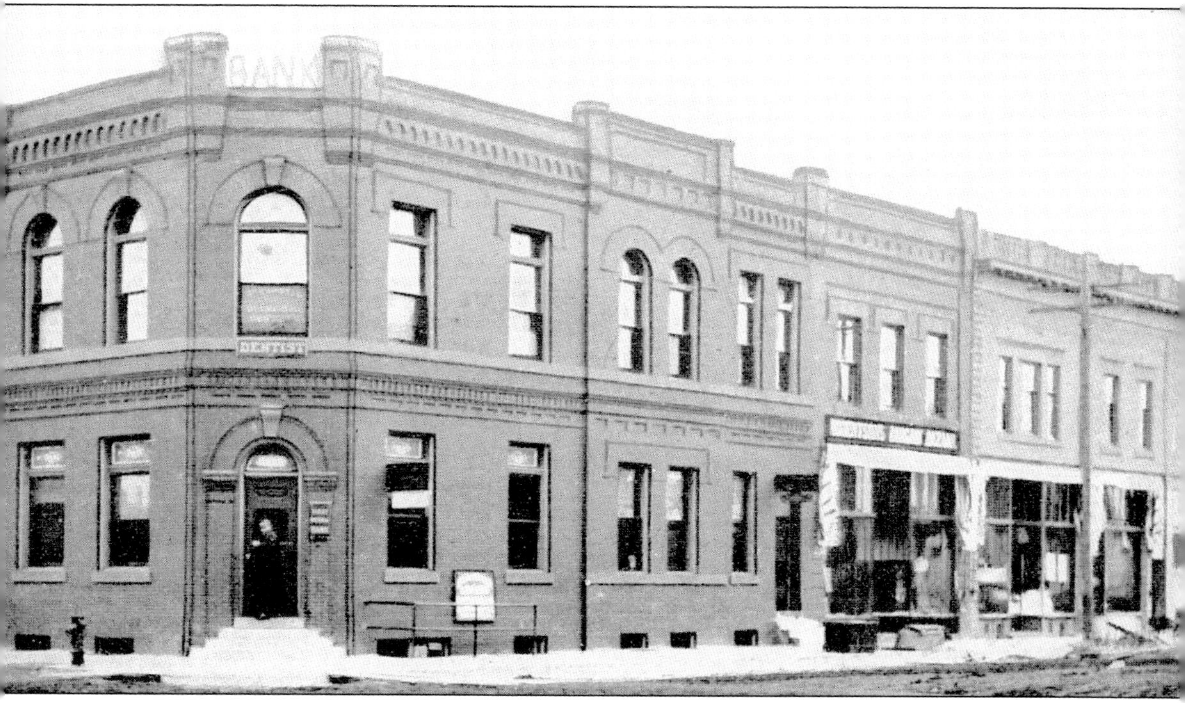

THIEF RIVER FALLS FIRST NATIONAL BANK, NORTHEAST VIEW. Shown in a view looking northeast on Third Street, the bank was on the corner at 302 La Bree Avenue North. Continuing east on Third Street, the other businesses were the Robertson Bargain Bazaar (205), Zeh and Curran Grocery (207), Langseth Shoe Store (209), and *Thief River Falls Press* (211) in 1909.

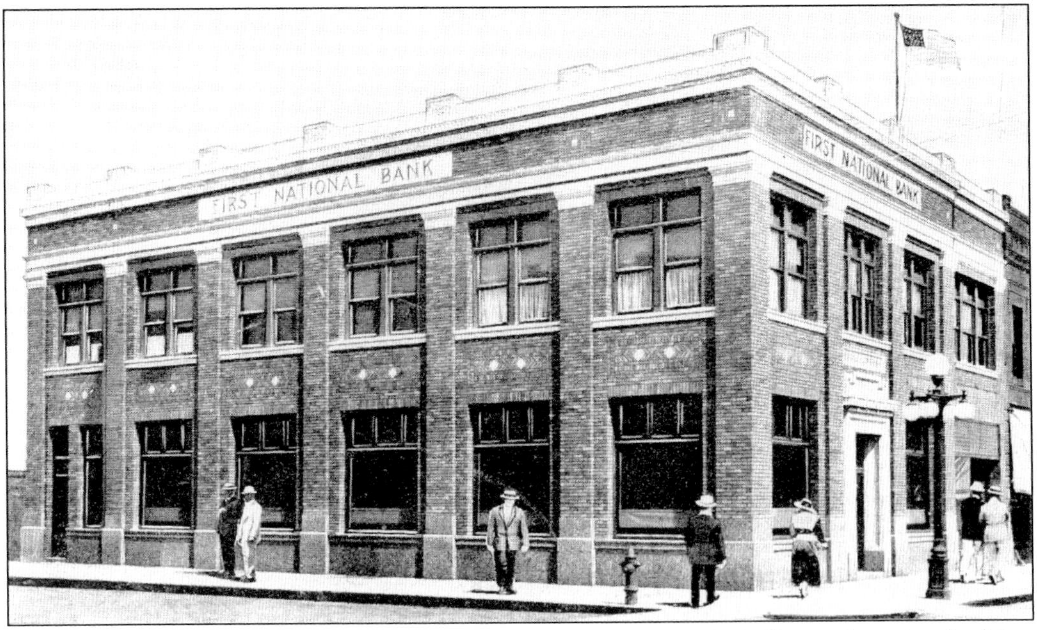

THIEF RIVER FALLS FIRST NATIONAL BANK, ESTABLISHED 1915. Shown in a view looking northeast, the building on the corner was remodeled to remove the sandstone corner door. The bank was established in 1915 and later became the Northern State Bank in 1935, with George Beito as president and chairman of the board.

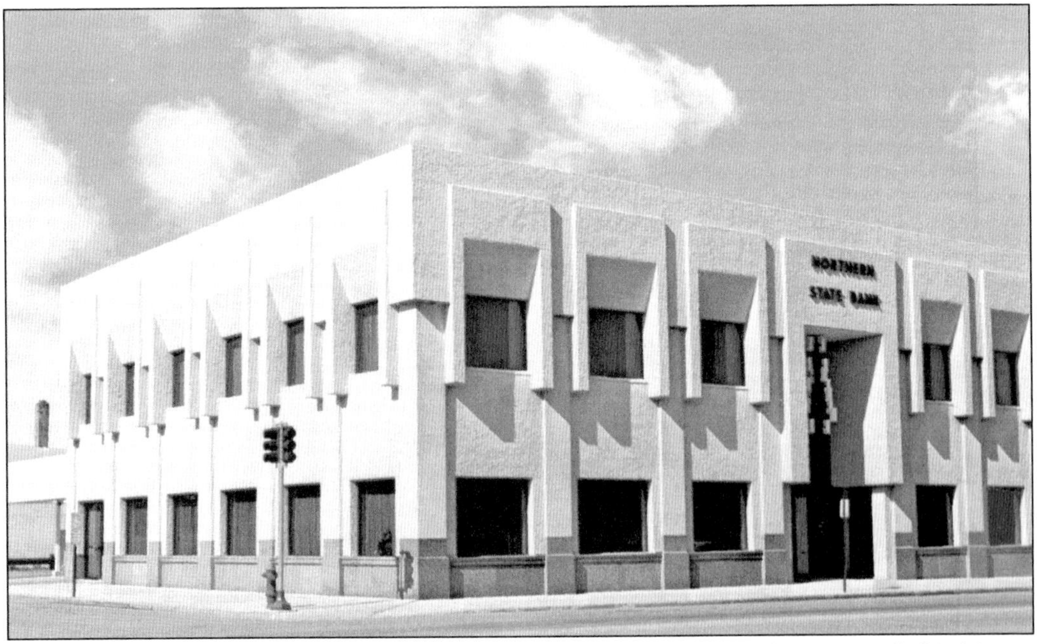

THIEF RIVER FALLS NORTHERN STATE BANK. Looking northeast at the corner of Third Street and La Bree Avenue, the bank is owned by the Beito Family. The building was remodeled again from 1970 to 1971 and in 1992.

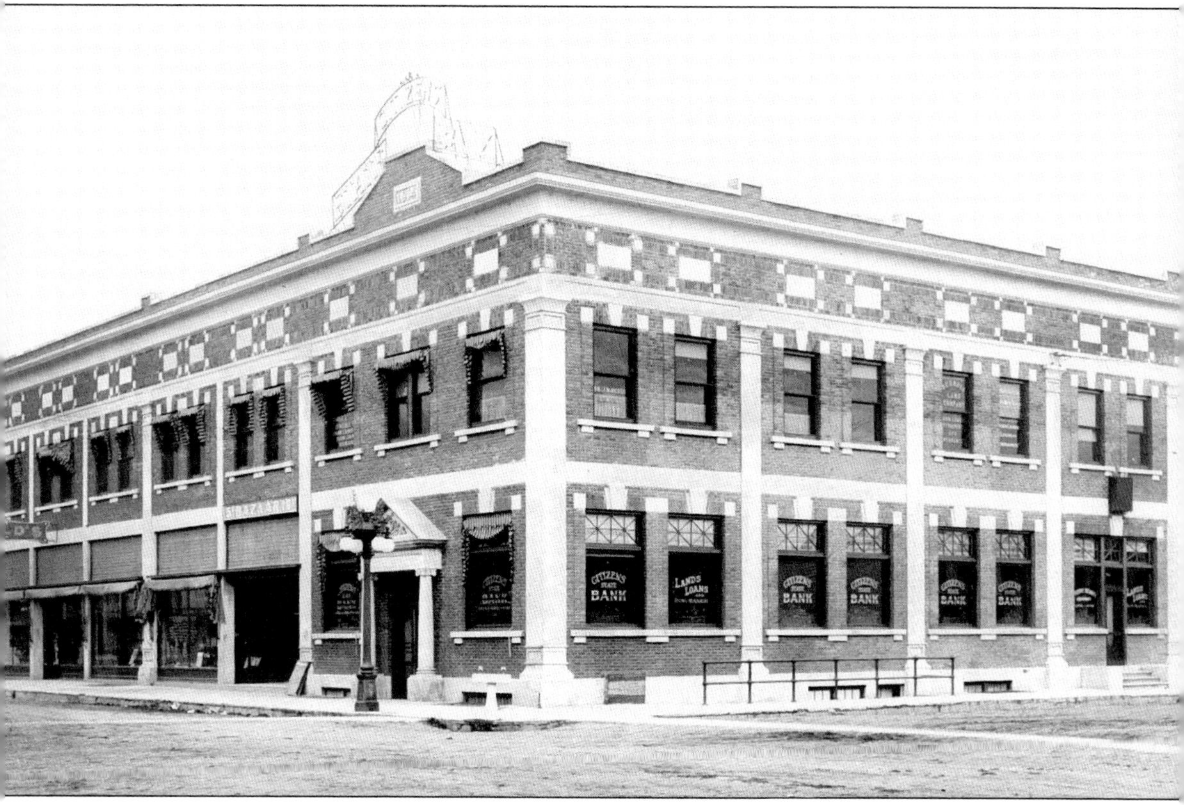

THIEF RIVER FALLS CITIZENS STATE BANK. In a view looking northwest at the corner of Third Street and La Bree Avenue, the bank was at 121–123 Third Street East after 1914. The first Citizens State Bank was previously located at 224 Main Avenue North in the Evenson Building, which burned in 1914. Wold's Clothing Store was included in this building. The B. P. O. Elks currently own the building.

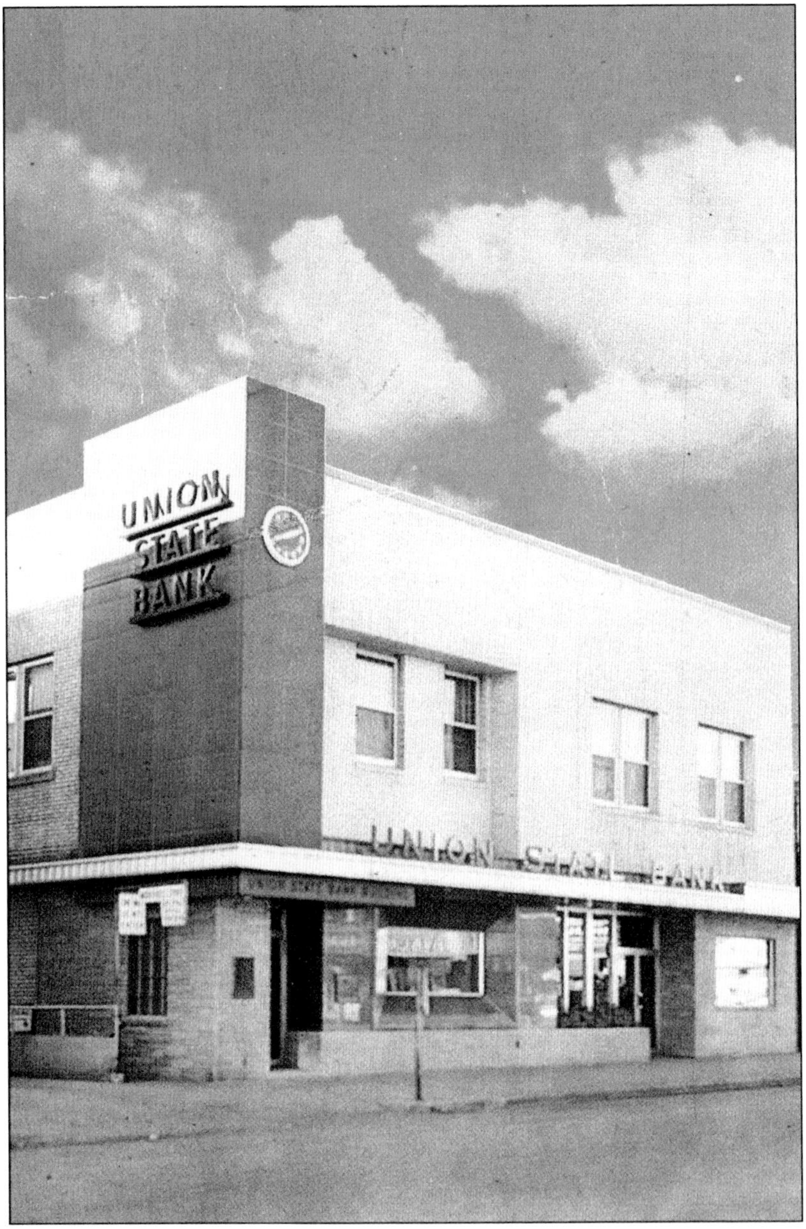

THIEF RIVER FALLS UNION STATE BANK. Shown in a view looking southwest, the bank began in 1930 at 110 East Third Street. The Union State Bank changed to the First Northwestern State Bank in 1974, Norwest Bank in 1988, and finally the Well's Fargo Bank, which was the building's last usage as a bank. The building is currently occupied by Lindahl's Furniture.

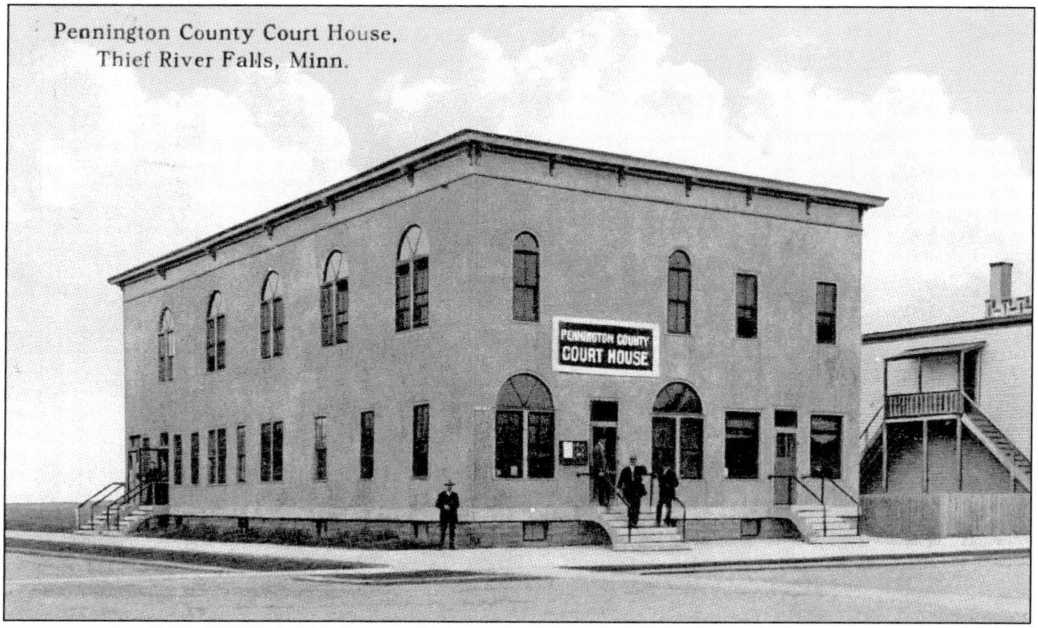

Previous Thief River Falls Pennington County Courthouse. Shown in a picture looking northwest from the corner of Main Avenue and First Street, the previous Thief River Falls City Hall was remodeled and occupied by the county on April 30, 1911. The building was demolished when the new courthouse was built.

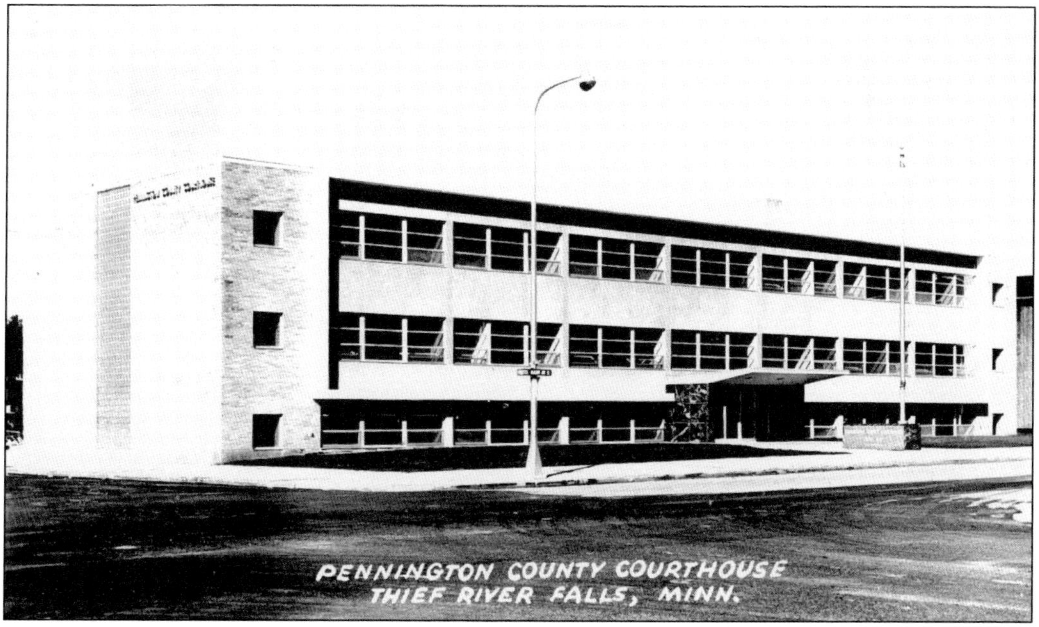

Current Thief River Falls Pennington County Courthouse. Shown in a picture looking northwest from the corner of Main Avenue and First Street, the current county courthouse was built in 1954 and also serves as offices for the motor vehicle license bureau, the University Extension Service, and the Veteran's Service.

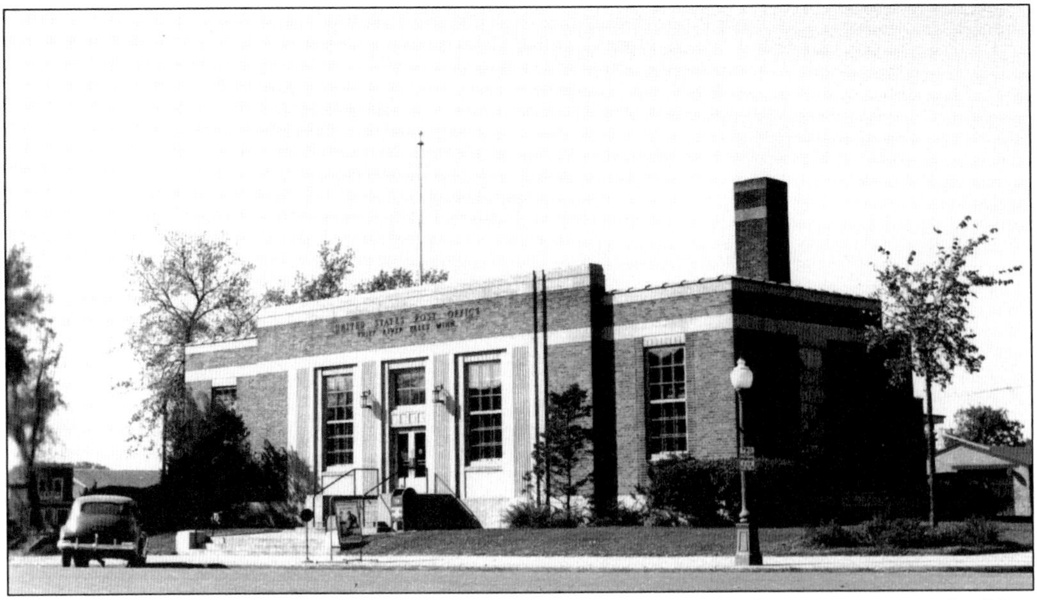

Thief River Falls United States Post Office, Built 1933. Shown in a picture looking southwest from the corner of La Bree Avenue and Second Street, a post office was officially designated in Thief River Falls in 1891 and was located at 111 Second Street East after 1909. In 1927, the post office was temporarily located at 123 Third Street East. The post office building was built in 1933.

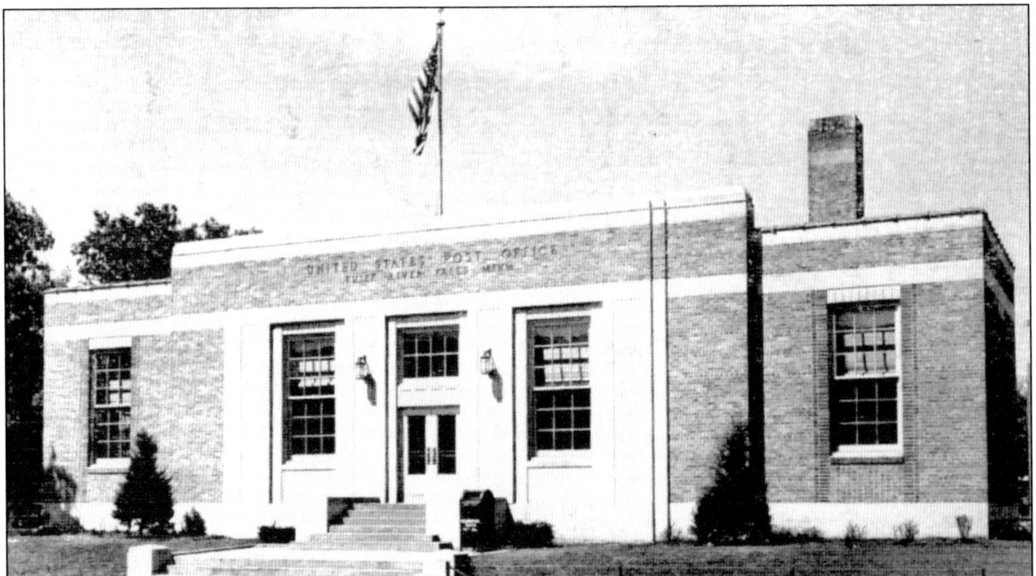

Thief River Falls United States Post Office. Shown in a view looking west from La Bree Avenue, the building at 115–121 has been remodeled to include a handicapped entrance and loading docks.

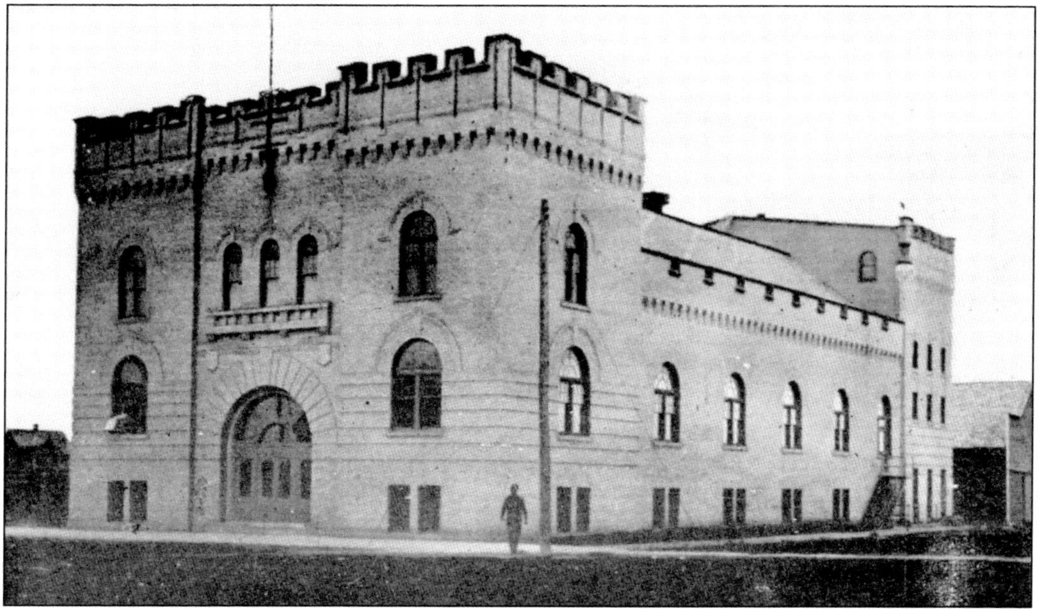

THIEF RIVER FALLS CITY AUDITORIUM, LOOKING SOUTHWEST. Shown in a view looking southwest from the corner of Main Avenue and Second Street, the auditorium building was erected in 1910 and served as the city armory, theater, opera house, and auditorium with a capacity of 6,000 people, a stage, and eight dressing rooms.

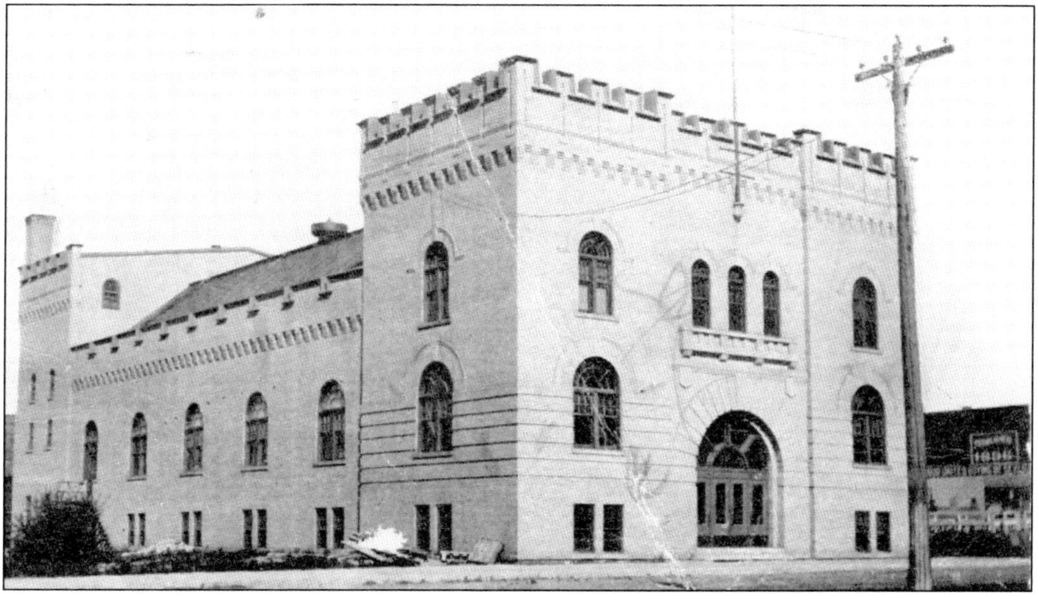

THIEF RIVER FALLS CITY AUDITORIUM, LOOKING NORTHWEST. In a view looking northwest, the building is located at 123 Main Avenue North and is viewed from the other side on this card postmarked February 2, 1911. On the reverse, Mrs. Gulrud wrote to Mrs. Christianson that she had seen a play, *The Burgomaster*, at the opera house. The play was on stage January 31, 1911. The building burned down in 1933.

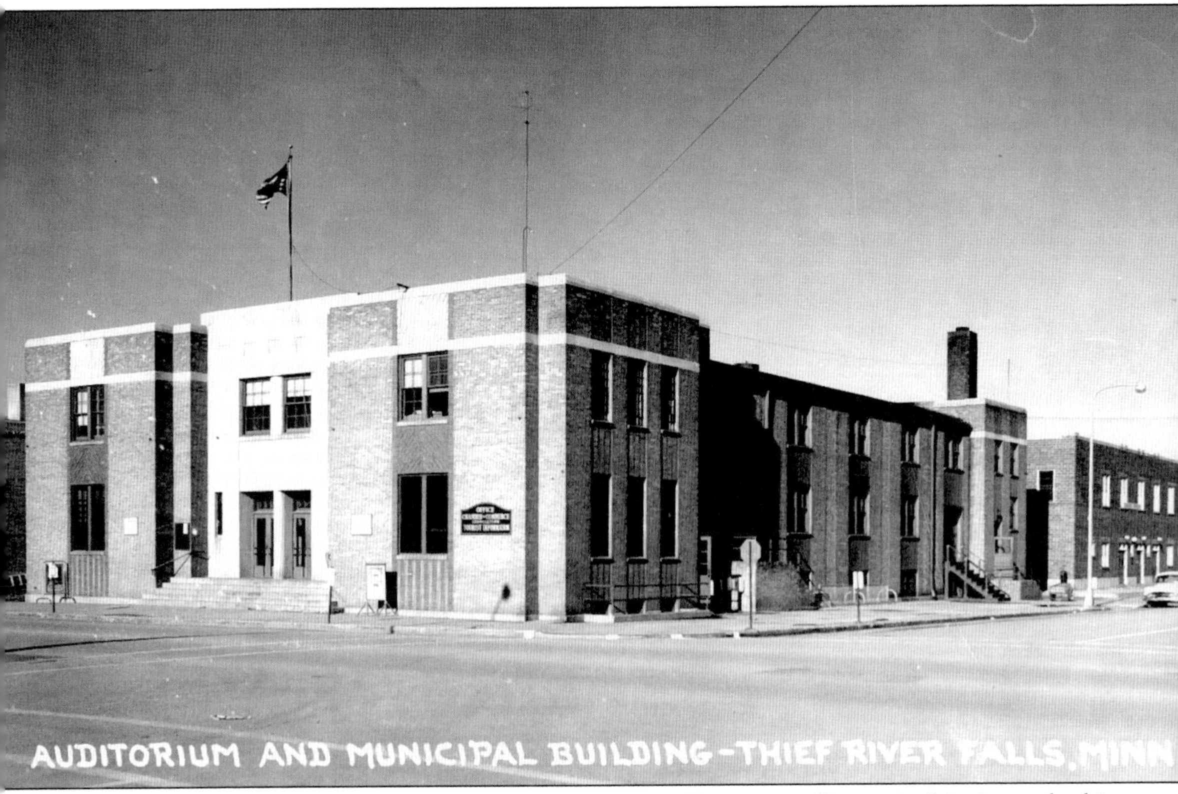

THIEF RIVER FALLS AUDITORIUM AND MUNICIPAL BUILDING. Shown in this picture looking southwest from Main Avenue and Second Street, the current auditorium was built in 1933. The Old Arena building on the far right at 118 Second Street West was built in 1936. It is currently one of three enclosed sheets of ice in the city.

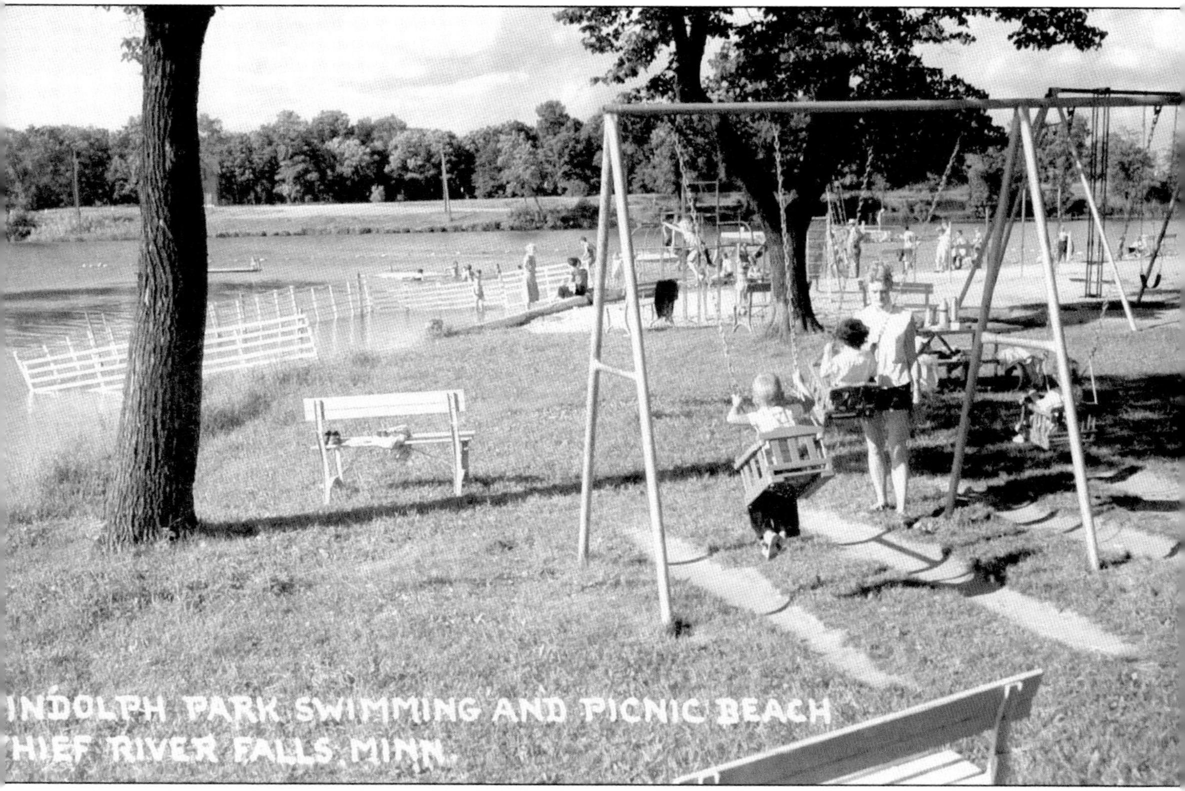

THIEF RIVER FALLS TINDOLPH PARK SWIMMING AND PICNIC BEACH. In this view looking northeast, the park is located where the Red Lake and Thief Rivers meet at the north end of Tindolph Avenue. The park was renamed as the La Fave Park.

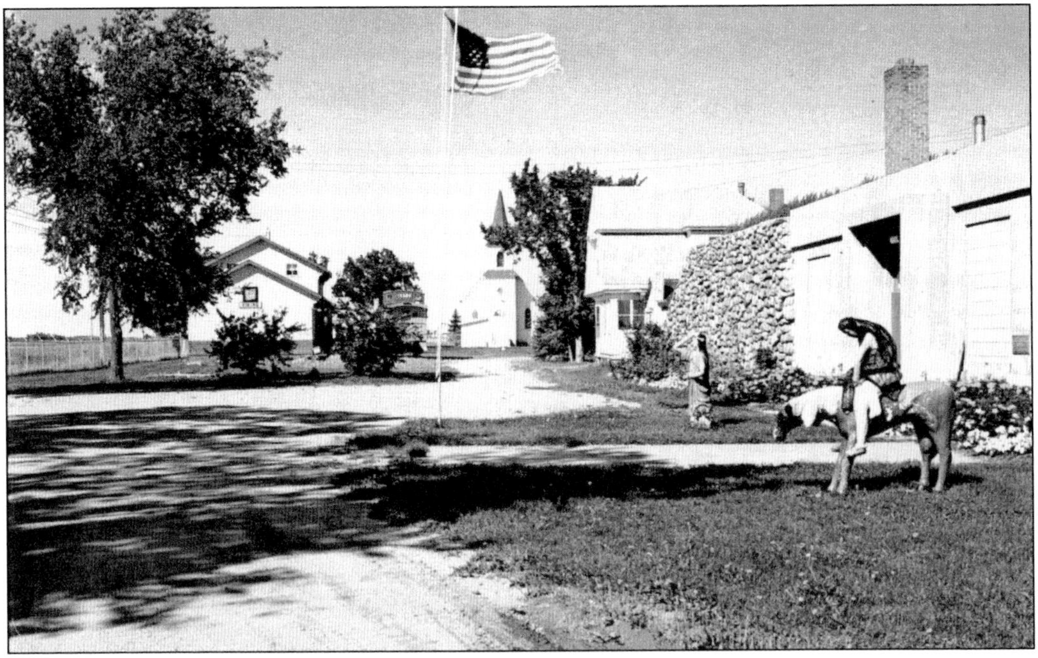

THIEF RIVER FALLS PEDER ENGELSTAD PIONEER VILLAGE, WEST VIEW. Looking west from Oakland Park Road, the village was created when the City of Thief River Falls vacated their sewage treatment plant and donated the land surrounding it to the Pennington County Historical Society. In its early development, the buildings were the Viking Soo Line Depot, Asphult Lutheran Church, Hamre Victorian House, and Geving Museum.

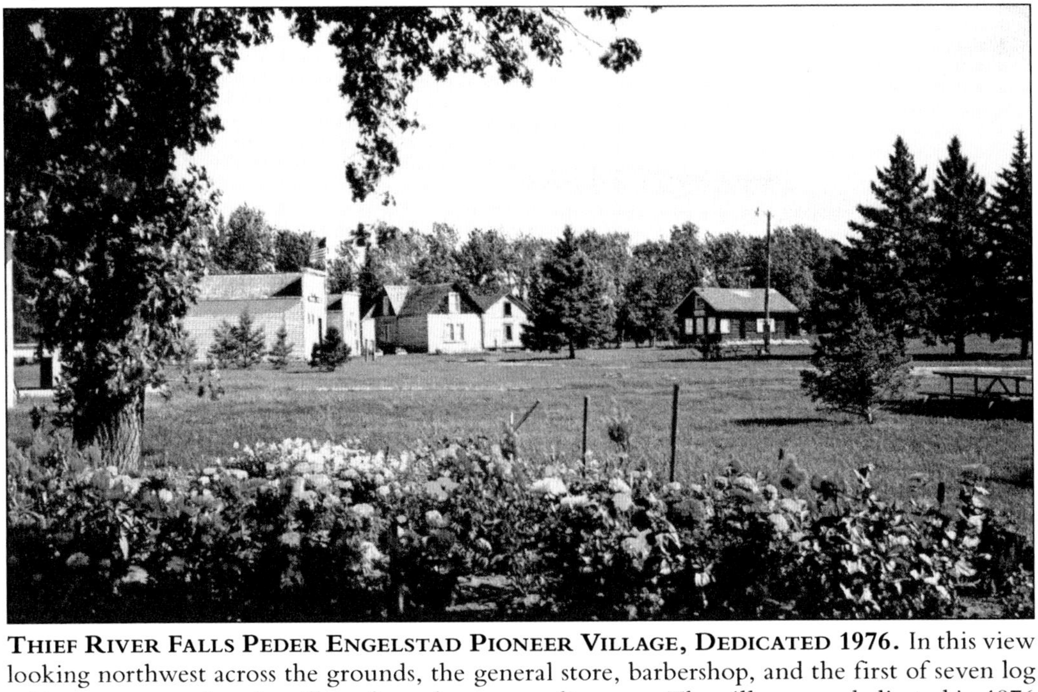

THIEF RIVER FALLS PEDER ENGELSTAD PIONEER VILLAGE, DEDICATED 1976. In this view looking northwest across the grounds, the general store, barbershop, and the first of seven log cabins were moved to the village from the surrounding area. The village was dedicated in 1976 and renamed in 1993.

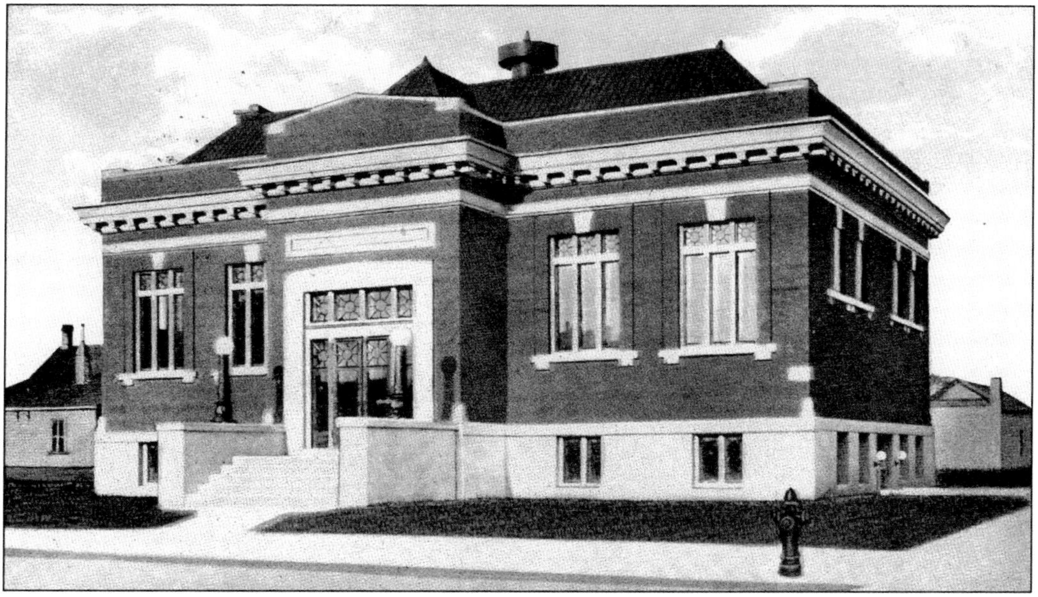

THIEF RIVER FALLS CARNEGIE PUBLIC LIBRARY, POSTMARKED 1915. This view looking east shows the library, located at 102 Main Avenue North, which was completed in 1915. The building was named to the National Register of Historic Places in 1983. It was constructed at a cost of $17,347.70, of which Andrew Carnegie donated $12,500. This card is postmarked 1915.

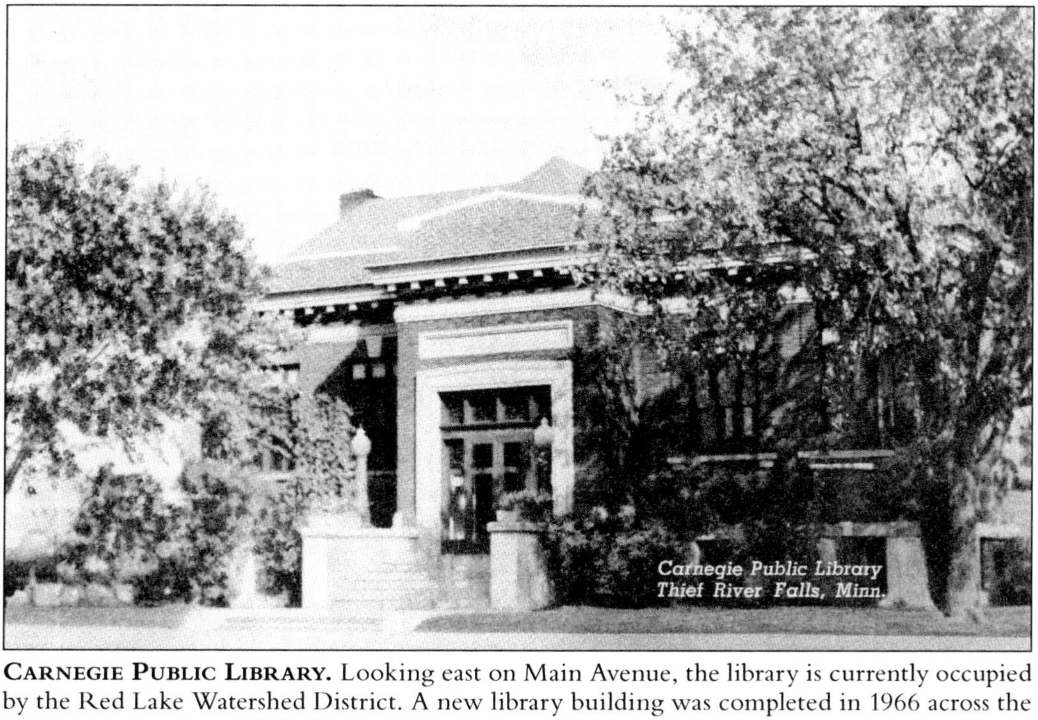

CARNEGIE PUBLIC LIBRARY. Looking east on Main Avenue, the library is currently occupied by the Red Lake Watershed District. A new library building was completed in 1966 across the street to the south on Main Avenue.

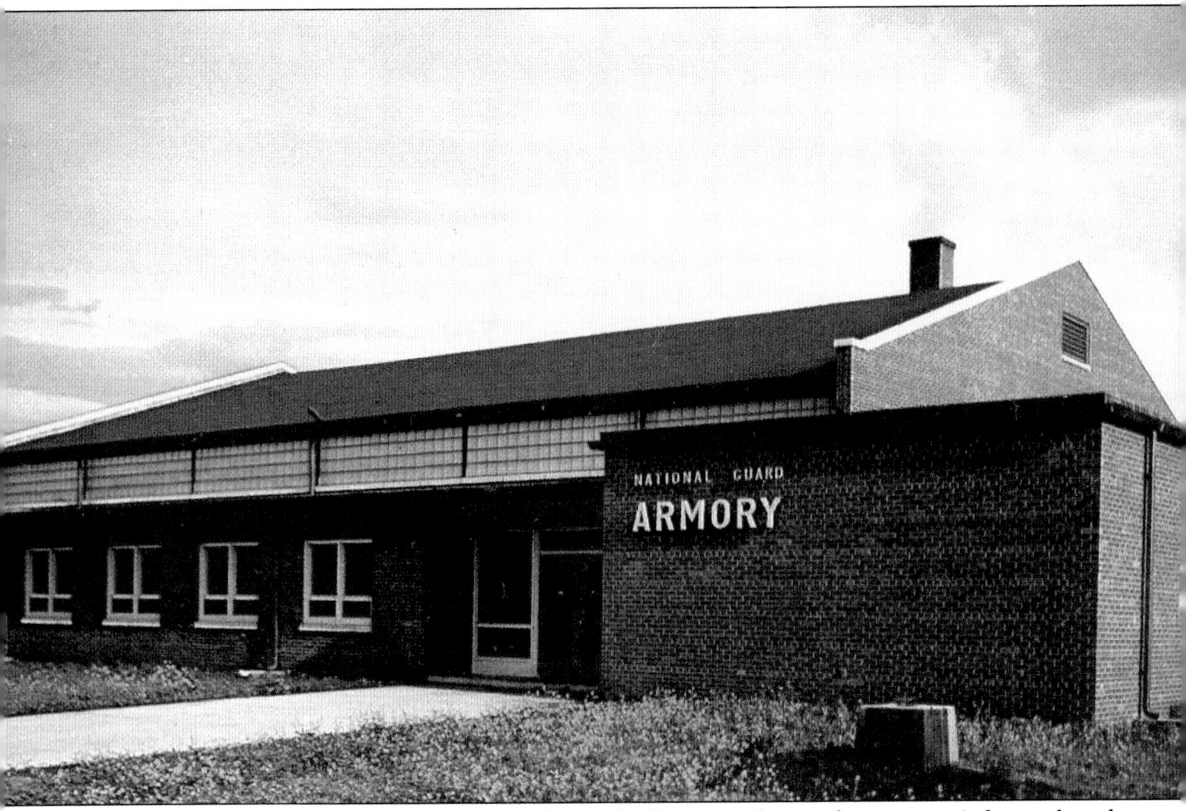

National Guard Armory. In this picture looking southeast, the armory is located at the intersection of Emil Street and Arnold Avenue South. The armory is the home of Company B of the 2–136th Combined Arms Battalion.

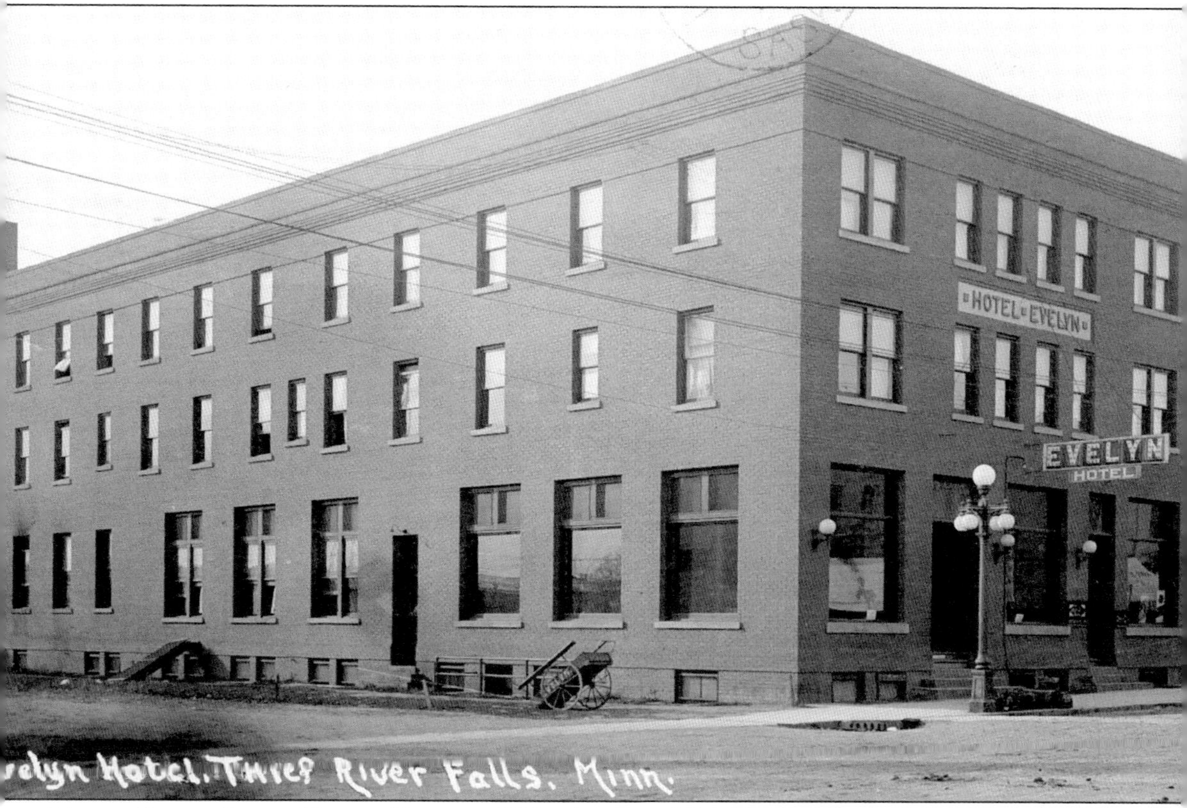

THIEF RIVER FALLS HOTEL EVELYN. This photograph looking southwest from the corner of Horace Avenue and Third Street shows the hotel that was built in 1915. It served as a bus station, had a restaurant, and housed a barbershop in the building at different times. The name was later changed to the Pennington Hotel, and the building was eventually demolished. Note the suitcases at the base of the light pole on this card dated 1915.

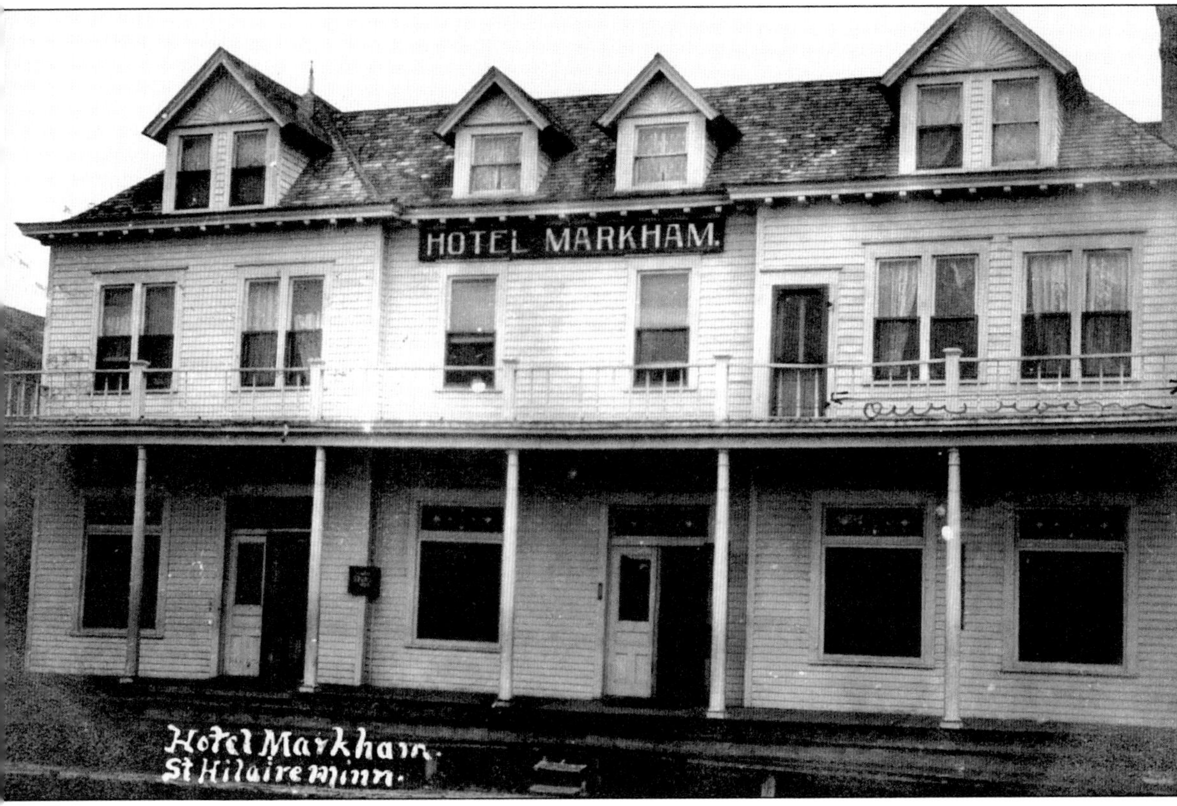

St. Hilaire Hotel Markham. In this view looking east from Broadway Avenue, the hotel was located between Second and Third Streets and had 32 rooms. The hotel was owned by Frederick Busse. This card was postmarked 1909.

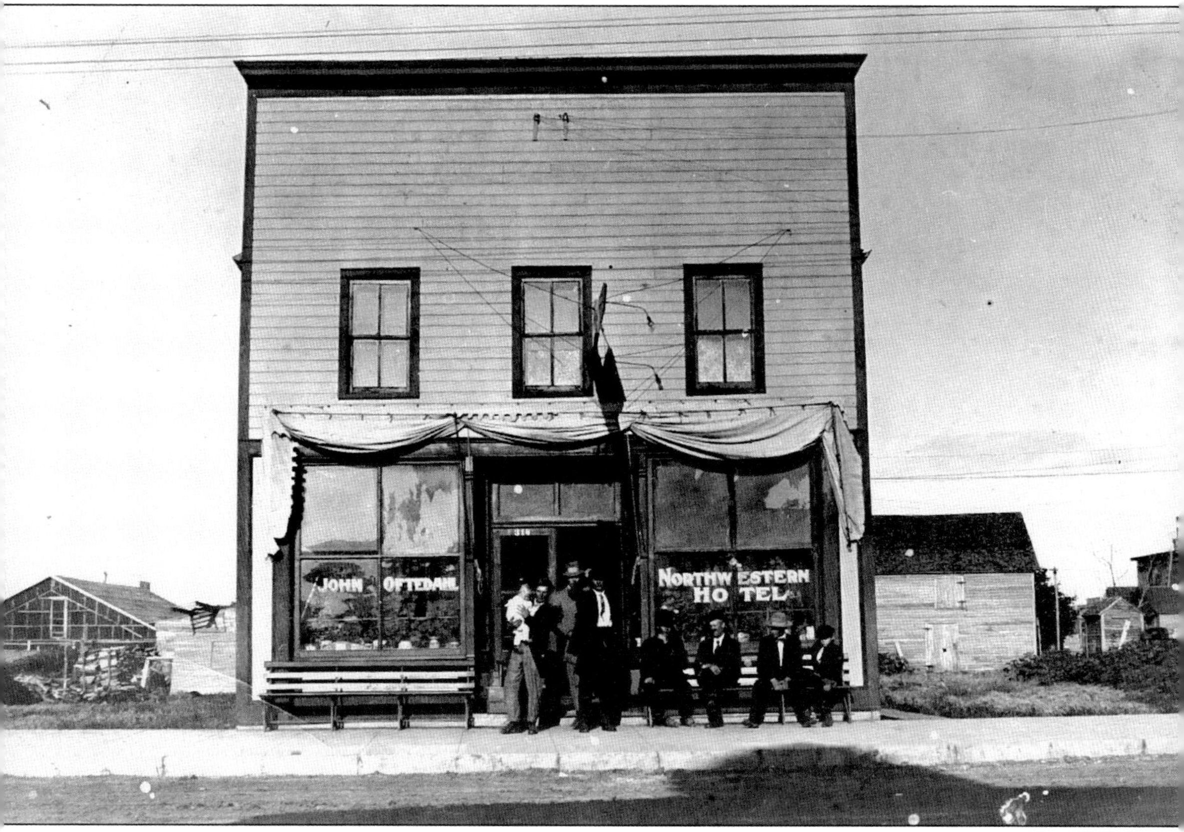

THIEF RIVER FALLS NORTHWESTERN HOTEL. In this view looking east from La Bree Avenue, the hotel was located at 316 La Bree Avenue. John and Tobine Oftedahl owned the hotel from 1911 until 1930.

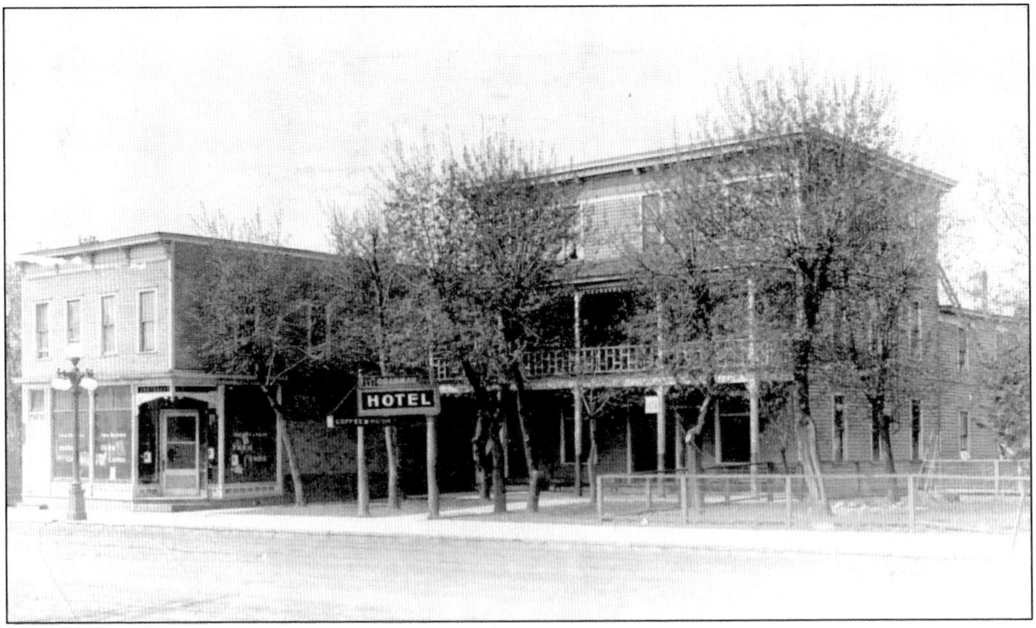

THIEF RIVER FALLS OGAHMAH HOTEL, POSTMARKED 1917. In this view looking southwest from La Bree Avenue, the hotel was located at 109 La Bree Avenue and was first owned by Charles Robbecke, and later George Leimers was the proprietor. The building on the left is the John Bratrud Farm Land Building.

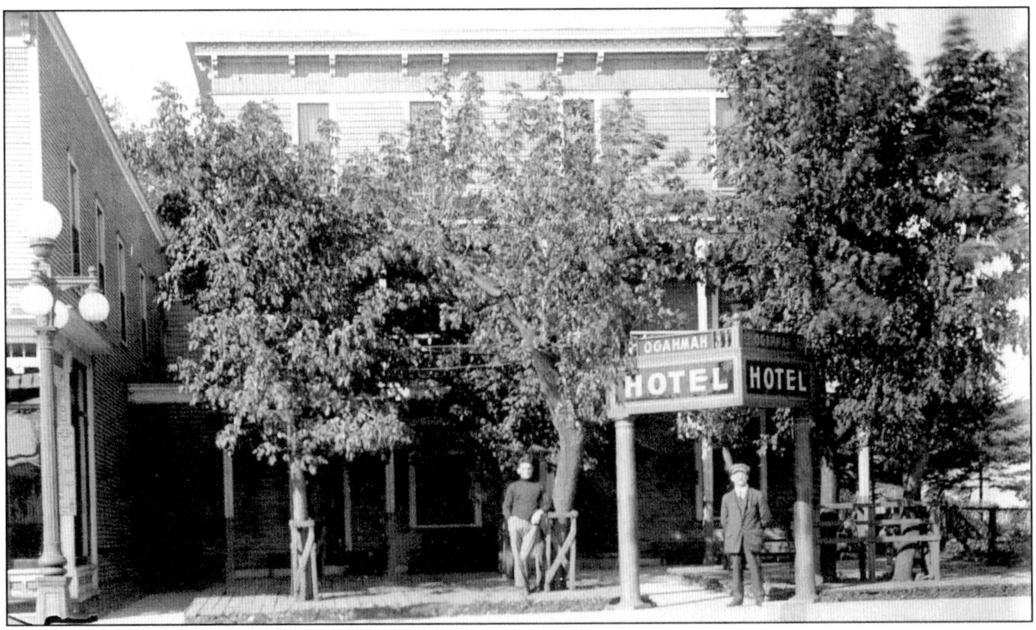

THIEF RIVER FALLS OGAHMAH HOTEL, POSTMARKED 1915. In the view looking west, the wood-frame building was behind several trees on this postcard. In 1888, Charles Robbecke moved to Thief River Falls from St. Hilaire, moving the Ogahmah Hotel along with him to be reconstructed as the city's first hotel.

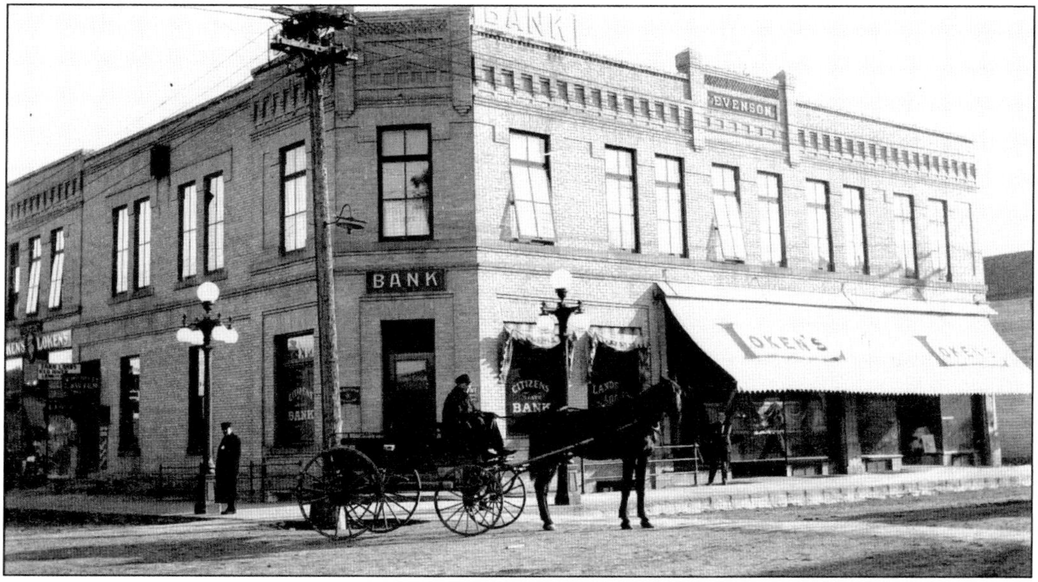

THIEF RIVER FALLS EVENSON BUILDING. Shown in this picture looking southeast from the corner of Main Avenue and Third Street, this building was erected by Charles M. Evenson. In 1902, the Golden Rule Department Store was located in the building. Loken Brothers, the Citizen's State Bank, and the J. C. Penney and Woolworth companies were later located on this corner. The Ben Franklin is currently at this site.

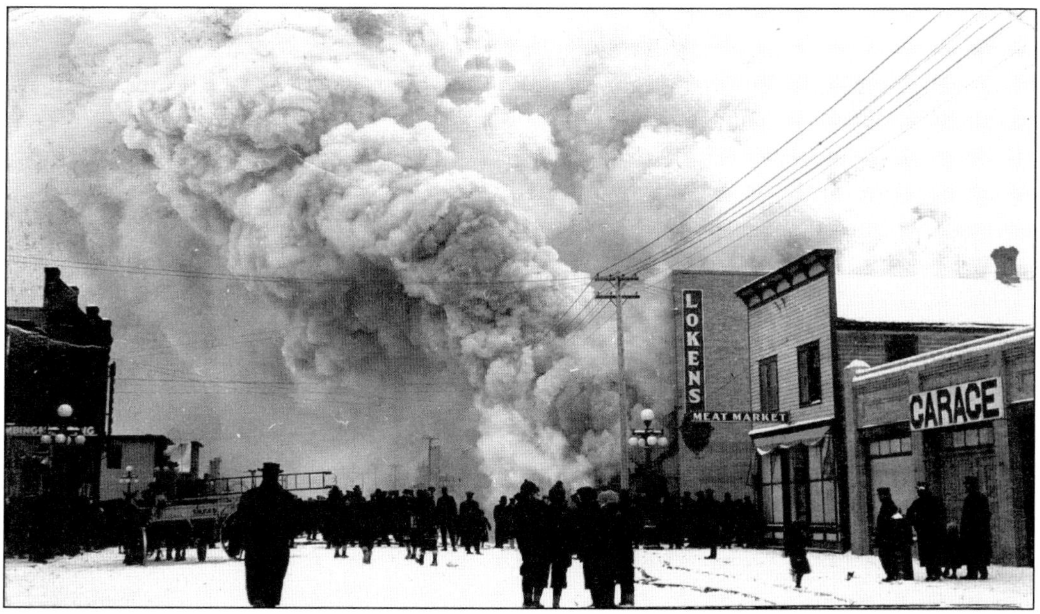

THIEF RIVER FALLS LOKEN BROTHERS. In this view looking north on Main Avenue, the Loken Brothers store is on fire in 1914. This card, postmarked February 2, 1914, has this message on the reverse: "Just a glimpse of last Sunday's fire." Decremer's Meat Market (216) and the Alf Borry Garage (214) were south on Main Avenue. Charles Evenson rebuilt the building, and the Citizens State Bank moved to La Bree Avenue after the fire.

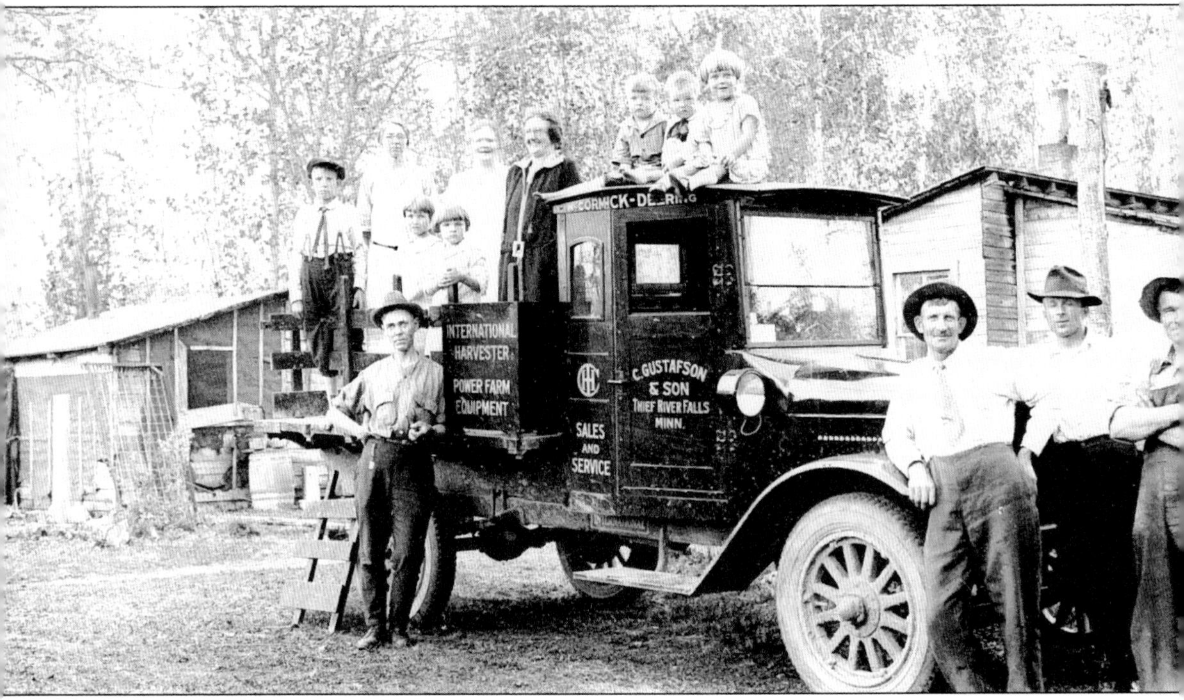

THIEF RIVER FALLS C. GUSTAFSON AND SON. Charles and C. David owned the farm equipment, tractor, and automobile company located at 324 Main Avenue North. Many members of the family worked for the company in the 1920s.

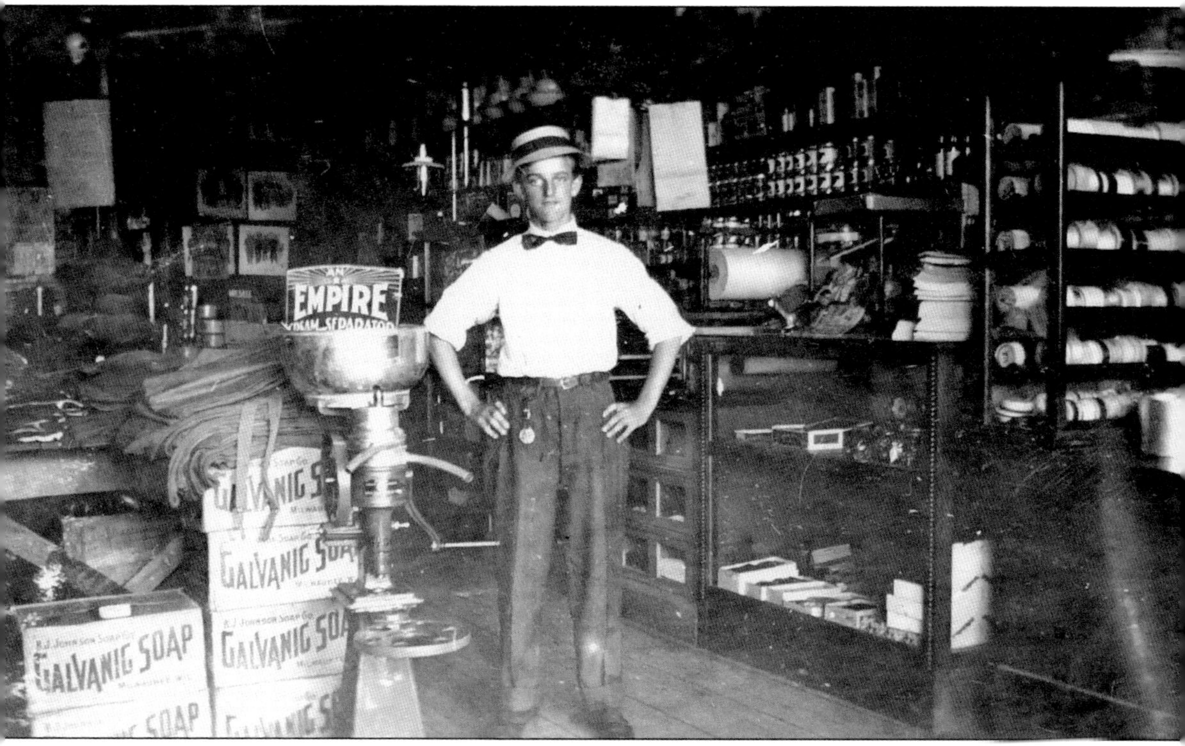

HAZEL MERCHANDISE STORE INTERIOR. The shadows of the town of Hazel are still present along the Canadian Pacific Railway tracks, where grain elevators stand east of St. Hilaire and south of Center Street. Walter Berg worked in the Hazel Store.

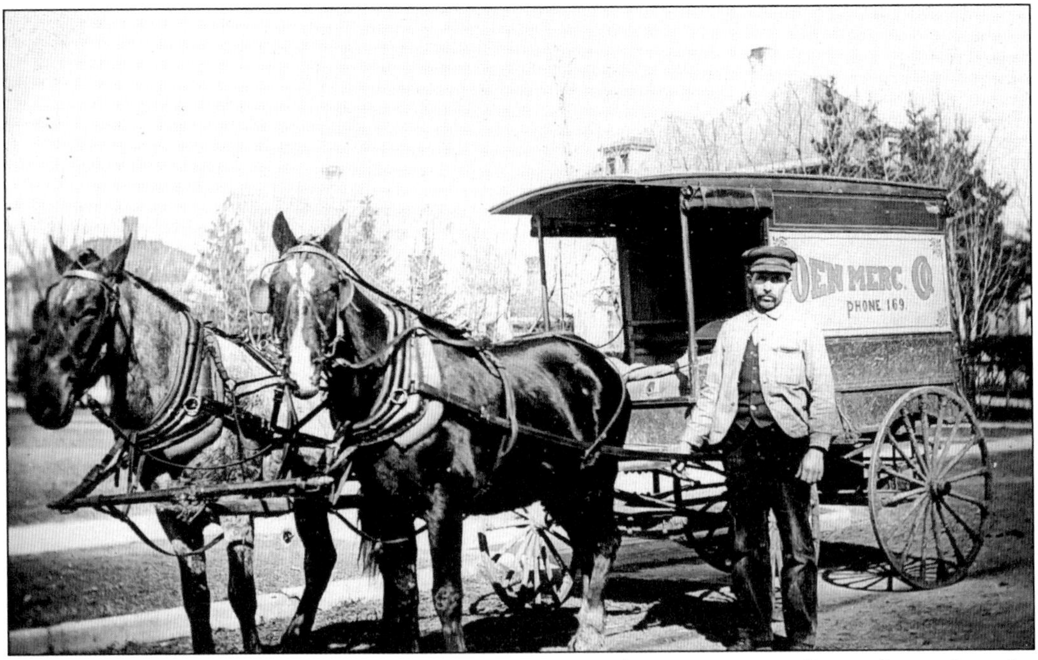

THIEF RIVER FALLS OEN MERCANTILE COMPANY. The Oen Mercantile was located on the southeast corner of La Bree Avenue and Third Street. Rasmus Oen was a tinsmith by trade, and his store advertised selling "Hardware, Farm Machinery, Furniture, Ladies' Ready-to-Wear, Dry Goods, Clothing, Shoes, and Groceries." As seen on this delivery wagon, the phone number was 169.

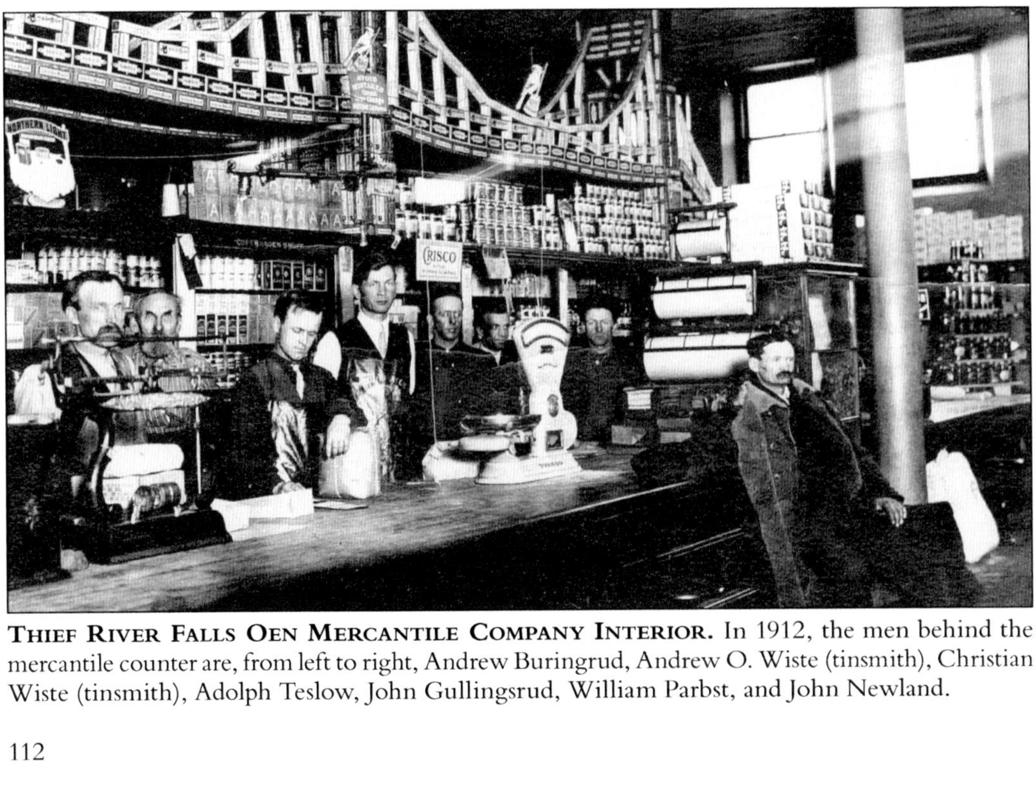

THIEF RIVER FALLS OEN MERCANTILE COMPANY INTERIOR. In 1912, the men behind the mercantile counter are, from left to right, Andrew Buringrud, Andrew O. Wiste (tinsmith), Christian Wiste (tinsmith), Adolph Teslow, John Gullingsrud, William Parbst, and John Newland.

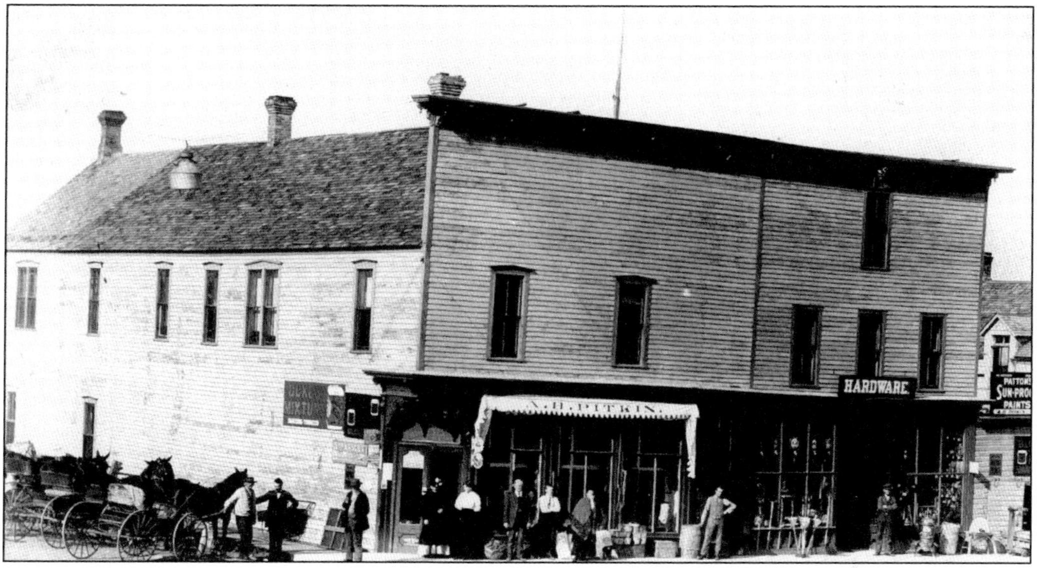

St. Hilaire A. H. Pitkin Store. Shown in this photograph looking northwest from the corner of Broadway Avenue and Third Street, the Pitkin store was established in 1909 and had a hitching rail on the south side of the building.

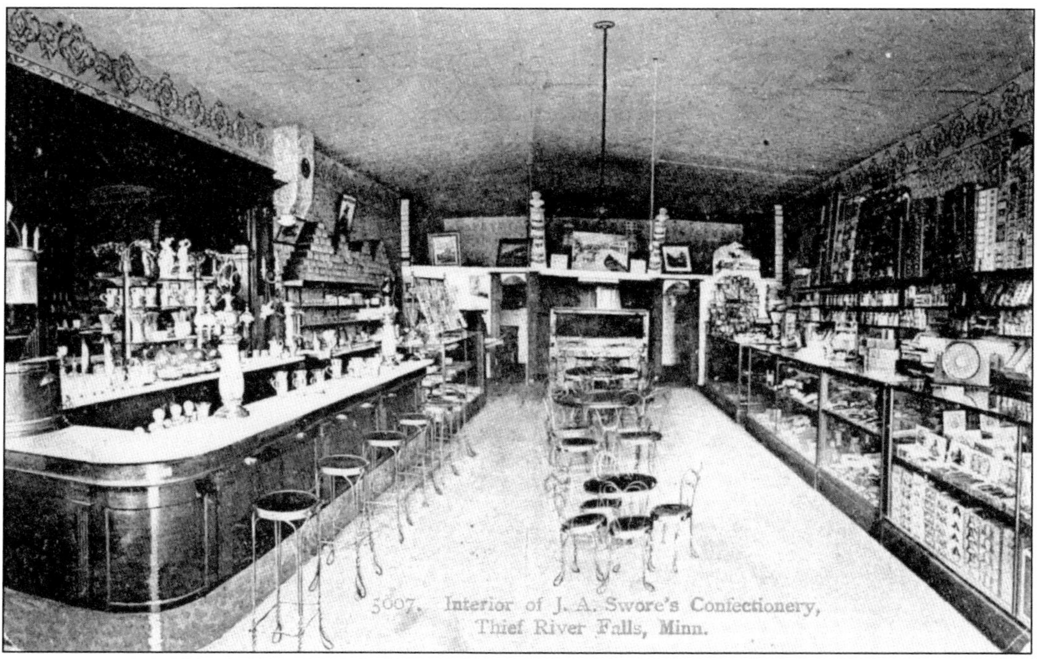

Thief River Falls J. A. Swore's Confectionary Interior. The confectionary was located at 207 La Bree Avenue and advertised selling fruits, ice cream, cigars, and tobacco. This card was postmarked 1909.

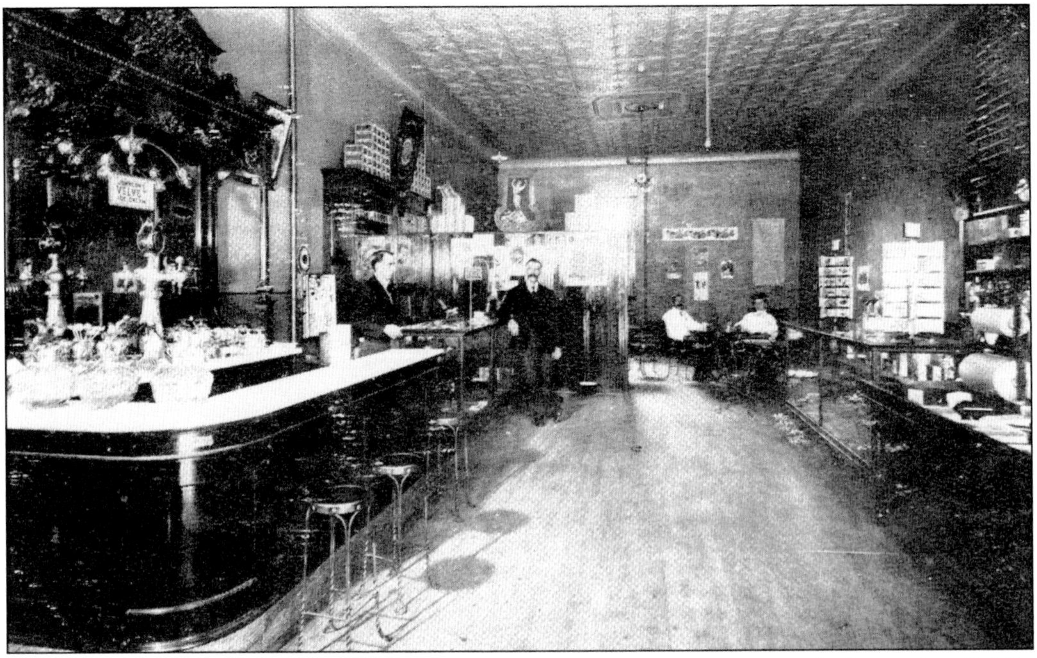

THIEF RIVER FALLS REX CAFÉ INTERIOR. The restaurant was originally located at 202 La Bree Avenue in the Odd Fellows building. Carl Christofferson and Lars Larson owned the café in the 1930s.

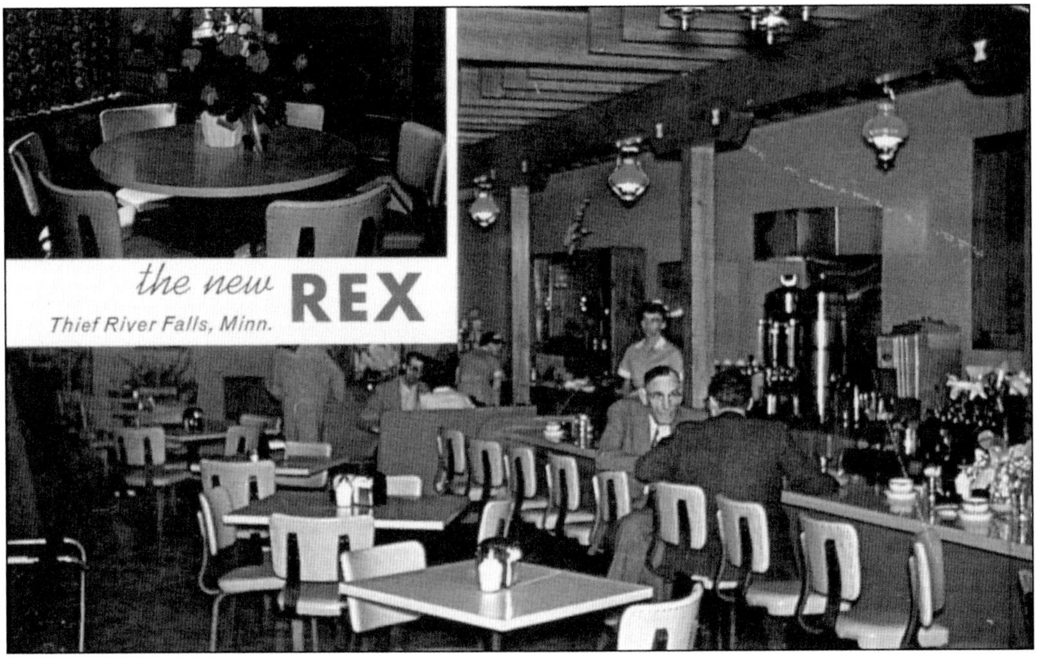

THIEF RIVER FALLS NEW REX CAFÉ INTERIOR. The restaurant moved to 218 La Bree Avenue in the 1940s. Lars Larson, John Curtis, and Phillip Larson owned the café, which was known for its sour cream raisin pie and lemon bars. The last owner was Ed Turenne, and the restaurant closed in the 1990s.

Five

People and Occasions

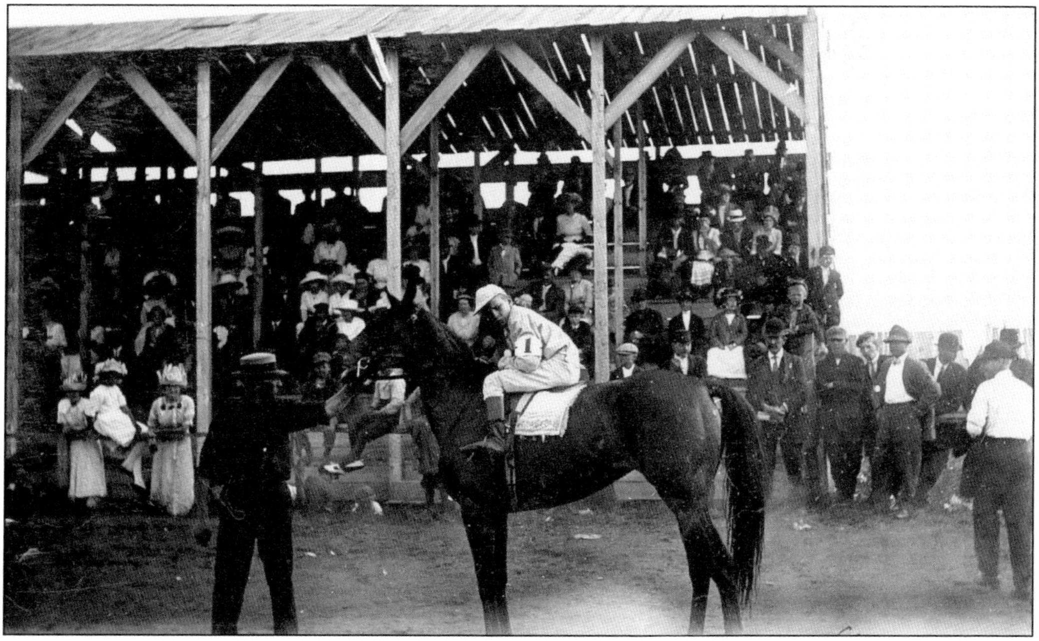

Pennington County Fair. George Brink is riding the horse Bill, held by Victor Brink in front of the grandstand at the county fair, which was in August 1912 in Thief River Falls.

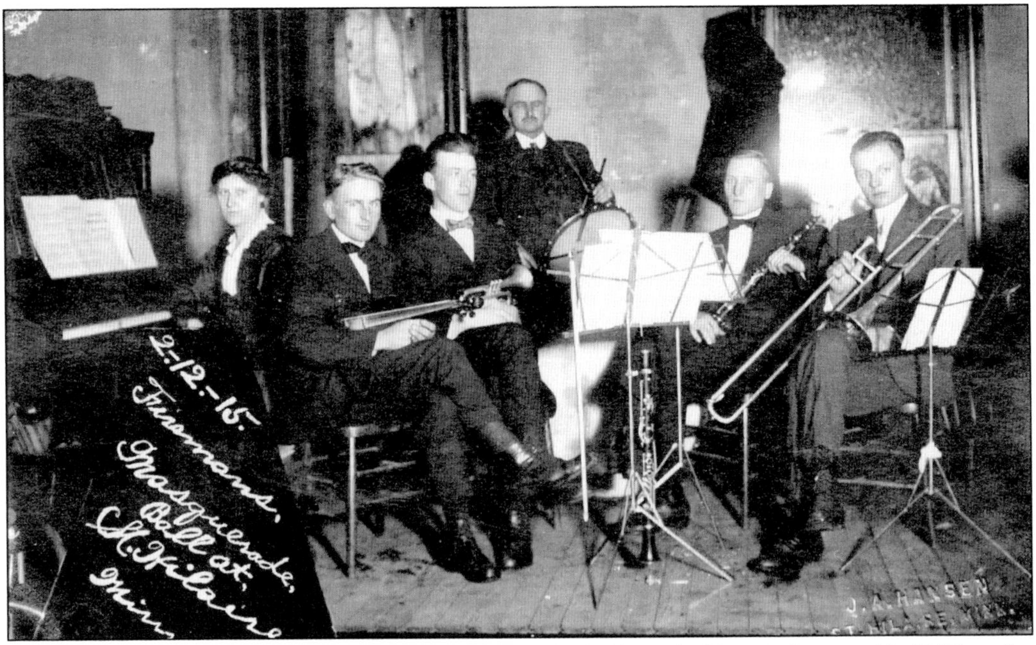

ST. HILAIRE FIREMEN'S MASQUERADE BALL. The ball was held on February 12, 1915, at the Imperial Opera House. The St. Hilaire Orchestra furnished the music. James King drew the prize for the best-dressed gentleman and Mrs. William Olson, the prize for the ladies. Delegations were in attendance from Crookston, Holt, Wylie, and Hazel.

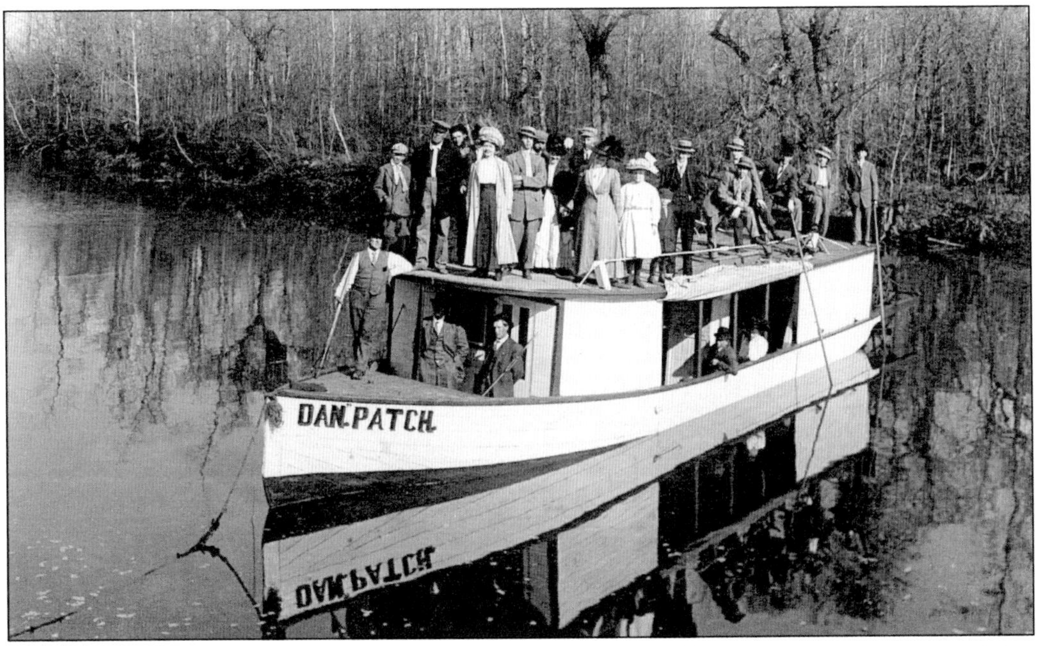

THIEF RIVER FALLS *DAN PATCH* RIVERBOAT. Joe DuChamp was the captain of this gasoline-powered riverboat, which towed a long barge and carried supplies and passengers between Thief River Falls and Red Lake. The cost of a ride was 75¢ each way. This card is postmarked 1912.

THIEF RIVER FALLS MAIL CARRIERS. Letters addressed to the city frequently traveled months before being forwarded to Rockstad, the first post office. In 1891, the post office was officially designated in the city, and the first daily delivery was in 1894 via the Great Northern Railway. Mail by carrier was established in 1911. From left to right, Harold McCrum, Walter Quist, and Fred Protz were the first mailmen.

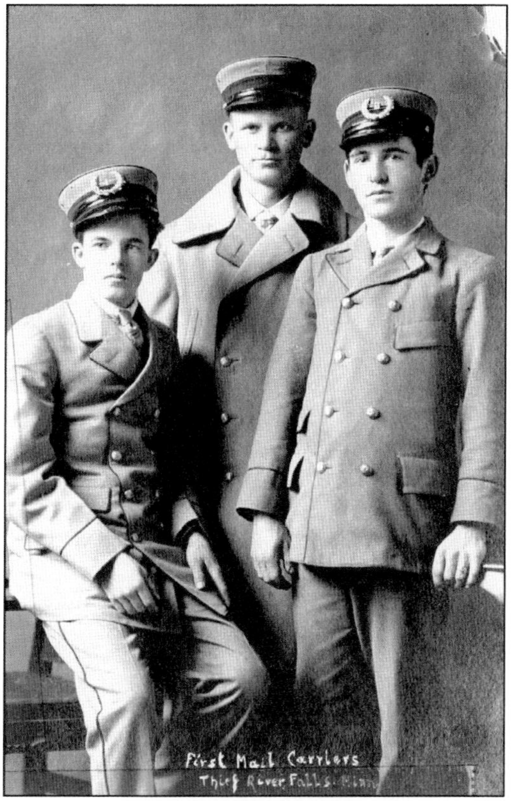

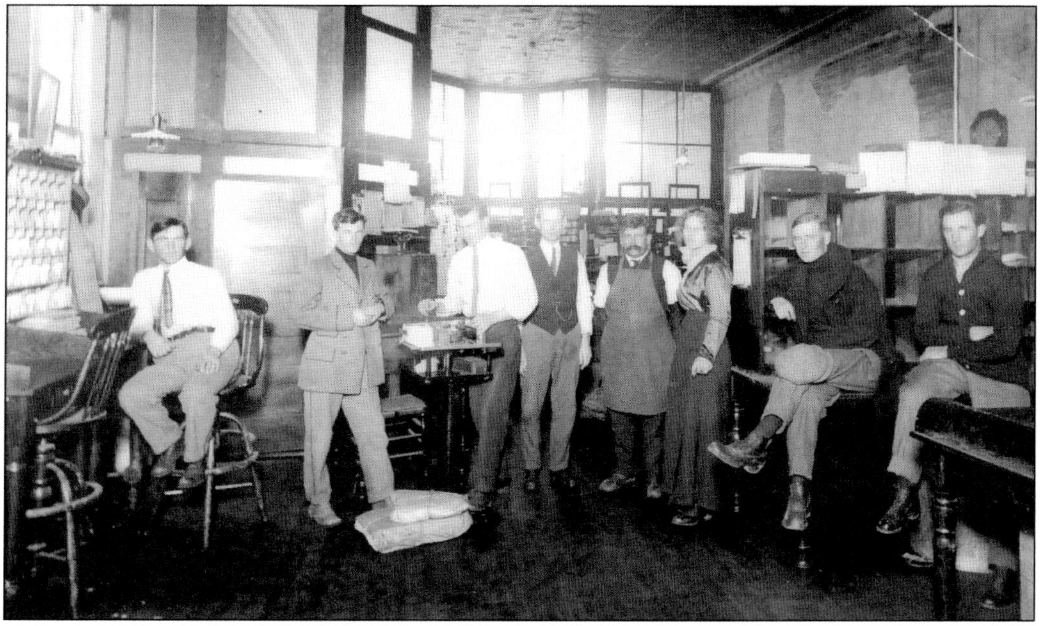

THIEF RIVER FALLS POSTAL EMPLOYEES. Although a post office was not built until 1933, a city post office was located in a number of buildings in the city. In 1914, from left to right, Fred Protz, Harold McCrum, Tom Chirtick, T. S. Brokke, E. W. Lown, Anna Brokke, Walt Smith, and Ray Pope were postal employees.

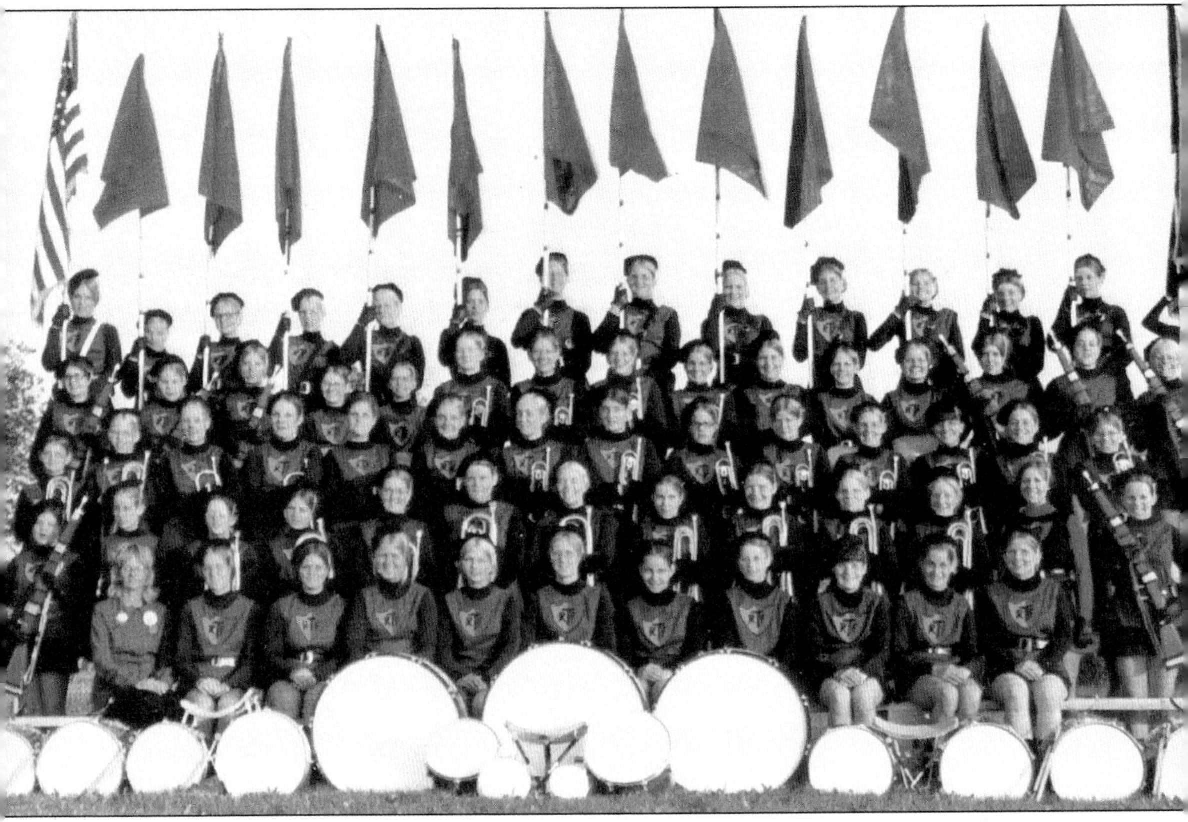

Thief River Falls TRFinettes Drum and Bugle Corps. The 72-member corps was comprised of female teenagers and directed by Gail Bergland (seated front far left) in the 1973 unit. The members played all ranges of bugles and drums, practiced twice a week, and performed approximately 10 times a year.

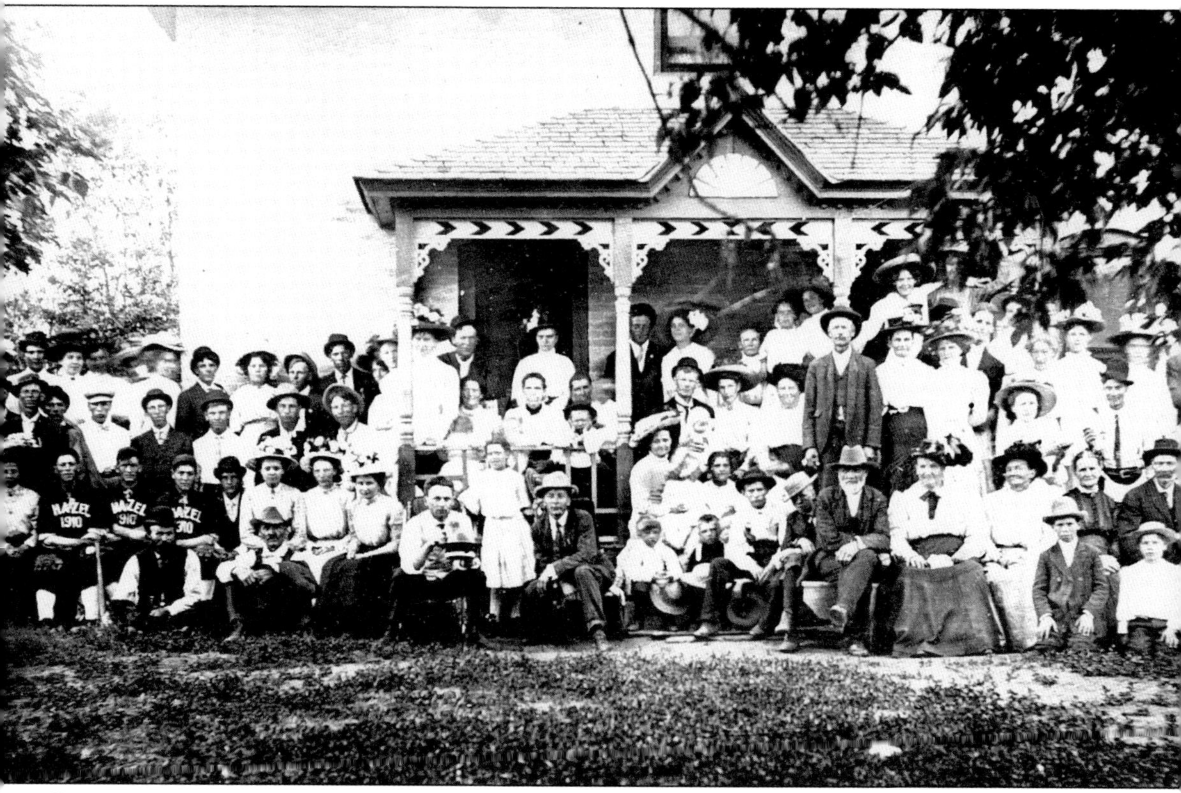

ROCKSBURY TOWNSHIP, S. O. LEE HOME. A gathering of people, including members of the Hazel baseball team of 1910, was in front of the S. O. Lee home.

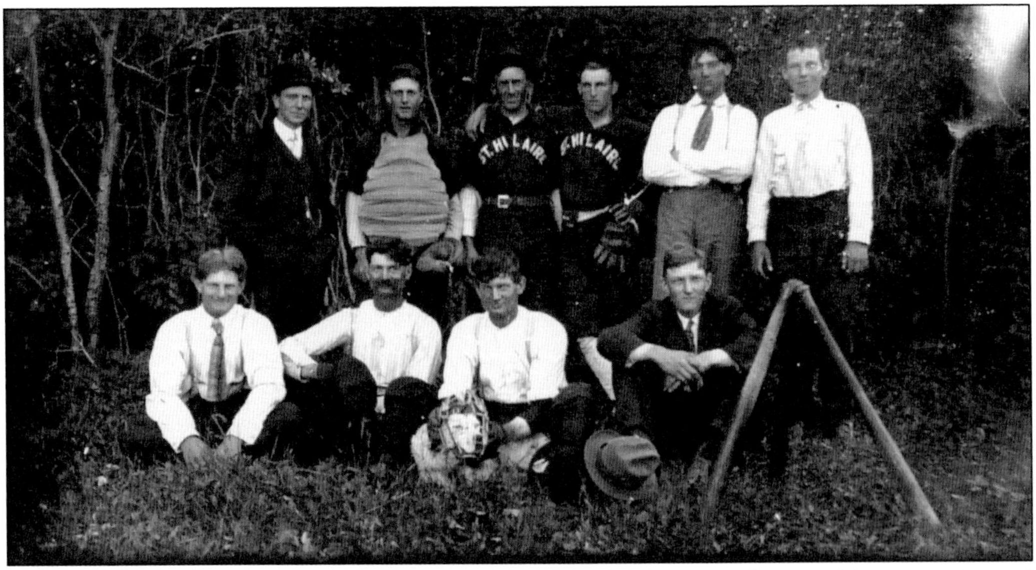

St. Hilaire Baseball Team. Although the names and positions of most of the team pictured are unknown, the equipment and dog were included in the team portrait. Some of the players are Albert Nellson, Louis Larson, and a Mr. Carpenter.

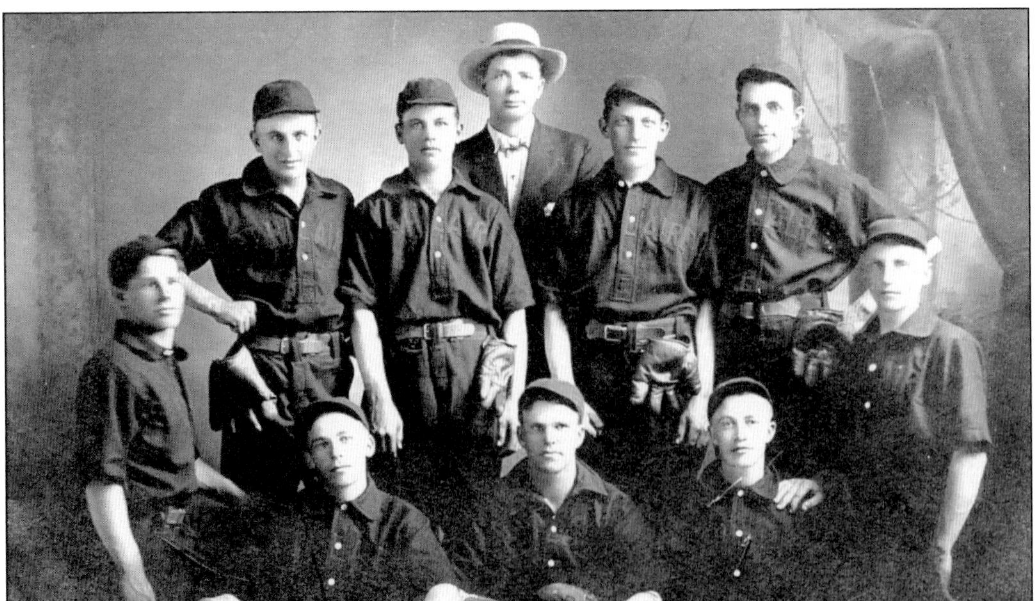

St. Hilaire Baseball Team *c.* 1910. One of the nine players was Myles Jackson, who was standing second from the right. The team is sporting team hats, shirts, and their gloves in the second decade of the 20th century.

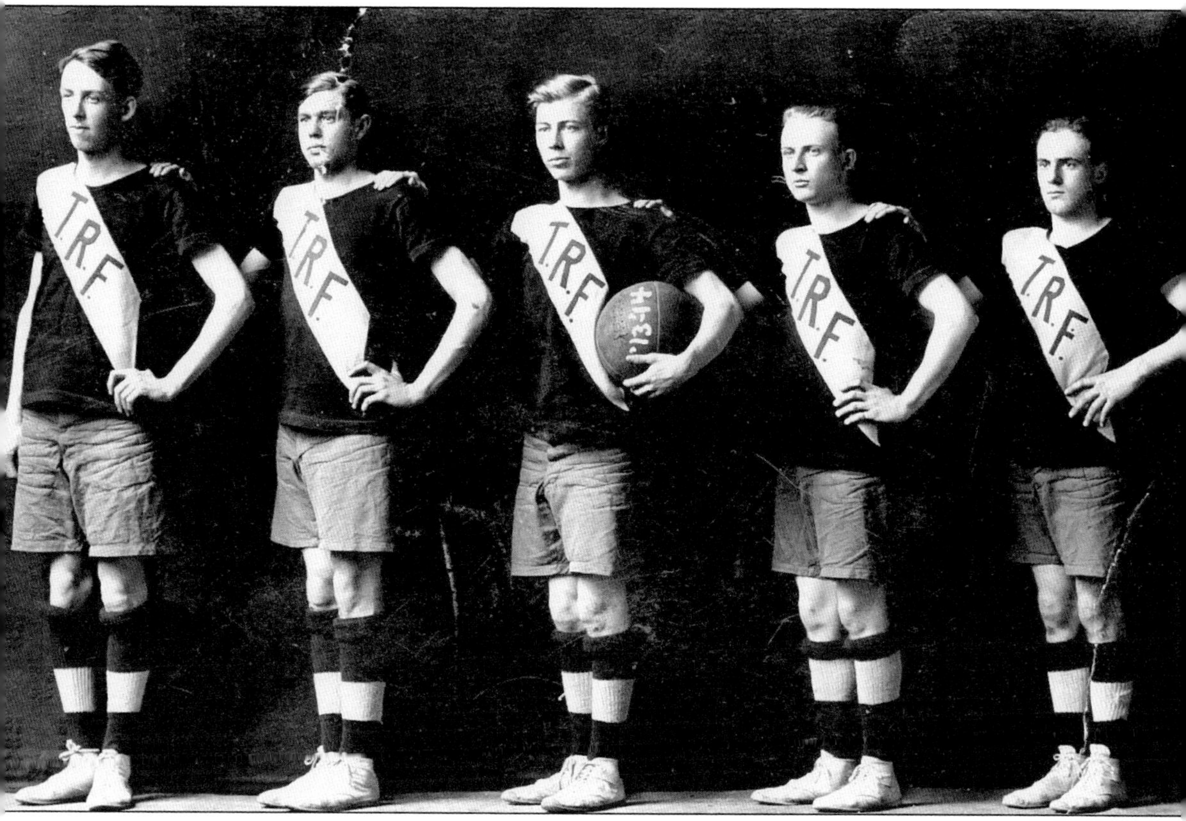

Thief River Falls Boys Basketball Team. Francis Burns, Ward Long, Oscar Paulson, R. Miller, and Lawrence Hermanson played on the team of 1913–1914. Francis Burns was the son of Michael Burns, who was one of the earliest settlers in the area.

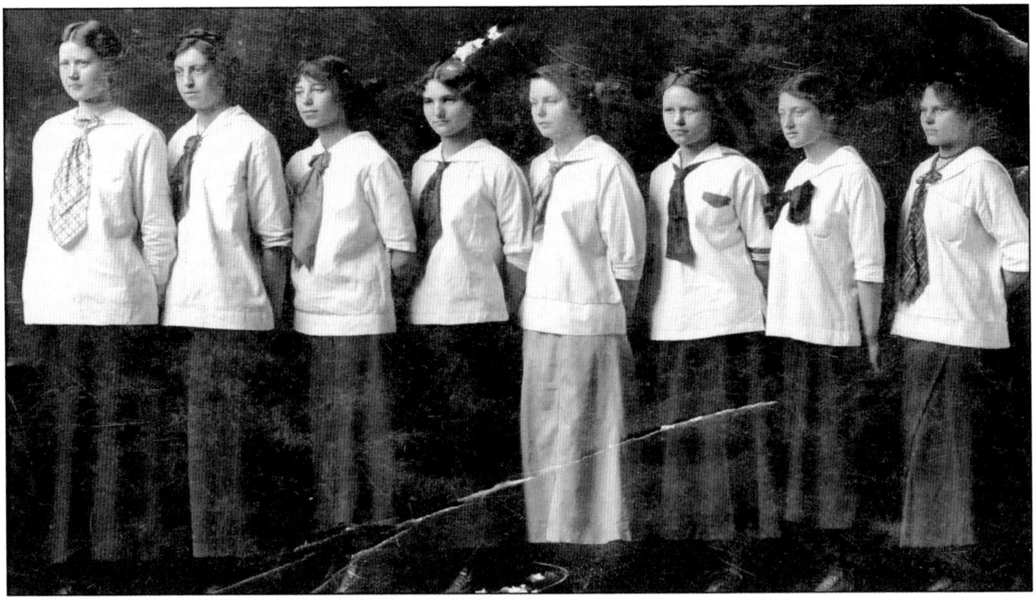

Thief River Falls High School 1913–1914 Women's Basketball Team. The young women on the team are, from left to right, Alice Elgesteon, Esther Tanberg, Esther Adolph, Lizzie LaCoe, Marjorie Cates, Eliz Kleppe, Susie Chettard, and Selma Lovas for the 1913–1914 school year.

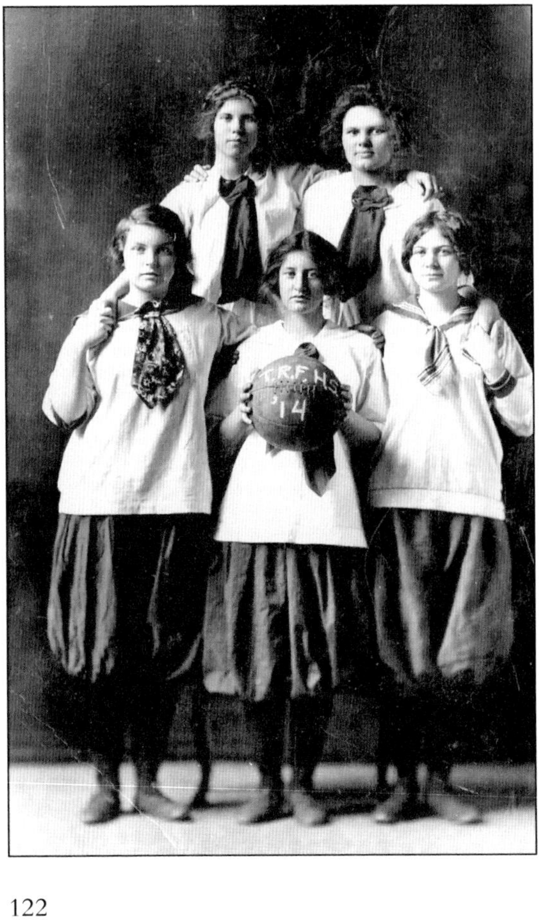

Thief River Falls High School Women's Basketball Team Graduates. Pictured may be five members of the team that graduated in 1914. Team members in the class of 1914 were Alice Elgesten, Esther Tanberg, Esther Adolph, Marjorie Cates, Susie Chettard, and Selma Lovas.

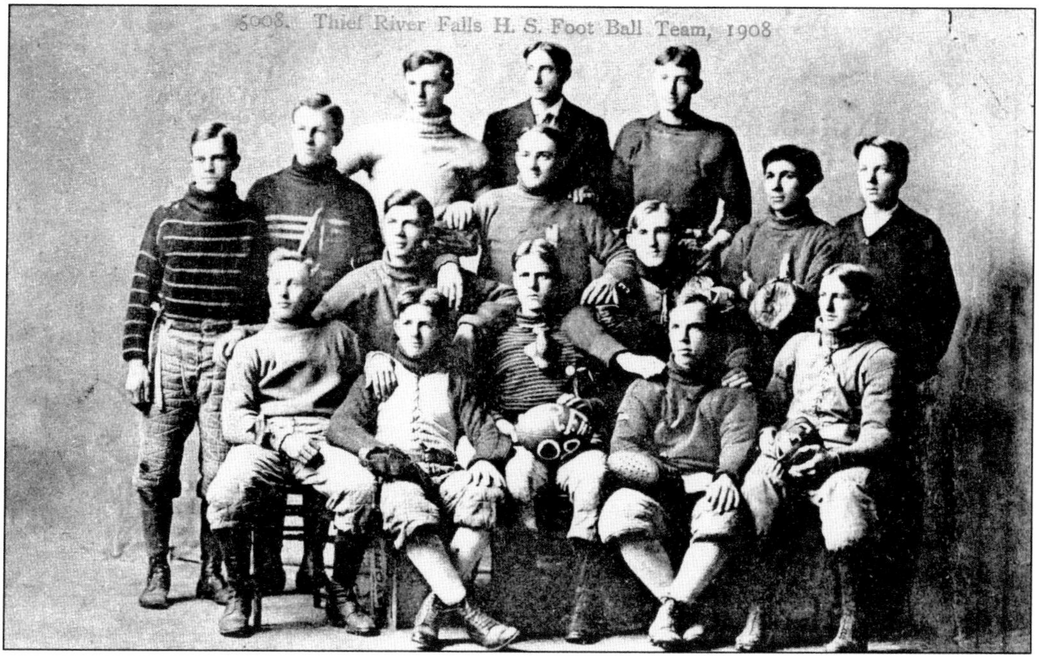

THIEF RIVER FALLS HIGH SCHOOL FOOTBALL TEAM. The members of the 1908 team, identified only with their last name, are Lipscomb, Curran, Jacobson, Brady, Iverson, Meehan, Curran, Brudie, Dolson, Johnson, Fossum, Ihle, Prichard, captain Hess, and Chittick. This card is postmarked 1910.

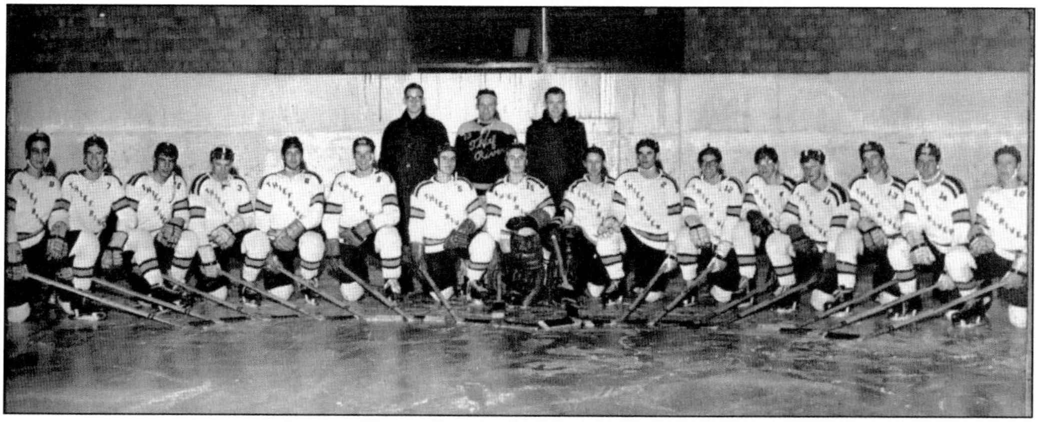

THIEF RIVER FALLS 1959–1960 LINCOLN HIGH SCHOOL PROWLER HOCKEY. The team state records on the reverse of this card were: 1951–third place, 1952–consolation, 1954–champions, 1955–consolation, 1956–champions, and 1959–champions. The players are, from left to right, (first row) Wes Halvorson, Jim Wegge, Jerome Larson, Dale Wennberg, Archie Schneider, Tom Melhoff, Tim Teal, Tom Teal, Babe Halvorson, Arlyn Hjelle, Don Waldera, Jack Goulet, Dennis Erickson, Jack Hofek, Gus Holmes, and Larry Poole; (second row) Gary Odegaard, coach Gene Sack, and Kern Olson. George Schlief, not in the photograph, is listed as the assistant coach.

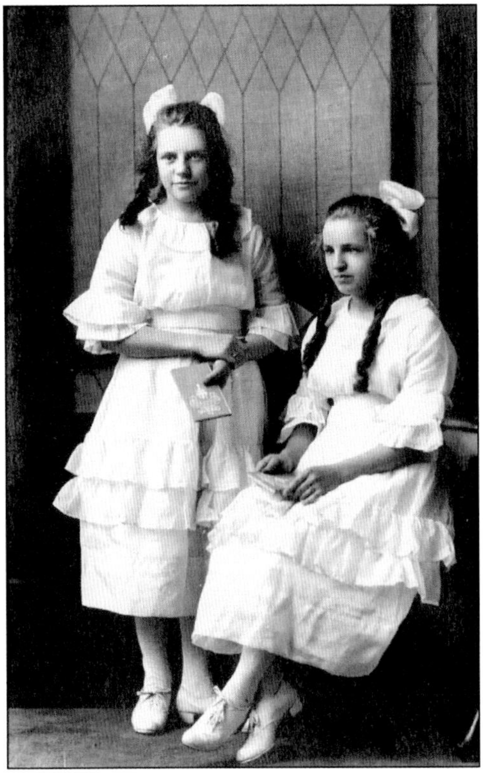

THIEF RIVER FALLS SISTERS. Josie Bugge and Hilda Bugge were the daughters of Peter and Petrine Bugge. Josie never married. Hilda married Carl Wennberg, and they had three sons, Jon, Don, and Dale. Dale Wennberg was elected mayor of Thief River Falls in 2002, began his first term in 2003, and was reelected in 2004.

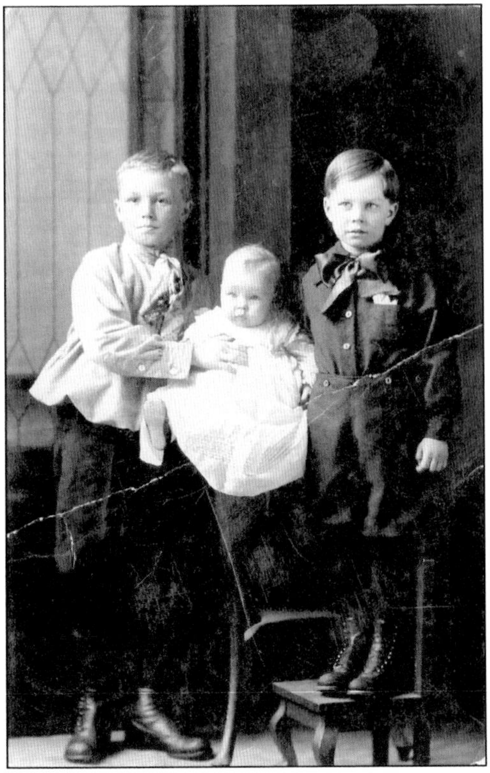

HAZEL'S ODEGAARD BROTHERS. Seen here from left to right, Oscar, Walter (baby), and Morris Odegaard were three of the five sons of Ole Odegaard who was one of the partners of the Hazel Mercantile. Rueben and Harvey were born later.

THIEF RIVER FALLS OFTEDAHL FAMILY. Standing in the back is Jeanette Oftedahl, who later graduated from Lincoln High School in 1918. In front of her are, from left to right, Agnes, Peter, and Inga Oftedahl. The Oftedahl family owned the Northwestern Hotel, which was located on La Bree Avenue in the early 1900s.

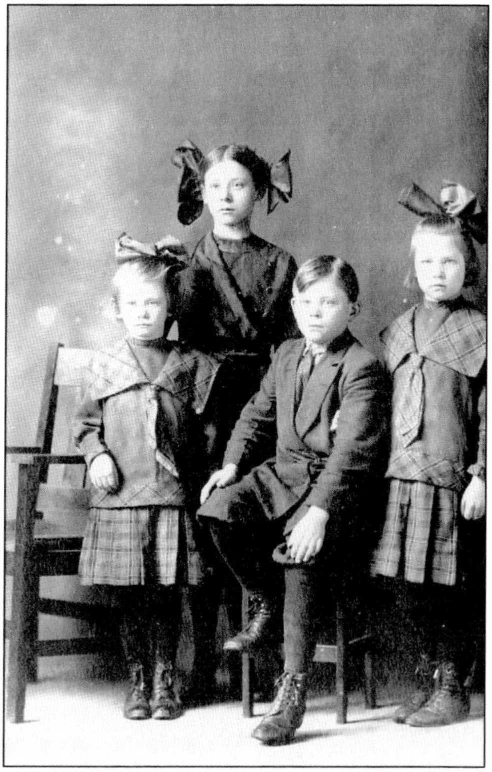

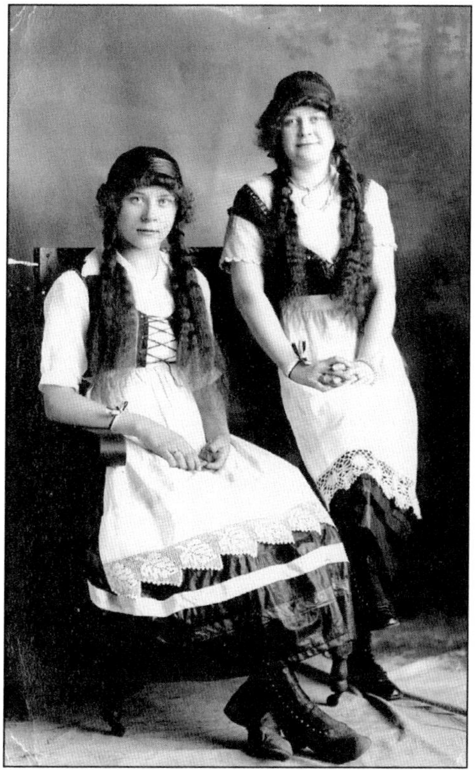

THIEF RIVER FALLS FRIENDS. Dressed for Syttende Mai on May 17, 1916, Jeanette Oftedahl (left) and Clara Oen were pictured on a card on which Jeannette wrote, "The best Pal I ever had in my whole life." Jeanette was the daughter of the Oftedahls who owned the Northwestern Hotel, and Clara was the daughter of the Oens that owned Oen's Mercantile.

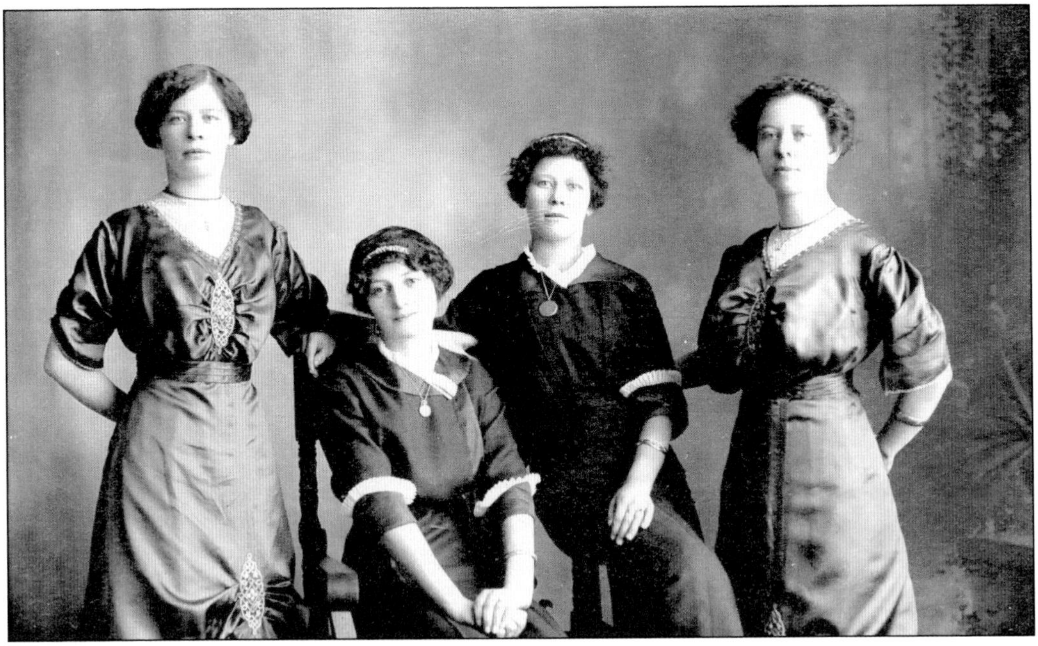

THIEF RIVER FALLS OFTEDAHL FAMILY. Seen here from left to right, Tillie, Olga, and Ella Oftedahl and the hired girl, who was seated, were the hostesses and employees of the Northwestern Hotel, which was owned by the Oftedahls.

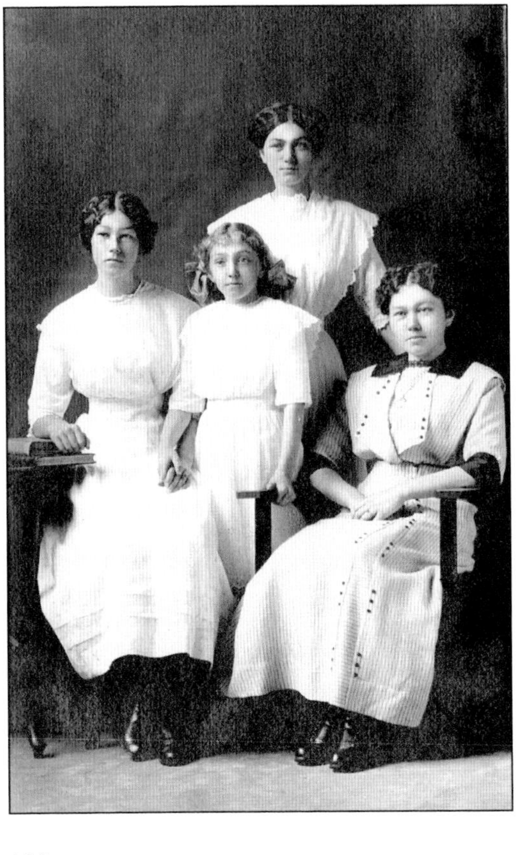

ROCKSBURY TOWNSHIP SISTERS. Standing in the back, Julia, and in the front, from left to right, Clara, Mabel, and Ragna Loberg were the daughters of Lars and Marie Loberg who farmed in Section 30.

ROCKSBURY TOWNSHIP SISTERS. Valborg and Louisa Engelstad were the daughters of Peder and Mathtilde Engelstad. Valborg married Edwin Hanson, and Louisa married Sigvard Anderson.

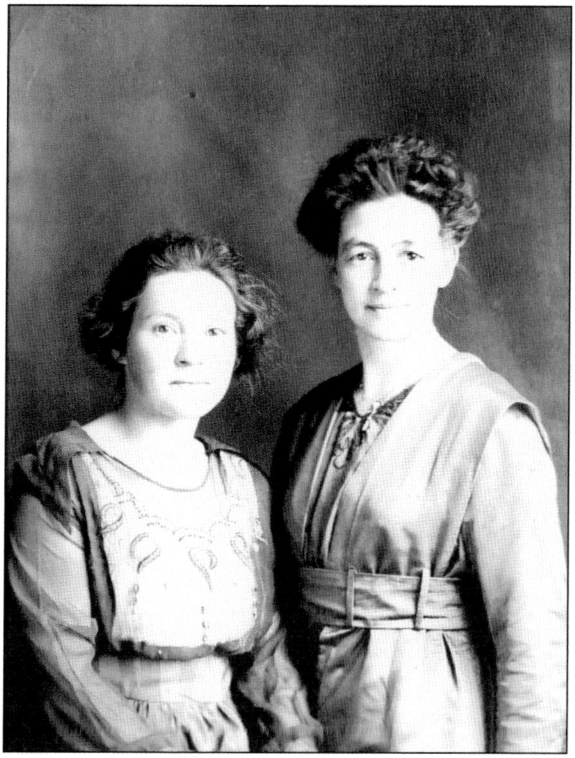

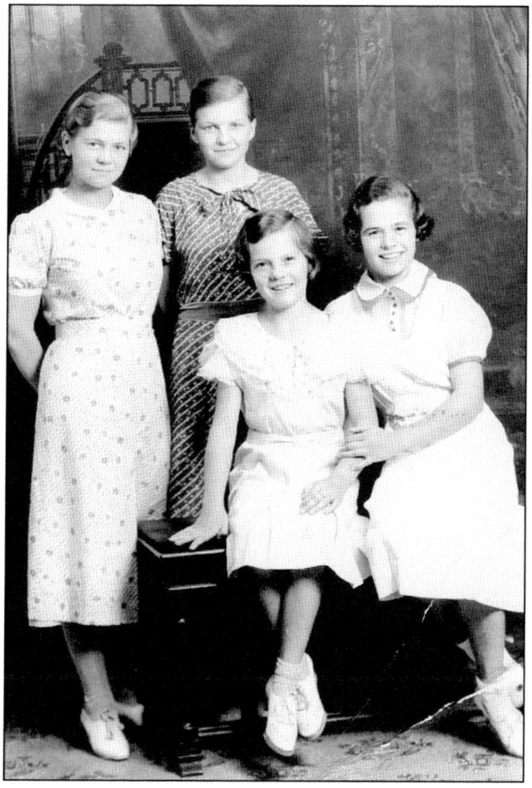

THIEF RIVER FALLS COUSINS. The older daughters of Valborg Hanson (née Engelstad) and Louisa Anderson (née Engelstad) were, from left to right, Violet Anderson, Pearl Hanson, Florence Hanson, and Helen Anderson.

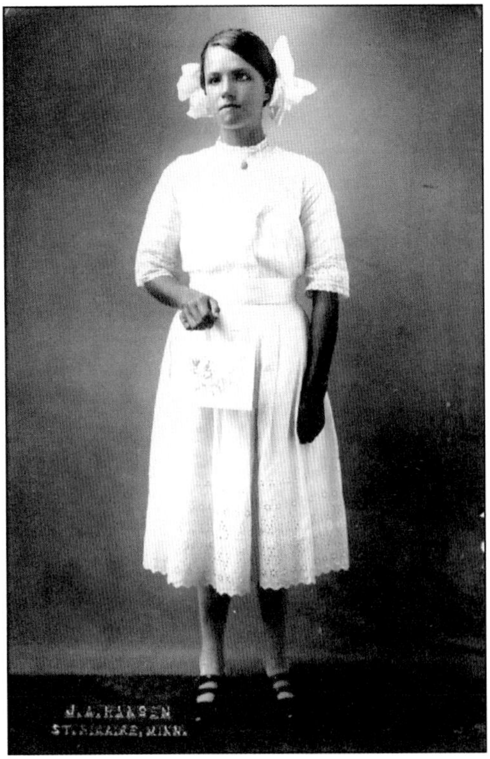

ST. HILAIRE CONFIRMANT. Selma Maland's confirmation from the Norwegian Lutheran Church on August 10, 1913, was celebrated on this postcard. Selma graduated from Lincoln High School in 1918, attended normal training, taught in many rural schools, and married Myles Jackson in 1926.

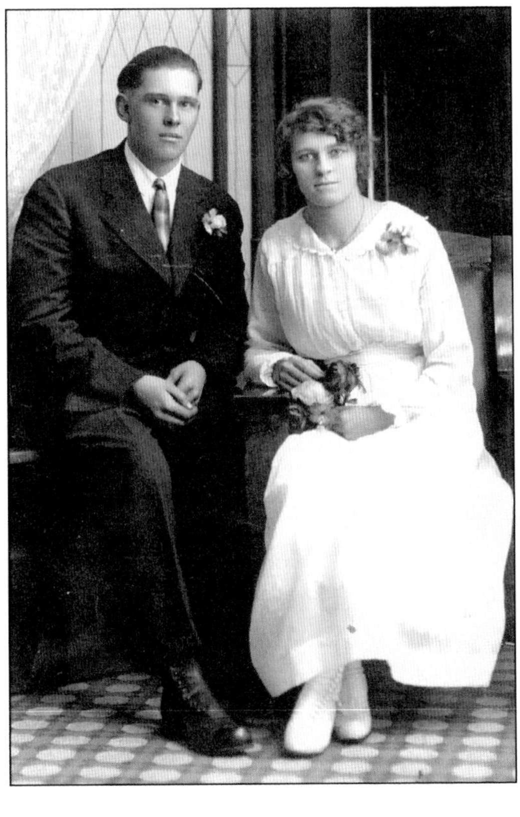

THIEF RIVER FALLS FAMILY. The wedding of Omer and Adlyn Williams was celebrated on this postcard. William was the son of George Williams who owned the Williams Bottling Company and later Williams Hardware.